P9-DEG-915

CONTENTS

PRAISE FOR
ON THE LINE

"*On The Line* is a fascinating case study of how a small business becomes a big business—and begins to act like one....It's written in an informal, quick-read style like a novel or a prime-time soap opera... and provides some of the best insights yet into the long-distance business....THE STORY OF ONE OF THE GREATEST BUSINESS BATTLES IN AMERICAN HISTORY."
—*Fort Lauderdale News and Sun Sentinel*

"BRISK, BRIGHTLY WRITTEN ...LUCID."
—*Publishers Weekly*

"A FASCINATING ENTREPRENEURIAL START-UP STORY."
—*Memphis Business Journal*

"AN AMERICAN BUSINESS SAGA."
—*Playboy*

"The engrossing text reads like a novel....EXCELLENT."
—*Library Journal*

ON THE LINE

HOW MCI
TOOK ON AT&T—
AND WON!

Larry Kahaner

WARNER BOOKS

A Warner Communications Company

Warner Books Edition
Copyright © 1986 by Larry Kahaner
All rights reserved.

Warner Books, Inc., 666 Fifth Avenue, New York, NY 10103

 A Warner Communications Company

Designed by Richard Oriolo
Printed in the United States of America
First Warner Books Trade Paperback Printing: August 1987
10 9 8 7 6 5 4 3 2 1

Library of Congress Cataloging-in-Publication Data

Kahaner, Larry.
  On the line.

  Includes index.
    1. Mass Communications, inc.—History. 2. American
Telephone and Telegraph Company—Reorganization—
History. 3. Telephone—United States—Long distance—
History. I. Title.
HE8846.M375K34 1987   384.6'065'73   87-10561
ISBN 0-446-38550-6 (pbk.) (U.S.A.)
    0-446-38551-4 (pbk.) (Canada)

ATTENTION: SCHOOLS AND CORPORATIONS
Warner books are available at quantity discounts with bulk purchase for educational,
business, or sales promotional use. For information, please write to: Special Sales
Department, Warner Books, 666 Fifth Avenue, New York, NY 10103.

**ARE THERE WARNER BOOKS YOU WANT
BUT CANNOT FIND IN YOUR LOCAL STORES?**
You can get any Warner Books title in print. Simply send title and retail price, plus 50¢ per
order and 50¢ per copy to cover mailing and handling costs for each book desired. New
York State and California residents, add applicable sales tax. Enclose check or money
order—no cash, please—to: Warner Books, PO Box 690, New York, NY 10019. Or send for
our complete catalog of Warner Books.

ON THE LINE

HOW THIS BOOK
WAS DONE

Most of the material in this book came from three sources: personal observations, taped interviews, and official documents. Except where it was impossible, information from interviews was corroborated by at least one other person or by documents. The bulk of the documents came from the Federal Communications Commission, Congress, the Securities and Exchange Commission, various federal and state courts, foreign Post, Telephone, and Telegraph administrations, and companies themselves.

It is almost impossible to reconstruct conversations exactly as they occurred, especially those that took place many years ago. However, conversations used here were reconstructed from information in court records or from the recollections of at least two of the participants or bystanders. The only exceptions were two-party conversations in which one of the two has since died or didn't respond to my requests for an interview. In many cases, one of the two participants didn't remember the exact conversation but believed it followed the spirit and intent of the dialogue as I have written it.

I approached Bill McGowan with the idea for this book in December 1983. At that time, he summoned his senior vice-presidents, and I gave them a three-minute synopsis of what I wanted to do: I wanted access to the company's records and its people, to sit in on meetings, and to travel with the senior officials. I would be free to write whatever I wanted, and no one at the company would see a word of the book until it was printed. Whenever I traveled, I would pay my own way. I also promised that all interviews would remain confidential, even from others in the company, until the book was published. I required an empty office to work in and an ID badge that would allow me to travel around the company's buildings freely.

McGowan and a few others liked the idea. Mostly, I believe they were intrigued and flattered with the thought of a book about the company done by an objective reporter. Some didn't like it one bit and tried to quash the project. Two months later, however, those in favor of the book prevailed.

Some people at MCI refused to talk with me. Others talked with me only after months of persistence. I was excluded from just a handful of meetings that were considered sensitive by virtue of the Securities and Exchange Commission's rules governing insider information and its effect on stock prices.

Although many AT&T officials wouldn't talk freely about their company as it related to MCI—mainly because of continuing litigation—some would talk candidly with me if the information they offered was worded so it wouldn't seem as if it had come from them in particular. I honored those requests.

I wish to thank my literary agent, Rafe Sagalyn, for his enthusiasm and hard work and my editor, Jim Frost, for his skill and guidance.

THE NEW BUSINESS—

Prologue
AUGUST 28, 1984

Bill McGowan walked into the most important meeting of his life. This wouldn't be like the hundreds of other ones. He wouldn't get bored and read some industry newsletter and listen with half an ear to other people. He wouldn't get up and leave after two hours, either. That was his usual limit. He got bored easily.

This was action, good action. He hadn't felt the need to visit Las Vegas in years. He satisfied his occasional gambling urges right here. He "bet the company" often. If you're not willing to take chances, why bother? If you can't try new things, make a couple of mistakes, what fun was it?

He didn't do it because the company was invincible. Some people thought it was. They figured the company had made it and would always be around. Hadn't it established once and forever its legal right to exist and compete in an industry once monopolized by AT&T, the world's largest company? And wasn't it pulling in almost $2 billion a year? Hadn't it been cited time and time again by business magazines and newspapers as having the best managers in the world, the most aggressive and unique strategies, and the fastest growth of almost any company ever? Wasn't it responsible for putting the entire telephone industry up for grabs, not only in the United States but overseas as well—$55 billion to anyone who had the guts to go after it?

No, McGowan knew better than that. The company hadn't made it.

13

Anyone who thought so didn't belong in the company. Sure, it was successful—in the past—at all the *other* businesses it was in. It had former lives, past businesses that it focused on and succeeded in before it moved forward to the next. That was McGowan's greatest strength, knowing what business the company was in, and even though other things had to be done, one business took priority. There was the "getting the license" business, the "litigation" business, the "survival" business, and others. Yes, it was successful at those, but now things were all new, all different. They were entering a new phase, a new business. The slate was clean, and whether the company would succeed or fail was unknown. What McGowan did know was that all the company's resources had to be channeled into the *new* business, the "equal access" business.

For the first time, the playing field was almost level. All competitors were the same. The ground rules had been written, and the contest was beginning. It was time to put up or shut up. No more luck, no more excuses. If this phase wasn't successful, the company would die. All those things that McGowan had said in the past would be lies. All that the company stood for, all the new management techniques it fostered would be relegated to a couple of pages in some business school's case study course.

The company was grounded in the belief that telecommunications was the vehicle of the information age. Much like railroads and trucks moved the manufactured goods of the industrial age, telecommunications would be the conduit of this new commodity—information.

McGowan had spent most of his adult life preparing for this new age. Now he believed the company was ready. Everything was in place for it to become the world's premiere telecommunications company. It had spent more than a billion dollars building a domestic long-distance network second only to AT&T's. It had begun service to other countries, getting ready for that "global community" where anyone in the world is just a phone call away. It had established an "electronic mail" business, allowing people to communicate over their computers. It had a finger in paging networks, car telephone systems, fiber optics, microwave networks, satellites—all the foundations of the new telecommunications infrastructure. He would tell you that it all came down to filling in a basic two-by-two matrix: Domestic/International: Voice/Data. Whatever it is, he wanted the company to do it. He was betting that there could never be too much capacity and that his company would be more efficient at handling it than anyone else.

He had established a company that businesspeople thought typified the new age. It was mean and lean. It gave employees the chance to grow along with it and rewarded those who made the company money. It provided a challenge to anyone willing to accept it. It broke a lot of corporate rules along the way and took a lot of flak for it.

McGowan had driven hard, working almost seven days a week for nearly twenty years. Unlike the typical corporate chairman, he never married; the company and its employees were his family. He smoked too many cigarettes; drank a bit too much as well, his colleagues used to tell him, until they finally gave up. He did stop once, cold turkey, about ten years ago, but he was hell to work with. They were happy, but also sad, to see him start again.

He had always told his top managers that they should look ahead five or ten years and then look back at now. "What do you wish you had done back then, to get where you want to be now?" he asked. It was a favorite game, one that allowed long-term planning often to the detriment of short-term gains. That had always been the problem with Wall Street. They looked at the short term; he believed in looking ahead. Short-term setbacks caused the stock to drop like crazy during some years, and that scared off investors. A year ago, McGowan was losing more than a million dollars a day from his personal portfolio. It didn't really bother him, though; he wasn't in it just for the money. He was in it for the challenge, the rush.

Now was one of those times when the company was out of favor with "the Street." After ten straight quarters of growth, the company that was called everything from "high flier" to "high-tech wonder" was losing money. Profits were down and would be down again the next quarter. The stock had slipped to its lowest price in nearly four years. Ardent company boosters, those who had been passionate cheerleaders in the past, were beginning to doubt if McGowan could really pull this thing off.

Even though AT&T was still reeling from its massive divestiture, it wouldn't take long for it to get up to speed. For now, AT&T was still partially regulated by the government because of its huge market presence, but that was changing. Other competitors were getting wise, too. They couldn't be laughed off anymore. Some people didn't think it was the best time to change the entire company. It might show they were really in trouble. How would it look to the outside world?

The biggest threat was not from the outside, though. It was from within the company itself. Bureaucracy was creeping in slowly, but surely, threatening to do to the company what its competitors could not—bring it to a dead stop. The company couldn't afford to move slowly now. It couldn't stand to get fat, particularly now when it would have to move fast to survive. It was heading that way, all right, and now was the time to stop it.

The company had once moved like lightning. It had seized opportunities and made quick decisions on the run while the others were still talking. That was the real secret of its success. Keep moving. Keep moving. Focus on the business. Focus on the business.

Three years ago, McGowan wanted to decentralize the company, put jobs out in the field where they belonged, but he was stymied. He wasn't convinced then that the company had the right people for these very special jobs. Each person would take control of a company, a clone of the big company but with a difference. Each would have absolute control. Almost all functions would leave the Washington, D.C., headquarters and reside in the field. Each president could organize it any way he wanted to, do things the way he wanted to do them, and no one at headquarters would argue or criticize as long as it worked. The company had to get close to its customers again. It had to get a handle on its tremendous growth. Most important, in an age of vicious competition, it had to do all the little things right. A big company just couldn't work anymore.

Unlike decentralization attempts at other companies that were merely cosmetic, McGowan wanted this one to be for real. Anything that didn't have to be done at headquarters went out. It was better to err on the side of letting them have too much control than too little. What he was really counting on to show that he was serious was the unspoken message he sent to the company's ten thousand employees by totally dismantling his management team in Washington and sending them out to run the regions. At most other companies, that move might be considered political suicide. A company chairman not surrounded by his deputies was often deemed impotent and crippled. Here it was a necessary risk if this idea was to work.

The details of the plan had been talked about for months. Everyone knew who was getting the new top jobs, but this was the first time that all the new presidents were assembled and told what was expected of them. Together, they would hear how the whole thing was going to work.

As usual, McGowan walked around, cracked some jokes. Business was serious, but it didn't have to be somber. Why shouldn't he and everyone else enjoy themselves?

He walked behind the podium, and everyone settled in. It was uncharacteristically bland of McGowan to use clichés, but on this occasion he did. He told the new presidents, "This is the first day of the rest of our life. MCI is a new company."

THE FIRST BUSINESS—

Getting the License
1960—68

Jack Goeken and his buddies were just trying to sell some more two-way radios. Shucks, they were just hoping to make a couple of extra bucks. They didn't know they were starting a multibillion-dollar company that would eventually break up the world's largest monopoly. Hatch a whole new industry? Geeze, they were just trying to keep their store open a little longer.

Jack and his Joliet, Illinois, crowd convinced General Electric to let them establish a two-way radio franchise in Springfield, about 190 miles to the south. It was the state capital, and it didn't have a GE dealer. With all the trucks traveling between Chicago and St. Louis along Route 66, it was a natural. They could sell lots of radios there.

Mobile radios had a range of about ten to fifteen miles. By building repeater stations on hills or high metal towers—to relay the signal over a larger area—they could extend the range to about thirty miles. The only trouble was that once a truck driver left Chicago or St. Louis and drove more than thirty miles, he was out of range. If he had to make a last-minute pickup, in Springfield, say, he was out of luck. So Jack and his pals figured if they could extend the range of those mobile radios to cover the entire 290-mile route, they could not only sell more radios but keep the Springfield dealership alive above the shouts of GE's franchisee in Champaign, who believed it was really his territory anyway. Besides, several of the gang had girlfriends in Springfield whom they visited on their weekly trips from Joliet. Keeping the dealership open became even more important.

So Jack devised a scheme whereby mobile radio repeating stations could be linked together along the route. Eleven, spaced every twenty-five miles or so, would do the trick. Wherever a trucker roamed, he could stay in touch. Even if he was somewhere in the middle, he could be contacted by a dispatcher at either end.

Something else dawned on the Joliet group but not until later. Not only could truckers use the two-way radio system, but the dispatcher in Chicago could talk to the dispatcher in St. Louis without going through the telephone system. His message would hip-hop across the farmland from repeater to repeater. If several different companies in Chicago and St. Louis wired themselves into the ends of this repeater network, the Bell System, which had the lock on communications in the United States, was out of the picture. The boys figured they had something here, but they weren't sure exactly what. They were still out to sell more radios.

About this time, the early 1960s, businesses were becoming increasingly unhappy with telephone service from AT&T. They couldn't get the services they needed; only what AT&T wanted to give them. It was not a matter of technology, but a matter of monopoly power. News organizations, for instance, were forced to pay for large-capacity circuits, even though they only needed a small portion of it a few times a day to connect their teletype machines. Take it or leave it. Airline companies that needed high-capacity lines to connect their busy computer terminals had to settle for less efficient transmission facilities. Tough.

In 1959, the Federal Communications Commission, a government agency set up in 1934 to regulate the telephone giant, had partially given in to complaints from large business users by allowing them to build their own private microwave networks. Companies such as Lockheed and Boeing could build the kind of customized system they needed but only for internal communications among branch offices.

For the first time, AT&T got worried and proposed a service called Tel-Pak in an effort to prevent these private-line networks from being built. The theory was simple: Give big businesses a service cheaper than they could build it, and they wouldn't build it. Even if it wasn't exactly what they needed, make it cheap enough, and they wouldn't leave Ma Bell's fold.

Tel-Pak was a sham. Even the FCC, which usually gave the

regulated company anything it asked for, winced at the idea. The plan called for large AT&T customers, the ones who could conceivably build their own networks, to get an 80 percent discount on their calls. Midsize companies, who could go either way, would get a 50 percent discount. Small companies and residential users who had no choice but to use AT&T wouldn't get any discounts at all. In fact, they would be making up the difference for the other users.

Tel-Pak was so unfair the FCC finally rejected it, even after AT&T changed it several times and gave it several different names to make it look respectable. It got people in Washington thinking, though. Perhaps there really was something wrong with the way AT&T ran its business. Maybe it really was a monopoly out of control, abusing its power.

Jack was starting to sense the growing unhappiness with AT&T, too, and he spent the next few months talking to small telephone customers to see what it was they really wanted. He discovered that they wanted flexibility. They wanted an "electronic pipe" that they could use to send any kind of information they had: voice, TV pictures, teletype, computer data, anything. He also realized that they all didn't need the pipe at the same time, and so it could be shared among a bunch of companies rather than sitting idle. They wanted a system in which you only paid for what you used and how long you used it. More important, Jack realized that AT&T didn't care about smaller users. Tel-Pak showed they wanted to woo the larger customers and let the smaller ones fend for themselves. He saw a latent market serving the small guy.

Jack figured the Bell System might even support him. After all, they weren't offering this type of service, and besides, he would be handing the local Bell Operating Companies a lot of business when he asked them to connect local customers into his pipe. He also knew that although AT&T had a de facto monopoly on long distance, it wasn't a legal monopoly. They could not stop him from building his service, which, if Jack was successful, would return maybe 1/60,000 of Bell's yearly revenue the first year.

What Jack didn't realize was that AT&T's arrogance and egotism would not let him take even a penny of its potential profits. They were to fight the Joilet farm boy with a high school education with everything they had. Ironically, it was that attitude that finally caused Jack's fledgling business to become successful. If AT&T had helped him or even ignored him, his business would have certainly failed.

Jack and the Joliet crowd were not the first to try to build a private microwave system that could be shared by many users. Some big companies had tried before and failed. Westinghouse and Raytheon, each hoping to sell companies its microwave equipment, had fought AT&T and lost, mainly because AT&T exerted tremendous political and economic pressures on them to quit. It just wasn't worth the trouble, and they gave up. By playing the game by the rules, rules which AT&T knew inside and out and even helped write, nobody could touch them. Jack, however, couldn't play by the rules because he didn't know them. His naïveté, unsophisticated manner, and primitive intuition were his greatest strengths. He also had nothing to lose.

Each of the Joliet Five contributed $600 each for a total of $3,000. That would be their war chest to fight the largest monopoly in the world.

After going to the Federal Communications Commission in Washington in December 1963 to apply for a license to operate the microwave system, Jack learned that he might need state certification. So he traveled to the Illinois Commerce Commission to get certified as a common carrier, a status given to government-regulated companies such as buses, taxicabs, electrical utilities, and gas companies. The state regulators were amused by Jack and his idea, didn't take him very seriously, but gave him two days of hearings each month anyway. Each day was cut short around 11 A.M. so Illinois Bell lawyers could take the regulators to a long lunch, leaving Jack and his group the equivalent of one day a month in which to argue their case.

Regulators in Illinois and other states didn't understand the telephone industry; most of their time was spent regulating trucks, electricity, and natural gas pipelines. Telephones were something you picked up and talked into. When Illinois Bell said they needed a local rate increase or wanted to change an offering, the Commerce Commission rarely said no. The figures they submitted to justify any sort of action were so complicated they had to be correct.

Jack was getting nowhere until he met Mike Bader, a Washington attorney. Jack met him through Mike Bader's neighbor in Georgetown during one of Jack's frequent trips to the Capital. Mike Bader worked on the cutting edge of law at the time. His specialty was communications, a rather new legal discipline. Because there was no communications industry outside of AT&T, he worked mostly on broadcast matters, filing licenses for TV and radio stations. He had, however, some experience with microwave licensing because he had written a tariff (a government term for how much and under what conditions a regulated industry may serve its customers) for the first operational microwave carrier company to serve cable TV. He also worked on some of the first tariffs for pocket-paging companies.

Mike Bader sensed there was a change in the air—that maybe, just maybe, if someone like Jack came along and challenged AT&T with a commonsense approach instead of trying to fight them on legal technicalities, he might have a chance. He knew it would take someone small, like the Joliet Five, to make it work. Large companies just didn't have the ability or tenacity to fight the long fight. They found it impossible to commit lawyers and money and justify to shareholders that they were going to compete with the Bell System. It sounded absurd. However, Mike Bader saw the seeds of competition in the FCC's 1959 decision to allow private microwave networks. More important, Mike Bader saw in Jack something else: a way to make a mark, to do good, to really make a difference.

Jack abandoned his battle at the Illinois Commerce Commission after Mike Bader told him that because the network crossed state lines, the FCC had jurisdiction and not the state of Illinois. The Illinois regulators were happy to see Jack go; they could get back to their lunches in peace and quiet.

With little formal education, Jack designed his microwave system out of Mike Bader's Xerox room. Sometimes, he would find an empty FCC office and drafting table and make believe he belonged there. Often, he would study AT&T's technical documents on file at the FCC and learn from them.

He didn't understand much of what he saw. His sole education had been gained during high school when he worked afternoons in a radio shop which was subletted from a Kirby vacuum cleaner store. Television was just arriving on the scene, and only bars had them. Jack was too young to enter the taverns, so he never saw a TV up close until a church youth club called his radio shop and asked if he could fix their TV set. "Oh, yeah, we do a lot of that," Jack told them. To avoid looking like he didn't know what he was doing, Jack brought the set into the shop to work on it. He took the set apart, studied how it worked, and fixed it. From that day on, they were in the TV repair business.

Kirby moved out, and Jack and his friends took over the entire store and wanted to branch out into the aircraft radio business. Joliet Municipal Airport was nearby, and it looked like good work. They began Mainline Electronics, Inc., at the airport.

Jack needed a government license to work on aircraft radios. The Federal Aviation Administration examiner refused to give Jack the license test, saying that he needed a college degree. Jack wouldn't take no for an answer. He found the rules, and although it implied that a degree was necessary, it wasn't the law. Jack persuaded the examiner to give him the test, and he passed. Persistence paid off.

With that same doggedness, Jack designed his microwave network. He learned about microwave towers as chief engineer of two local radio stations. He also picked up experience hanging around the airport microwave stations. His system was crude, but it would work— and cost a lot less than AT&T. He said that AT&T didn't care how much it spent on its network. The costs would be passed through to the rate payer, who had no choice but to pay his bill. In addition, the more AT&T spent, the more it got back as part of its guaranteed rate of return. At that time, it was 7 percent. No one at the FCC or anywhere else could knowledgeably argue that AT&T spent too much money because no one knew how much a network was supposed to cost. Only AT&T knew that. No yardstick existed to judge whether AT&T was spending its money wisely. Jack would provide that yardstick.

Jack claimed he could lease the land for each of eleven microwave sites for $560 a year. He would spend $250 for an enclosure (a Sears, Roebuck shed), $700 for an antenna, and $150 for a tower to hold the antenna. He would use $13 guy wires to hold up the tower. Jack proposed that his towers be erected where four properties met and the tower built adjacent to the crisscrossing of existing fences. Therefore, he didn't use valuable farmland, and farmers wouldn't charge him very much. The total cost, excluding radio equipment, would be about $1,100 a site plus $560 a year rental.

AT&T said it couldn't be done. They had been in this business longer than Jack, longer than anyone in the world, in fact, and the cost, they had sworn to the government for years and years, was higher. AT&T would buy a section of prime farmland for $50,000, build a $30,000 building complete with rest room facilities and, for protection, a $20,000 fence. Total cost was $100,000 per site.

During hearings at the FCC, Jack said his system didn't need washroom facilities. His technicians were raised on farms and knew how to go in the fields.

AT&T also attacked Jack's technical ability, saying that his system could not possibly work on the ground that he was not an engineer. AT&T said his network was flimsy and poorly designed. They were prepared to produce streams of expert witnesses to testify before the FCC that Jack and his crazy company, Microwave Communications, Inc., or "MCI" as it became known at the federal agency, was a waste of everyone's time and that the FCC had better things to do than pay attention to this buffoon who talked like Casey Stengel, had little education, and didn't own more than one suit.

That's when Jack and Mike Bader knew they had a winner. If AT&T hadn't decided to fight MCI's application, he would have faded away like all the rest. Just the mere fact that AT&T was ready to stop him legitimized his idea automatically. Whether it would work or not, or whether people would buy the service, almost didn't matter. Potential financial backers, who had at first dismissed Jack's crazy scheme, began to take another look.

Mike Bader knew the story of Hush-A-Phone and how AT&T had tried to crush a small company over an insignificant device that had been used since 1921. As the story goes, in the late 1940s, a young, ambitious AT&T lawyer was strolling in downtown Manhattan when he saw in a store window a device called Hush-A-Phone. The Hush-A-Phone clamped over the mouthpiece of the phone and allowed someone to talk softly into the phone without people nearby overhearing him. It sold for a few dollars and required no electrical connections to the phone at all.

The lawyer bought one and took it back to AT&T headquarters at 195 Broadway to show his co-workers, who became incensed that anyone had the audacity to connect anything to the sacred Bell network. Absurd as it sounds, AT&T fought Hush-A-Phone with the claim that someone using the non–Bell-manufactured device in New York City, for instance, would destroy Bell's long-distance network so someone in Texas wouldn't be able to call his mom in California. AT&T took its case to the FCC, which believed AT&T's claim that little Hush-A-Phone would ruin the nation's phone system. The Hush-A-Phone Corporation took the case before the U.S. Court of Appeals, which decided that just because AT&T didn't make something for its phone system was no reason to prevent others from doing so. It ordered the FCC to change its decision.

AT&T shot itself in the foot, as lawyers like to say in Washington. The Hush-A-Phone case, because it was formally brought before the FCC and the courts, set a legal precedent that allowed harmless non-Bell equipment to be connected to the network for the first time. Anyone could manufacture and sell such telephone equipment and connect it to the Bell System. Later, companies cited the Hush-A-Phone case when they wanted to connect more intricate devices to the phone system. AT&T, which manufactured telephone equipment through its Western Electric subsidiary, brought competition upon itself by trying to destroy Hush-A-Phone.

Mike Bader knew he was in for a fight. If AT&T resisted Hush-A-Phone, imagine how they would respond to Jack's idea. Just how much of a fight, or how vicious it would become, neither he nor anyone else could have ever envisioned.

While fixing radios at Joliet Airport, Jack and his friends learned how to fly. No matter how poor he was, Jack always had a plane to fly—either his, one he borrowed, or one he rented. Somehow, he always had wings.

By now, Jack was flying all over the country, meeting with people about his plans, trying to raise money, and learning all he could about engineering from AT&T documents filed at the FCC. He was getting ready for the long-drawn-out process that always followed any FCC filing.

Jack knew that one of AT&T's main arguments against him was how much his system would cost to build and how much he would have to charge for the service. Although he couldn't get any information at the FCC, he heard about a confidential report that AT&T had commissioned about owning and operating microwave systems. That report, if he could get it, would help Jack's case.

On a cold Sunday night, Jack had flown to Hartford, Connecticut, on a whim. Someone had put a bug in his ear that insurance companies had lots of money to invest in new ventures. Moreover, they were large users of communications and might find merit in Jack's plans to save them money on their phone bills. Jack knew that Hartford had lots of insurance companies, so he went to visit them. He was taken aback when the several people he talked to didn't understand what he was trying to accomplish. Fight the Bell System with no assets? They couldn't get over it. "No, we have assets," Jack said very seriously. "I have this plane, and in five years it will be paid for."

Jack wasn't discouraged and set off to New York City to call on communications managers of companies and also to get a copy of the AT&T pricing report. In his own naïve way, he thought if he asked nicely, they might just give it to him.

Hartford experienced a blizzard that Sunday night and Monday, and by Tuesday the city was covered with several feet of snow. Jack borrowed a shovel to dig out his plane so he could taxi it to the plowed runway. The sun was hot and bright despite the low temperature, and after a few minutes of digging, Jack found himself sweating and took off his heavy overcoat. After he finished digging, he fueled the plane on a borrowed credit card and took off for New York, but he forgot his coat.

That turned out to be one of the best mistakes he ever made.

New York was clear, the sky was blue, and Jack got by with just a sports coat. He took a taxi to his meetings in Manhattan, and after talking with several managers on Tuesday and Wednesday, Jack prepared to call on AT&T.

On Thursday, a storm like the one in Hartford hit New York. Jack was cold and wet and stopped off at a diner for soup to shake off the chill. When the waitresses saw this wet mass of a man, they offered to buy him a coat. "Here I am trying to fight the largest company in the world, tell the government I'm financially stable, and some waitresses want to buy me a coat," he thought. "No thanks; I got one. I just forgot it," he said, embarrassed.

When he got to the AT&T building, Jack went to the bathroom to wipe his clothes with paper towels. He had the name of someone to see about the study and headed for his office. When he arrived, the man was out, so he asked a woman in the office how he could go about getting the document.

She thought Jack worked there. It was snowing outside, and he had no boots, no hat, no scarf, no overcoat. He had to be an AT&T employee. She said the report was in the library, and when Jack asked where—meaning where is the library—she thought he meant where *in* the library and gave him an official interoffice request with the document name and number. Something told Jack to keep his mouth shut except to say thank you.

Jack handed the librarian the paper, and she came back with the report stamped "for internal use only." Jack knew he would have to give the original to the FCC, but he wanted one for himself, so he asked for another copy. Why not?—he was on a roll. Moments later she returned with an extra copy, including the paper wrapper marked "confidential."

The report was to become pivotal to Jack's presentation at the FCC. MCI said in its application that if the Chicago-to-St. Louis route worked, it would expand nationwide. AT&T claimed that MCI's cost estimates were too low, that it would end up costing them five times what they claimed. That being the case, AT&T argued, MCI would be forced to charge higher rates than AT&T, nobody would use them, the public wouldn't be served, and therefore, their license shouldn't be granted. Knowing that no one really knew the true figures except them, AT&T thought they had Jack stymied.

But they didn't take into account Jack's forgetting his overcoat. During subsequent filing and appeals before the FCC, AT&T produced economists who confirmed their five-times-too-high figures. AT&T even denied they had any studies to the contrary.

That is, until Jack showed the report to the FCC.

The application and hearings process dragged on for more than four years. MCI filed its application, then AT&T filed to deny the application; then MCI filed to deny AT&T's file to deny their file. Western Union Telegraph Co. and General Telephone & Electronics also opposed Jack and filed petitions against him. They didn't really care much about MCI. Its impact was minuscule, but they pay their lawyers to routinely oppose anything at the FCC that affects their businesses. When lawyers die and go to heaven, some people think they go to Washington.

During that time, Jack, now deeply in debt, relied on his street sense to live. People felt sorry for him and let him use their offices. Mike Bader, only sometimes getting paid, helped Jack in his spare time and let him use his law library. Jack could often be seen walking into large companies and using the Xerox room before anyone asked if he worked there. His wife turned in soda bottles at the store for food money. Jack flew his plane and charged the gas to credit cards cajoled from friends. One of his favorite ploys was to charge a rental car to travel from the airport to the city and back and abandon the car somewhere at the terminal. He would argue with the rental agency later. Anyway, when Hertz cut him off, there was always Avis and Budget and on and on.

The more the Bell System fought him, the stronger Jack's resolve became. Corny as it sounded, Jack truly believed that he had a constitutional right to try his system. If it failed, fine, okay, he would drop it. But he believed he had the right to fail.

Jack would stay away from home for weeks at a time to avoid the cost of flying back to Joliet. When he got home, stacks of mail, mostly bills from people threatening to sue him if he didn't pay, greeted him. In fact, the state of Illinois once sued Jack for $286.70 in back taxes on his radio company, Mainline.

On one of his trips home, Jack approached the mountain of mail with apprehension. Which credit cards would be useless now? Who is going to sue me? He received a letter from Dr. Manley Irwin at the University of New Hampshire, who wrote that he had been following Jack's case at the FCC, and would he send him some copies of the filings? "All I need now is to start sending stuff to some goofy professor," Jack thought. With that, he threw the letter in the wastebasket.

About two hours later, it bothered Jack. This guy was nice enough to show interest in the case; the least he could do is answer him. So Jack retrieved the tossed letter and sent Irwin some copies of filings.

If he hadn't pulled that letter out, there might not be an MCI. Irwin was the kind of person Jack would have given his right arm to know. He did consulting work for the FCC and the Senate Committee on Small Business. Because of Irwin, the subcommittee pressured the FCC not to charge Jack $1,200 for a minor change in his application. At that time, MCI didn't have $1,200, and had the FCC insisted, Jack and MCI might have gone bankrupt.

Jack didn't have to learn the lesson of being nice, but the Irwin incident taught him never to close any avenue of possibility. He had to talk to anyone who would listen.

Toward the end of his paper chase at the FCC, Jack was feeling down, depressed over whether the FCC would really grant him a license after coming this far. It was down to the wire, and the only thing left to do was prepare himself for the formal hearing process where he would be questioned by attorneys from the Bell System and elsewhere.

Feeling tired and lonely, Jack went into an Irish bar that he had passed many times before. He figured he would drink some beer, listen to some lively music, and forget his troubles.

As it turned out, the tavern wasn't Irish, and it had no music. Jack walked to the bar and had a beer anyway. All of a sudden, he felt a tap on his shoulder. "Hey, don't I know you from Joliet? Don't you have a

radio store?" the man asked. Jack was startled. Here he was in
Washington, meeting a guy who had once come into his radio shop in
Joliet.

They became beer friends, and Jack would stay at his house outside
of Washington whenever he was in town. That would at least save Jack
from staying at the President Hotel, where he had to sleep with his
jacket on to keep the cockroaches from crawling on him.

One day, he was having a drink at his pal's house waiting for two
dates to show up. One of the girls, Jack had been told, was unmarried
and pregnant. She wanted an abortion but didn't know where to get it.

When the dates arrived, Jack's friend and his girlfriend left, leaving
Jack and the other behind. Jack felt awkward, but they got to talking,
and Jack said he could help. It was the TV repair story all over again.
He didn't know what to do, but he would do something. He told the
woman to give him a urine specimen the next day—that sounded like
something someone who knew what he was doing would say—and
asked her where she worked. "The FCC, Common Carrier Bureau,"
she said. Bingo! Jack was living right, it seemed.

The next day, Jack was working at the FCC hunched over a drafting
table tracing AT&T's microwave routes so MCI's system wouldn't
cause it radio interference. She brought in the specimen bottle in a
paper bag and put it on the edge of the table. Jack said thanks, that he
would take care of it, even though he still wasn't sure what to do with
the bottle. He thought he might fly it back to Joliet, where one of his
contacts at the sheriff's department might know what to do.

Fortunately, Jack didn't have to do anything with the specimen after
all. The woman miscarried shortly thereafter but was so grateful to Jack
that she said she owed him one.

The payoff came months later when she gave Jack a confidential
document outlining the exact concerns the FCC's Common Carrier
Bureau had about MCI's application.

Jack showed the document to Mike Bader, who immediately told
him, "What, are you crazy? Don't you see what this says: 'Confidential'? Do you know what they'll do to you if they know you have this?"
Jack figured that was the least of his worries, and after he calmed Mike
Bader, the two went through the document point by point being
careful not to be too well prepared to answer the FCC's questions when
the time came.

The FCC decided to hold formal hearings, which were to begin in February 1967. The odds seemed stacked against MCI: Jack and Mike Bader against AT&T attorneys and attorneys for each of the local Bell Operating Companies, not to mention Western Union and a few other interested parties. More than a dozen against two. Jack couldn't find any companies willing to testify on his behalf. He understood the pressure that AT&T could heap on them if they opposed Ma Bell. AT&T probably wouldn't retaliate against a customer, but companies weren't willing to take the risk of alienating the only company that provided telephone service.

Jack didn't hold any grudges against communications managers who supported him privately but not publicly. He understood that their jobs were at stake. He also didn't bear ill will against the AT&T lawyers who were against him. He knew they were just doing what they were supposed to do. Jack made sure to be polite and say good-bye to them at the end of each hearing day. Only one lawyer took it all personally, Jack thought: Gordon Winks, an attorney for Illinois Bell. Mr. Winks knew Jack from Springfield, where he had tried to prevent his certification by the Illinois Commerce Commission. He couldn't forgive Jack for going against the sacred Bell System. Moreover, Mr. Winks didn't want to be remembered as the lawyer from the Bell region that allowed the first outsider to penetrate. It was a matter of honor.

One day, he refused to ride in an elevator with Jack after a hearing. Winks was also the one who told the FCC that Jack was once sued for back taxes.

At FCC hearings, once a lawyer asks all his questions, he can't ask any more. He is done, and the next lawyer gets his shot. But AT&T double-teamed Jack. When someone from a Bell company would ask a question and was satisfied with the answer, he would sit down. If he got an afterthought about another question, he would whisper it to the next Bell attorney, who would ask the question. Jack's testimony alone filled three thousand pages.

During that same period, Jack and Mike Bader testified before the House Subcommittee on Small Business about Jack's fight to start a business. He told them that so far he had spent $110,000 just on paperwork and travel and expected to spend about $50,000 more before he even received a license.

Despite the importance of Jack's battle, he received little notice in the press except for trade journals. Later, Jack befriended a reporter who covered the telephone industry for *Business Week* in Washington and tried to get him interested in the case. Perhaps he just wanted the reporter to take him to lunch. Bill Hickman, who wrote *Talking Moons*, a prophetic look at the communications satellite industry, was fascinated by Jack's concept, but couldn't sell the idea of coming competition in the phone industry to his New York editors. They just didn't believe it was possible.

During the FCC hearings, the hearing examiner, Herbert Sharfman, heard much conflicting testimony from both sides. Both sides, naturally, offered self-serving testimony, and no one knew who was telling the truth. AT&T, however, had been caught rather blatantly several times, while Jack seemed unflappable or, at the very least, consistent.

One time, for example, during examination by AT&T attorneys, a Bell Labs engineer was asked how far apart microwave towers could be placed for proper transmission. AT&T was trying to show the examiner that MCI's towers were too far apart to work because two sites were over twenty-six miles apart, and that was beyond accepted practice. After offering credentials establishing himself as an expert and saying that he had designed many microwave systems, he stated that he wouldn't go over twenty miles, but that you could stretch it to twenty-two. He added that some engineers would tell you twenty-four miles was the limit.

Jack took the stand in rebuttal and stated that he had no formal engineering credentials and that this was the first microwave system he had built. When asked about the engineer's contention that MCI's microwave towers were too far apart to work, Jack produced exhibits showing that AT&T's own system, according to FCC maps, used towers that were thirty-two, thirty-four, even thirty-six miles apart.

The entire hearing went like that. Finally, Sharfman called a halt in mid-April, two months after the hearings began, and the docket was closed. All that remained was for each side to summarize its arguments and let the FCC rule. The seven FCC commissioners would vote on Jack's license, and they usually followed the recommendations of the Common Carrier Bureau and the hearing examiner.

There was nothing left to do but wait. What Jack didn't know was that the FCC Common Carrier Bureau was planning to recommend to the full commission that they deny his license application.

Dr. Irwin and Jack met in Washington one Monday, and Jack was filling him in on the latest progress over dinner that night. That afternoon, the two visited Bernie Strassberg, who was then chief of the Common Carrier Bureau. The three had a nice chat and talked about everything but MCI. As they turned to leave the office, Bernie told Dr. Irwin that the bureau was going to turn down MCI at the Wednesday FCC meeting. Dr. Irwin was shattered but didn't show it. He just said, "Fine, okay," and caught up with Jack, who was already down the hallway.

That night, Irwin felt terrible about this poor bastard who had no idea what was going to happen to him in just two days. Jack was telling him about all the progress, how well he thought things were going, but Dr. Irwin never let slip what he knew.

After dinner, Jack saw Irwin, who rarely drank, get rip-roaring drunk. He was holding such bad news in that he got smashed to relieve the tension. This straight-arrow professor even got up and danced onstage with a go-go dancer. Jack had to put him to bed that night.

The next morning, Irwin met with Bernie Strassberg and told him that he shouldn't turn down MCI. Bernie said for him to come in Wednesday with his version of why they shouldn't, because he already had his staff's version as to why they should, and he would take it all into consideration. He would make his decision the morning of the meeting.

Jack's luck held. On Wednesday, Bill Lesher, chief of the FCC staff and the only bureau member adamantly opposed to MCI, was making a speech at the University of Michigan. He wasn't there to persuade Bernie that morning, so Dr. Irwin's arguments carried more weight. He was there, after all, doing a strong selling job. The Common Carrier Bureau recommended that the commissioners vote to give Jack his license.

A few months later, in October 1967, the hearing examiner filed his report in favor of granting MCI a license. Now, for the first time, almost four years after it began, the signs were there. It looked like the FCC would give Jack the right to begin his service between Chicago and St. Louis.

Some loose ends still needed to be tied, i's had to be dotted and t's had to be crossed, and the full FCC was not to vote and grant the license until August 1969. Jack was getting ready, however, trying to raise money, preparing for the business to begin.

He knew that once they won, others would try to do the same thing. So the winner would be the firstest with the mostest, and that required large amounts of money.

Brilliant man that he was, Jack never had a head for big money, and the amounts he would have to raise were out of his league. A lawyer named John Worthington, from Jenner & Block, a Chicago law firm that had worked for MCI, wanted Jack to meet Bill McGowan—a wizard, he said, at getting companies started. He knew how to talk to bankers. His speciality was raising venture capital.

Jack resisted. He believed that he could do it himself. He put off meeting McGowan several times, but at the insistence of others at MCI—especially Tom Hermes, a vice-president of Rand McNally—Jack finally gave in. Hermes was not an original partner but took control of his brother's estate when he died. As he went through his papers, he saw documents saying that his brother, George, owned a quarter of something called Microwave Communications, Inc. Hermes also saw the names of Kenneth Garthe, Leonard Barnett, Nicholas Philips, and John Goeken.

When they met, Jack didn't like McGowan. He was too sophisticated for him, too polished, a Harvard Business School graduate who might one day take control of MCI and leave Jack behind. He didn't trust McGowan.

McGowan saw in Jack a future-thinking genius with so much common sense but so little business sense it could make you cry. He also saw a man who was honest and down-to-earth but couldn't balance a checkbook because he misplaced it all the time. He saw in MCI a company that needed his Midas touch for managing and raising money and a company that might make some big bucks.

Both first impressions would be absolutely right.

THE SECOND BUSINESS—

Raising Venture Capital

1968—71

1

Bill McGowan was born in Ashley, Pennsylvania, near Wilkes-Barre/Scranton. The town didn't have very much going for it except some coal mines and the railroads that carried the coal away. His father was an engineer on the Central Railroad of New Jersey, one of six lines that went through or ended in Ashley. As the coal became exhausted, the railroad companies continued to use Ashley as a place to exchange their freight cars to route them to different lines. McGowan worked on the railroad at night and went to high school during the day. He had many different jobs—dispatcher, car checker, clerk, weigh-station attendant—and the idea was to qualify for as many jobs as possible so his name would show up on many different lists when it came time for the "shape-up."

All of the five McGowan children, one girl and four boys, were taught that they could do anything they wanted as long as they put their minds to it. There was a strong emphasis placed on independence and education. Their mother had been a schoolteacher, and their father finished high school at night, having begun as a railroad braker boy at age twelve. It was expected that all the children would not only finish high school but attend college as well. By age fifteen, McGowan's sister, Lenore, had already graduated from high school.

McGowan went to the University of Scranton and majored in chemistry. He didn't particularly like the subject, but he found that he could easily memorize the formulas and equations and pass tests without much trouble. The goal was to get a college degree, and this seemed like a painless way to do it. After being drafted and serving in the Army, he returned to the area and enrolled in Kings College under the G.I. Bill. Kings was a newly formed school in Wilkes-Barre, near his home, and it allowed him to continue working on the railroad at night. The best job was station clerk because a train might go past once an hour and in the times between trains he could sleep on the stationmaster's big desk or indulge in his greatest passion: reading. Even as a young child, McGowan would slip away from family gatherings to read. The family understood this quirk, and nobody felt insulted by his leaving. And nobody disturbed his quiet time. Later, as an adult, he would read at least four hours every day no matter where he was. It was up to those around him to understand that he wasn't necessarily bored with a conversation (although his attention span *was* very short), and he wasn't being rude. It was just his time to hide out and read.

Because Kings College was new, McGowan was able to form a chemistry club and organize field trips to see chemical plants in New Jersey. During one of those trips, he asked one of the guides, "Who runs this thing? What are their backgrounds?" He discovered that chemists didn't run the show; it was always someone with a degree in business or finance. All the chemists worked in laboratories far away from what he perceived as the real action, the fun part. Back home, he hadn't been exposed to business except for the railroad. He didn't know any businessmen. His father didn't know any, and there weren't any in his neighborhood. All he knew, after visiting the plants, was that people called businessmen ran things.

Partially because he wanted to run things, and partially because he didn't know what else to do after college, he applied to Wharton, Harvard, Columbia, and Kent State to become a businessman—whatever that meant. Both Harvard and Wharton accepted McGowan, and he chose Wharton, because Harvard had sent him a form letter saying that if he had any military obligations he should take care of them before going to school. McGowan was annoyed that Harvard apparently hadn't read his application where he stated that he had already served three years in the Army.

A friendly dean at Kings had taken an interest in McGowan, mainly because it was important for a new school to encourage its alumni to continue on to graduate school. He met McGowan in the hallway and asked what school he was going to attend. McGowan said, "I've been accepted to Wharton, and I'm going there."

The dean said, "Well, look, don't be disappointed about not getting into Harvard."

"Oh, no," McGowan answered, "I've been accepted there, too."

"Listen, do you have a couple of minutes to talk about this thing?" the dean said, and the two went to see the college president in his office. There, the president and the dean convinced McGowan that if he got through Harvard he would be better off than if he finished Wharton. It was better respected, its curriculum was sharper, it would open more doors, and so on. (They didn't tell him that it would look better for Kings, too.) They told him to forget that the students were East Coast big-city snobs with names that ended in Roman numerals whose fathers had hospital wings named after their wives. It would be worth it, the president told him, and McGowan was convinced.

The first year at Harvard, McGowan didn't work on the railroad, the first time since he was a teenager that he didn't have a job. He was intimidated by all the Ivy Leaguers and figured he would have to work very hard just to keep up with them. He had put aside enough money to last him for the year. He still had his railroad pass, too, so he could ride home for free whenever he wanted.

At the business school he enjoyed working on "case histories." These were real-life scenarios and problems that had been posed to companies, and students had to figure out the solutions, not necessarily the ones that the companies picked.

To McGowan, many of the answers seemed simple, although not always obvious. He learned quite early that businesses often did things that were much too complicated when simple answers were usually the best. He also discovered that many businessmen didn't understand what business they were really in. The railroads that McGowan knew so well were the perfect example of what not to do. Many went bankrupt because they didn't know what business they were really in. It wasn't the train business; it was the transportation business, and had they addressed themselves to being transportation companies, maybe they would have survived.

In the histories, there was usually more than enough information to come to a reasonable and workable conclusion. McGowan's trick to solving them, which he learned by trial and error, was to absorb as much information as he could, overloading his brain like crazy, then cast aside all the information that wasn't relevant and make decisions based on what was left. The times that he got confused were those in which he didn't see into the heart of the matter but instead got sidetracked by all the peripheral information. Some of that reasoning skill came from his upbringing. All the McGowan children were encouraged to make their own decisions.

During his second semester, McGowan received all D's. In those days, A, B, C, D wasn't used. D was the highest mark possible. It meant "distinction."

During the summers, McGowan found himself a job at Shell Oil in New York City working in a think-tank group that analyzed capital expenditure requests from divisions before they went to corporate headquarters. At Shell, he learned a lesson that would stay with him the rest of his life.

Oil companies had an unwritten policy of not hiring from each other. They did that to prevent "raiding," but what McGowan saw were people who detested their jobs but couldn't take it out in the usual way—by leaving the company—so they stayed on and just hunkered down and became less productive and more unhappy. They knew only one industry, the oil industry, but because they couldn't get hired at another company, they were forced to stay where they were and be miserable. They were trapped. McGowan was fascinated but not surprised by the lack of interest these people had in their company. The job seemed interesting to him, and these were bright people, but during breaks, for example, they talked about their crabgrass, their houses, their children, everything but business. McGowan, who really didn't know anything about the real business world outside of the railroad, wondered, "Is this what happens in business? They didn't tell us about this at the Business School."

Although the oil industry eventually changed that practice over many years, it made a strong impression on McGowan. He decided that if he ever ran a company, employees would have an absolute right to transfer within the company no matter what, and if an employee wanted to leave altogether, there would be no bad feelings. He could even come back at a later time without prejudice if he wanted to.

McGowan graduated in the top 5 percent of his class. Because of his good grades, he received a lot of job offers, mostly from large, dull corporations. He wasn't thrilled by any of them. They didn't seem exciting enough.

Through someone at the Business School, McGowan was put in touch with Malcolm Kingsberg, who had been president of RKO

Theater Division in the 1930s. Earlier, Kingsberg had also been a partner in the investment firm of Goldman, Sachs, where his job was to oversee that firm's business with Mike Meehan, a flamboyant stock manipulator. Kingsberg was bent over with spinal arthritis and was looking for someone who could be his arms and legs in a new business he and others were trying to start.

Kingsberg and McGowan met in New York City at the Harvard Club and Kingsberg told him what he was trying to do. He gave McGowan the names of four people to talk with about him, almost like a list of references. Kingsberg wanted to make certain that McGowan knew what he was getting into. One of the people he spoke with told him, "You'll be working for the meanest, nastiest bastard you'll ever meet. But I'll tell you what, if you've got the stomach for it and are willing to put in a couple of years of sheer hell, you will learn more than you learned in all your years at school."

McGowan called the next person. He was a little more polite about it, and simply said, "Mr. Kingsberg has certain expectations about the people who work for him."

The others gave him similar stories about this intolerant, unforgiving taskmaster. But McGowan, looking for a challenge, something out of the ordinary, took the job. Before he began, however, Kingsberg suggested to McGowan that he not tell anyone at the company that he had gone to Harvard. He thought that they would give it negative connotations, that they would think McGowan had book learning but no common sense. It would be a lot easier for McGowan to get along, he said. McGowan agreed and told everyone that he went only to Kings College.

The new company was called Magna-Theatre Corporation. The company owned, and was trying to develop, a film process called Todd-AO. That stood for Todd, as in Mike Todd, one of the partners, and American Optical, the company that had engineered the special camera lenses. Todd-AO was a 70-mm process that allowed widescreen projection with only one camera. Rogers and Hammerstein had joined the company and used the technique for *Oklahoma!* and *South Pacific*. McGowan's job was to negotiate contracts with movie theater owners and persuade them to rip up their projection booths and rebuild them to accommodate the new projectors. He was very good at it.

After three years, McGowan realized that although show business was fun, it wasn't an industry he could succeed in. It was too crazy for him—all the egos, all the insecure people, all the glitter. One event typified it all for him. He saw moviemakers pay $120 for custom-made jeans for cowboy actors while they could have bought a good pair for $19. He would always ask the producers, "How can you tell the difference on the screen?" And the producers would always answer, "That's not important. These people are actors." That stuck in his mind, and McGowan said that if he ever had his own company, he wouldn't pay for trappings that didn't matter.

McGowan didn't know it at the time, but these two personal case histories—the lesson of the high-priced jeans and the story of the unhappy Shell Oil workers—would play a prominent role in the running of MCI.

McGowan stayed in New York City and became an independent consultant. His techniques were simple. Often, he would go into an ailing company and do the opposite of what they were doing. Fifty percent of the time, naturally, it worked. If for example, a company was using first-in, first-out accounting, he had them switch to last-in, first-out accounting. What the hell. It was like the rainmakers in the Midwest who promised farmers they could seed the clouds and cause it to rain. If the rain clocked in at more than average, they would collect a fee. If not, the job was free. They didn't really have to do anything because half the time, the rain would be higher than average. That's what an average means, after all.

McGowan made a lot of money bailing out companies. In one case, his fee came in the form of 25 percent of a loft on New York City's Fourth Avenue. McGowan had never owned real estate before, so he would go over to it every once in a while just to look at it. About nine months later, Mayor Robert Wagner, just before he left office, signed a law that changed the name of that part of Fourth Avenue to "Park Avenue South." Two things happened because of that move. Mail got screwed up for months afterward. Letters meant for Park Avenue South went to Park Avenue addresses. Second, property values on Park Avenue South shot up like crazy because of the prestigious Park Avenue name, and McGowan sold his share of the loft about a year and a half later for $200,000.

Part of that money went to pay a debt that McGowan was forced to cover when one of his business partners went wrong.

Ed Cowett was a Harvard Law School graduate and coauthor of the "Blue Sky Law," a body of regulations that was supposed to prevent investors from putting their money into companies that had about the same value "as a patch of blue sky." Unfortunately, laws varied from state to state, and no definitive guidelines existed. Along with Harvard professor Louis Loss, Cowett analyzed statutes of all states and drafted a model Blue Sky Law that became the standard text on the subject. Blue Sky Laws are used widely in company annual reports and prospectuses. They take the form of disclaimers like: "This company will make money if so and so happens, but it doesn't look good." Then if an investor still wants to invest his money, he can't complain to the Securities and Exchange Commission that the company misrepresented itself or that he wasn't warned.

Cowett's uncle was Malcolm Kingsberg, and he got Ed started in New York by introducing him to the firm of Strook & Strook & Lavan, a Wall Street law firm. Cowett hoped to use law as a business tool and left Strook after he had learned as much as he could.

As coauthor of the "Blue Sky Law," Cowett was an expert in the legalities of marketing and promotion of new, sometimes flimsy, companies. Early in 1959, through his uncle Malcolm, Cowett met McGowan and they started a company called COMAC. CO stood for Cowett, and the MAC stood for McGowan. COMAC invested in new companies making electrical gadgets like intercoms and cordless shavers.

A friend of McGowan's at Harvard Business School had a brother who was an engineer for a company that had developed a jewelry cleaner. The device consisted of a small tub of water into which ultrasonic vibrations were emitted. The water would shake almost imperceptibly and loosen dirt from the intricate detail of jewelry placed in the water. The company, Powertron, needed financing, and it looked like the type of business McGowan might be interested in.

Although the engineers thought Powertron was a technology company, McGowan knew better. There was nothing amazing or sophisticated about the product at all. It was really a matter of marketing and selling. If investors wanted to think it was cutting-edge "high technology," a buzzword of the early sixties, that was okay with him. It would make his job easier. A decade later, McGowan applied the same idea to MCI. There was nothing magical or mysterious about MCI's network. It was just plain old microwave towers using the same technology as World War II radar. If investors and the public felt better investing in a company they thought was high tech, McGowan wasn't going to argue. During the early sixties, anything having to do with computers or electronics was a hot item on Wall Street.

When Powertron was formed, McGowan and his associates took 150,000 shares at 6/10 cents each for a total of $900. Cowett got about 3,000 shares. The first year, Powertron lost about $100,000, and by the summer of 1960, it was ready to go public and raise capital. That's where Cowett's knowledge of Blue Sky came into play. The prospectus had all the necessary legal language, including the Blue Sky disclaimer, so investors knew that they were buying stock of a company whose product may or may not be accepted by jewelers and that the technique itself might work as well as wiping the jewelry with a plain old rag.

Investors loved it anyway. Shares sold for $2 each, and the company hit $13 a share in March 1961. Eventually, the company's glitter dulled, and it was sold to a company called Conrac. McGowan learned a great deal from Powertron. He learned about the stock market and how to take a company public.

Cowett had one company called Geriatric Services, which operated close to forty nursing homes. Cowett's idea was that it could profit from the Kennedy Administration's Medicare program. Around 1961, McGowan and a stockbroker named John Zeeman took an interest in Geriatric Services and were appointed to the board. Because the proposed Medicare program took a long time to get going, Geriatric Services went bust, but not until it had gone public at $4 a share, making McGowan a tidy profit—though only on paper.

Cowett had other business deals going. He was a partner with the infamous Bernie Cornfeld in Investors Overseas Services, which sold mutual funds to overseas investors. The whole idea behind IOS was not to make profits for its clients, but to launder hot money by getting it out of the United States and into foreign securities. McGowan had never met Cornfeld until years later, even though their offices were near each other.

McGowan had nothing to do with IOS until the summer of 1962, when he started getting calls from brokers who hadn't been paid by Cowett when some of his investments went sour. Apparently, Cowett was putting COMAC money into IOS. McGowan called another partner, Al Feldman, and the two entered Cowett's office to see what they could see. In the bottom drawer of Cowett's desk, they found mail from brokers still unopened. Cowett was in Switzerland at the time, and when McGowan telephoned him, he said he couldn't come back just yet. Cowett and the Securities and Exchange Commission weren't seeing eye-to-eye on certain matters, and it was best to stay away from the United States. McGowan was forced to cover his partner's debts. McGowan paid $100,000 to keep his reputation intact. McGowan came out of the affair poorer but much wiser. His reputation was untainted, but Cowett never fully recovered, financially or otherwise, and later died of a heart attack while on a plane between Houston and Miami.

McGowan spent about four years as a consultant in New York City, and he gained an excellent reputation for saving failing companies and for knowing how to deal with the Street. To McGowan, it was all very flattering, but something was wrong. He wasn't happy. It all seemed too easy, too pat, and he began to see that most people in business were bored with it. In fact, he was bored with it. He had done so much, so many things, that he didn't know where to go next. "Where's the payoff besides money?" he kept asking himself. "There's got to be something more, something more challenging, more rewarding. Otherwise, what's the use?"

McGowan decided to take a sabbatical. College professors got them, and he figured he worked just as hard as they did, so he gave himself some time off. He traveled around the world, visiting Europe, Asia, Japan, and generally knocked about. He did some business along the way, justifying the trip to the IRS, but it was really a way to get his head clear. Naturally, instead of clothes in his suitcases, he packed books.

When he arrived home, he still didn't know what else to do. Sure, he could do consulting, but he had already done that. He was still unhappy. He needed action.

He got a call from a former independent sales agent for Powertron in Chicago who had gotten involved in a real estate maintenance firm called Marx Industrial Maintenance, Inc., affectionately known as MIMI. Among other things, MIMI kept airport rest rooms clean.

MIMI needed some financing, which McGowan was able to get, and during that time, he needed some legal assistance. A friend steered him to Jenner & Block and a lawyer named John Worthington.

After McGowan was finished with MIMI, John asked him if he would be interested in other deals, and McGowan said yes. That's when he was introduced to the guys from Joliet and Jack Goeken.

McGowan and the MCI partners met for lunch at the Italian Pavilion, a restaurant in Chicago. They told McGowan that they wanted to raise $35,000. McGowan asked to see some financial statements, and they said they didn't have any. Then McGowan asked what their assets and liabilities were, and they said they really didn't want to discuss it. Then McGowan asked, "What are your debts?"

Jack did most of the talking and said that they owed $35,000, at which point McGowan said, "I'm a little confused. Didn't you tell me before that you wanted to raise $35,000?" They all said yes. "Well, if your debts are $35,000, why do you want $35,000? Why don't you raise more? What are you going to build the business on?"

They all said that they didn't need more than that.

McGowan said to himself, "Advanced financial planners I'm not dealing with here."

The debts were with Mike Bader's law firm, an outside economist, an engineer who had testified before the FCC in MCI's behalf, and American Express for some air travel and hotel charges.

Although Jack wasn't a financial genius, McGowan at least knew that Jack was an honest man. Even if MCI was a crazy idea, it was on the up-and-up. During one of their following luncheons, Jack had to get to the airport, so he borrowed ten dollars from McGowan for a cab. Although McGowan tried to stop him, Jack insisted on writing

McGowan a check for the money. The check bounced. McGowan knew that a con man suckering you into a scam would have made sure the check didn't bounce to gain your confidence for the big sting. Now all McGowan had to figure out was whether or not the plan would work and whether he wanted to get involved.

McGowan liked the fact that he would be fighting AT&T, the world's largest company. That would certainly be different from anything else he had ever done. He would also be able to use his financial skills. And because the phone industry was highly regulated by government rules, he could practice using law as a business tool, a technique he learned from Cowett. He was very excited. Still, he approached MCI as he had approached all the other possible deals that came his way. He studied and asked questions and, of course, he read.

During the spring of 1968, he read everything he could get his hands on about communication, the telephone industry, the Bell System. McGowan went to the FCC and read through thousands of pages about MCI, the applications, the petitions, the hearing transcripts. He talked with Mike Bader and with the Joliet crowd a few more times. He realized three things: one, AT&T had a de facto monopoly on long-distance service, not a government-mandated monopoly, even though the government regulated the company; two, until Jack came along, no one had really challenged AT&T's monopoly; and three, if done right, MCI could be big.

While in Chicago talking to Jack, McGowan took a side trip to St. Louis to see Dick Sayford. Sayford and McGowan had been roommates at Harvard.

Sayford was working for IBM in sales. He had made a name for himself within IBM by being one of the first in the company to sell computers to the Bell System while he was stationed in Philadelphia. McGowan asked Sayford if he knew about MCI and what they were trying to do, and Sayford said that he had heard about them. He told McGowan that MCI's plan could work and that for years AT&T had ignored the computer companies that needed special long-distance networks to send their information. In addition, he said, AT&T was vastly underestimating the future of computer-to-computer communications, a market that was just beginning to grow in the late 1960s. Sayford also thought these computer companies might support an idea like MCI, and they wouldn't be afraid to piss off AT&T. They were antiestablishment anyway.

McGowan also learned about other companies with plans similar to

MCI's. One was Interdata in Washington, D.C. The system was to span Washington to New York City. In Lincoln, Nebraska, another group calling itself Nebraska Consolidated Communications Corporation, which later changed its name to N-Triple-C, was funded by independent local telephone companies, not connected with the Bell System. They had built a private microwave system for the state of Nebraska and wanted to build a shared system for public use like MCI. However, neither group had had an FCC hearing. Although their applications may have been technically and financially sounder than MCI's, the latter's application was much further along. These two potential MCI rivals would later play a crucial role in MCI's survival when MCI bought them both.

The more he learned, the more fascinated McGowan became, but still, now approaching the crisis age of forty, he didn't want MCI to become just another notch in his gun. If he took it on, it would have to mean something special, something different from all the other companies he had begun or bailed out of trouble with his sharp business skills.

McGowan decided to take another short sabbatical, this time with his brother Joe, a priest in Scranton. Over the years, Joe had been his brother's sounding board for many of his ventures, so when the two decided to take three weeks off and travel in Europe, Joe knew it would also serve as a way for his brother to think about MCI and decide whether he would go ahead and do it.

What his brother told him, however, took Joe by complete surprise. For the first time, he talked about quitting business for good. He said there was a futility in it all, that there really was no point in starting a business just to sell it later at a profit. There had to be more to it. If there wasn't, he might as well do something else. He confided to Joe what had been troubling him for several months.

McGowan's preoccupation didn't mar the trip. They drove through the German countryside, France, and Italy, making sure to thoroughly read about each city before they entered it. They had no schedule, no agenda. They just took in the sites and sampled wines. Occasionally, they would stop along the road long enough for McGowan to point out a microwave tower to Joe and explain what it was. He told him about the coming "information age" and how communications would play a vital role but only if there were no restraints, only if there were competition with the Bell System. He talked about how AT&T

ignored the computer industry, small users, and others who needed special communications services.

He also knew that attitudes about the Bell System were changing. Back home, another Jack Goeken–like character named Tom Carter neared the end of his fight with AT&T. Carter had invented a device that enabled truck dispatchers to connect their two-way radios to the phone system so drivers could make telephone calls while on the road. Carter convinced the FCC, above AT&T's objections, that his equipment would not harm the Bell network and that he had every right to connect his non–Western Electric gear. Although Bell insisted that any device connected to the Bell System use an AT&T-manufactured coupling device, Carter's "Carterfone" company opened up the huge telephone equipment industry. Maybe this was the right time for a company like MCI after all. (That coupling device turned out to be another AT&T tactic to deter competition. Years later, the FCC ruled that any appropriate device could be connected to the phone system as long as it met certain technical standards. Being manufactured by Western Electric wasn't one of them.)

By the trip's end, McGowan didn't have to tell Joe about his decision on MCI. Joe knew just by looking at him that he had made up his mind.

John Worthington was already putting MCI's papers in order, getting it all shipshape from a legal point of view. He had been brought in by Tom Hermes to do just that. When Hermes had inherited his brother's share of MCI, he had the feeling that the company may have unwittingly violated some securities laws in the way it was organized and kept books. It took Worthington only a short time to realize that Hermes was correct. Fortunately, the records were sparse instead of complicated and wrong, and that allowed Worthington to construct, almost from scratch, papers that would hold up to securities rules and regulations.

By now, Tom Hermes was convinced that McGowan could do some good for MCI, and he pushed the others to let McGowan in on the deal. Worthington had drawn up an agreement between McGowan and Jack saying who would own what. Jack and McGowan never signed it, however. They were supposed to ink a fifty-fifty deal, but every time the paper was drawn up, Jack was out of town. Or McGowan was out of town. As a result, the two just started working together, McGowan being forced on Jack by the partners, especially Tom Hermes.

At first, Jack and McGowan made a good team—the unsophisticated farm boy and the savvy businessman. Jack would travel around looking for customers, and McGowan would look for money. They complemented each other.

However, the two began to drift apart over the company's direction. McGowan soon realized that if MCI were to be a successful business, it would have to bring in large amounts of revenue in a hurry. It could only do that if it went for existing markets. Jack's idea of serving specialized, small markets just wouldn't cut it. The market did not yet exist; it would have to be nurtured. McGowan, however, saw a market already there: AT&T's traditional long-distance voice business, a $7.5-billion pie from which MCI could take a sliver.

McGowan didn't touch MCI, the Chicago-to-St. Louis company that Jack had established. If he did, it would mean changing FCC applications and more delay. Instead, he set out to form a lot of little MCIs that would link together major cities with high traffic between them. If all went as planned, those regional companies could one day be connected into a single nationwide company. While Jack tended to MCI (the Chicago-to-St. Louis company), McGowan was lining up venture capital for the newborn companies. He set up the regional system because he knew it was the only way to raise money. A banker in New York would be more apt to invest money in a business in his area than one in Texas or California. Investors like to invest locally. More important, the FCC had always stressed localism in granting TV and radio applications, and McGowan believed that local ownership of the networks would increase chances of getting a license.

McGowan copped the idea from Theodore Vail, AT&T president in the 1880s, who built the basic framework of the Bell System which lasted until the company's divestiture in January 1984. Vail licensed patent rights to the telephone to local investor groups for a 30 to 50 percent piece of the company. They set up the companies, sold stock, used the telephone, and gave AT&T a piece of the action. McGowan would sell local investors the knowledge of how to set up a company and file applications at the FCC. He would give a name to John Worthington, who was still involved with the company through his law firm, Jenner & Block, and Worthington would draw up the proper incorporation papers: MCI New England, Inc., MCI-New York West, Inc., MCI Indiana-Ohio, Inc., and so on.

McGowan established Microwave Communications of America in August 1968 to sponsor these smaller companies. Jack and McGowan each got 25 percent of the company, the investors got 25 percent, and the company, nicknamed "Micom," held on to the other 25 percent.

McGowan traveled around the country getting money for Micom. In Chicago friends introduced him to Baker, Fentress & Co. That relationship blossomed as James Fentress became a member of Micom's board of directors to keep an eye on his investment. They in turn introduced him to people at Hornblower, Weeks. McGowan knew the Allens at Allen & Co., a well-known venture-capital group, from his days at Magna-Theatre, and they invested $1 million. Ray Shultz, who was running Holiday Inn's reservation system, was always looking for ways to cut the company's phone bill, and he invested money in Micom. Sam Bodman, who later became president of Fidelity Management in Boston, was also an early investor. McGowan's strongest asset was his enthusiasm. He had the ability to make people *believe*, to jump up and down along with him whenever he got excited about a project. He charmed potential investors into giving him money, and he played one against the other until he had raised $5 million.

With the MCI companies now almost ready to go, McGowan spent the summer and fall of 1968 lobbying the government to grant MCI's license for Chicago to St. Louis. That consisted mainly of talking with people at the FCC and Congress. McGowan, who gave himself a quick education in communications, was amazed to see how little Congress knew about the subject. While watching a House of Representatives hearing on telephone service, McGowan heard Torbert MacDonald, chairman of the Telecommunications Subcommittee, conduct a rather routine oversight hearing on the FCC. Usually, they were held once a year or so to make sure that the budget Congress gives to the FCC is well spent.

McGowan was dumbfounded when MacDonald asked FCC Chairman Rosell Hyde about AT&T and how it related to the local Bell telephone companies. Hyde, knowing where his money came from, began to explain in a serious manner that American Telephone & Telegraph Company, which was the long-distance company, owned the local phone companies, which only handled local calls. The local companies, except for a few like Chesapeake & Potomac Telephone in Washington, D.C., used the word "Bell" in their company names.

MacDonald asked, "So they're almost like the same thing?"

"Yes," said Hyde politely. "That's a good way to put it."

By now, McGowan had moved to Washington from New York to be

near the FCC. Even though the FCC record was closed, the FCC had not yet voted. In December, the President's Task Force on Communications gave a boost to MCI by endorsing the concept of specialized common carrier networks, Jack's original MCI idea.

The following summer, in 1969, Jerry Taylor—who knew Jack from Joliet—showed up at Micom in Washington to see Jack about a job. Jerry had been a physics professor at Berkeley but had run a business with his brother selling planes in the same Joliet airport where Jack kept his plane. Jack and Jerry got along well, and Jack invited him to Washington to take a look around. Perhaps he would like to work for him. Jerry was getting tired of the teaching life and wanted to get into the business world again. Actually, Jerry needed some quick money, so the two set a date to meet in Washington.

As usual, Jack was out flying around somewhere when Jerry arrived. Nobody knew where Jack was. Jerry had paid his own airfare to Washington and no Jack. "What kind of deal is this?" he thought. Jerry interviewed with McGowan, whom he had never met before. In fact, he didn't know anything about McGowan or MCI but ended up taking a job working for Jack and McGowan anyway. The company employed about ten people, and Jerry handled many different jobs, but he spent most of his time writing applications for the regional companies and getting them through the FCC. McGowan soon learned that Jerry had a knack for getting new projects and products off the ground. And what started as a way for Jerry to make some quick cash would lead to a career.

Shortly after Jerry arrived, the FCC voted on MCI's application. The FCC said that MCI's service had merit and that the public could benefit from such an offering. That may have been government lingo for saying that MCI was harmless and would probably fade away in a short while so why not give them a chance? Meanwhile, the FCC would look like heroes, giving "Jack the Giant Killer," as he had become known, the right to fail.

The vote was close because of the political makeup of the FCC. On August 14, 1969, when MCI was born, the vote went along party lines: four Democrats for; three Republicans against. One of those Democrats voting for MCI was Commissioner Ken Cox, who would later join MCI as a regulatory counsel.

The FCC noted in its decision that the local phone companies must give MCI "interconnection"—access to the local phone network— which, unlike long-distance service, *was* a bona fide monopoly.

Without that last-mile connection to the customer, MCI's service could not work. Even if they wanted to, MCI could not build a local phone system. There could be only one to a city. The AT&T-owned local phone companies, which served 85 percent of the population (independents served the rest), told the FCC that interconnection would not always be technically feasible, but the FCC warned them that until it learned differently, the local companies better not balk when the time came to connect MCI.

Neither McGowan nor anyone else knew what to expect from the local Bell companies on interconnection. They would find out several years later, however, when Bell pulled the plug and pushed MCI to the edge of bankruptcy.

A few weeks after MCI won its right to build Chicago to St. Louis, Micom filed the first of its regional applications with the FCC. Other companies did the same. McGowan wasn't worried, though. He had a head start.

Dean Burch, chairman of the FCC, saw trouble ahead if the FCC had to hold hearings on each applicant that wanted to mimic MCI, so he and the other commissioners decided to make things easy on themselves. In July 1970, the FCC began a "rule-making procedure" to see what the public thought about other companies getting into the phone business as well. It solicited comments from the public and received 176 separate groups in favor of the idea, and 10 opposed. In a unanimous decision in May 1971, the FCC voted that anyone could enter the long-distance market as a specialized common carrier without hearings or other red tape. From start to finish, the whole process took less than a year, surprising everyone that the FCC could do it in so short a time when most other procedures of its kind took years.

Applications poured in, although only a handful of companies actually followed through. Southern Pacific Railroad, which hoped to capitalize on knowledge gained from their internal microwave network that ran along their tracks' right-of-way, filed for permission to build a network. It formed Southern Pacific Communications Company, separate from the railroad's communication system, and focused on California and the Southwest.

That company later became Sprint and was bought by General Telephone & Electronics, one of the companies that originally opposed Jack's application. Next to AT&T, Sprint would become MCI's strongest competitor.

THE THIRD BUSINESS –

Building a Company
1971 – 73

1

To those at Micom, it was obvious that McGowan was slowly taking control from Jack. Even though they had an unspoken fifty-fifty agreement, McGowan seemed to be doing all the work. Jack was always traveling around or in Chicago overseeing his original Chicago-to-St. Louis system while McGowan was in Washington making all the decisions.

The two of them had still not solved their disagreement over the direction of the company, so it went McGowan's way by default. Jack was rarely around to pitch his point of view.

McGowan knew that the future of MCI hinged on managing the regulators, the FCC. He had learned from Cowett that you could build a business by thinking of regulatory bodies such as the FCC as something that had to be managed, the way you would manage any other item that affected your business. Lumber companies managed natural resources like forests; MCI would manage the FCC.

McGowan had to find someone who could do that for MCI. He needed someone who knew the FCC inside and out, someone who spoke their language, someone who had impeccable credentials. That person was Ken Cox, who became available because of Richard Nixon and his hatred of the *Washington Post*.

President Nixon wanted to assert his control over the FCC. He didn't like the newspapers, and he liked TV reporters even less. During his administration, the FCC succeeded in passing a rule that prohibited a newspaper from owning a radio or TV station in the same city. The FCC said it feared media concentration, but some observers said the rule was aimed mainly at the *Washington Post*, which was forced to trade its local TV station for one in Detroit. Nixon and the *Post* never got along.

On the morning after Nixon's election in 1968, FCC Commissioner Ken Cox knew that, because he was a Democrat, his days were numbered. By law, the President's party could control a majority of FCC seats, and Ken was the next commissioner up for reappointment. President John F. Kennedy appointed Ken to a seat on the commission in 1963 while Ken was serving as chief of the FCC's Broadcast Bureau. He was to pull a seven-year term, but with two years left to go, Ken figured he better start making plans. He called his old friend from Seattle John Ehrlichman to see what he knew about Nixon's intentions: When the time came, would Nixon keep Ken or replace him with his own man? Ehrlichman never called back, but one of his aides did and told Ken that Nixon had a very hot prospect, someone named Sherman Unger. Ken began looking around.

As it turned out, Nixon nominated Unger for the FCC, but Unger got into trouble with the Internal Revenue Service, and Nixon was forced to withdraw his name. During the House Judiciary's investigation of Watergate, Unger's travel records and testimony provided proof that hush money had been paid to E. Howard Hunt. Under President Ronald Reagan, Unger became general counsel for the Department of Commerce, and later the President nominated him to be a federal judge. The American Bar Association tried to stop the nomination, saying that Unger was unqualified. He died of cancer while the nomination was pending.

While Nixon searched for a replacement, Ken stayed at the FCC two months after his term expired.

Mike Bader telephoned Ken and said he had a client who would be interested in hiring him. Ken thought it was a broadcaster he knew, so Ken agreed to meet with him. Mike Bader, Ken, McGowan, Jack, and Alex Buchan, who would later become president of Radio Free Europe, had breakfast at the Mayflower Hotel, a classy joint a few blocks from the FCC. Ken immediately liked McGowan and Jack, and the job sounded challenging and promising. He would work half-time at Micom, the other half at Mike Bader's law firm. He took it.

The next person that McGowan needed was someone to build Micom's network. Engineers were a rather conventional bunch, and McGowan knew that he had to find someone who wasn't afraid to be unconventional, to do things a little differently than they had been done before. AT&T had written the book on building long-distance networks. McGowan needed someone who had read the text but wasn't afraid to change it to suit Micom's needs. The network had to be inexpensive, and it had to work.

Tom Leming had had trouble holding a job. From McGowan's point of view, that made him perfect for Micom. Leming was outspoken, smart, liked to shake things up, wasn't afraid to try new ideas, and wasn't scared to tell anyone in the company he was full of crap. McGowan liked that. He would be perfect for a company like Micom that had to be the opposite of its staid rival, AT&T, in order to survive.

Leming had worked for Western Electric, but that didn't take, so he left. He hired on at Motorola, and that didn't work out, so he left. Leming then became director of engineering at Collins Radio, a leader in radios used in airplanes. They also manufactured shortwave transmitters and receivers that were considered the Cadillac of radios. Leming worked in the microwave division for about thirteen years. He was a graduate of the University of Illinois but got most of his knowledge about microwave systems in the Navy teaching radar to new operators. In 1967, he and Art Collins, the chairman of the company, got into a fight over whether Collins should go into the computer business. Leming said no, Collins said yes. Leming was out. Later, Collins lost his company pursuing his ultimate dream of getting into the computer business.

So Leming went to work for Hughes Aerospace. He didn't get along there either and left after three years.

Leming then got an offer from Continental Telephone to begin an MCI-type service using cables buried along highways instead of microwave towers. The advantage of cable was that it didn't use radio channels. Therefore, because it couldn't interfere with any other microwave services, it didn't need FCC approval. That had been one of Jack's major stumbling blocks: trying to find frequencies for his microwave system that wouldn't interfere with other established microwave operators like AT&T. Continental officials figured that if they didn't need FCC approval, they could build their system rather quickly. Phil Lucier, Continental's president, was hot for the plan and hired Leming to carry it through.

Leming was there about six months when a mobster knocked off Lucier. Police believe the hit man was trying to scare an attorney representing a St. Louis businessman into having his client pay some money owed the mob. He thought Lucier's car belonged to that attorney and wired it with a small bomb.

Jack McGuire took Lucier's place, and shortly after the mistaken murder, Leming and others were called to Bakersfield, California, where McGuire had his office. McGuire wanted to know exactly what Leming had planned to do with this cable system project that the late Lucier had liked so much. After Leming explained the plan, McGuire was horrified and said, "How can we possibly consider this? The Bell System is our partner!"

Because Continental was an independent phone company, not owned by AT&T, it relied on AT&T to carry its customers' long-distance calls. The agreement to handle long-distance traffic from non-Bell phone companies was forced upon the Bell System in 1913 after the death of J. P. Morgan, who financially controlled the Bell System. He pushed President Theodore Vail to continue gobbling up small independents to complete AT&T's monopoly over all telephones. By not giving independents the long-distance connections they needed, Morgan forced many of them to sell out to AT&T at rock-bottom prices. That didn't sit well with the government, and they were ready to break AT&T's monopoly on grounds of antitrust—using its virtual monopoly power to force other companies out of business. With Morgan out of the picture, however, Vail was free to deal in a conciliatory manner with the government and prevent a breakup.

AT&T Vice-President Nathan Kingsbury wrote a letter to Attorney General James Reynolds agreeing that AT&T would dispose of its stock in its competitor Western Union, purchase no more independents, and, most important, connect all independents to AT&T's long-distance network for a reasonable fee. The Kingsbury Commitment, as it was called, stopped AT&T's expansion but kept the company intact.

Leming's response to McGuire cost him his job. "My God," he told him. "We've got the Mohave Desert, and they've got downtown Los Angeles. One more partnership like this and we'll be dead."

Leming began looking for another job.

Through some friends, Leming knew McGowan and Jack. He had lunch with them once or twice, but there was no talk of a job. In the meantime, Raytheon offered Leming a job for $50,000—good engineer's pay for 1971—and he was all set to take it. First, though, he wanted to take a small vacation.

When he got back home, the phone was ringing. It was McGowan. He had heard that Leming left Continental. "Yes, that's right," he told McGowan. "I'm going to Raytheon."

McGowan said, "We're going to be one of their biggest customers for microwave equipment. Before you take that job, if you want to sell us anything, I insist that you talk to us."

Leming said okay, he would, but added, "I'm going to take the job at Raytheon. I already have a badge. I've taken my physical. I'm not sworn onto the payroll yet, but I'm all set to start."

McGowan, Jack, and Leming met and talked for a long time, and they convinced Leming to join Micom. In 1971, at age forty-six, for $10,000 less than the Raytheon position, Leming took charge of Micom's microwave network. His first task was the Chicago-to-St. Louis construction project, which had been behind schedule since its start several months before.

Both Jack and McGowan liked Leming's style. He was an odd mixture. He was gruff, cursed a lot, and ran his shop with incredible precision and an iron hand. He didn't pull his punches; he told his workers what he thought. They did things the way *he* wanted them done. This was in contrast to his other side, a gentle side. He loved the grandeur and sweetness of the opera and symphonies. He surrounded himself with Oriental tapestries, jade carvings, and intricate water-colors.

Leming didn't think Micom would be huge. He just hoped it would grow to be a few-hundred-million-dollar company and he could make some money and enjoy the challenge of running his own shop. If someone had told Leming that he would one day have the distinction of building more miles of microwave networks than any other human being, he would have slapped him on the back, grabbed a drink, and had a damned good laugh.

McGowan didn't know it, but AT&T was getting ready to decide what to do about Micom. Every year, AT&T's top brass met for its Presidents' Conference. This year, the eighty-sixth annual conference, they got together at the Ocean Reef Club in Key Largo. For four days in May 1972, they discussed what AT&T should do about the changes they saw around them. Although MCI was never mentioned by name, it was clearly on the minds of those who attended.

John deButts, AT&T's chairman, opened the meeting that set the tone for how AT&T would deal with new competitors.

Like many others, deButts was virtually born a Bell employee. He started as a traffic student in Virginia at the Chesapeake & Potomac Telephone Company in 1936 and stayed with Bell his entire working life. He worked his way up to become president in 1961 and chairman in 1972. He was one of the company's most forceful chairmen, taking the reins at a time that would be remembered as the most important in the history of the Bell System. For the first time, Bell would suffer loss of integrity in the public eye and low investor confidence because of a series of scandals.

During his tenure, T. O. Gravitt, vice-president of Southwestern Bell, committed suicide after he was accused of stealing money from AT&T. Before he breathed deeply from his car's exhaust pipe, he left behind a note accusing AT&T of making illegal payoffs to politicians, illegally wiretapping and getting approval for high phone rates in Texas by providing regulators with false data. His note ended: "Watergate is a gnat compared with the Bell System."

Two weeks after his death, Southwestern Bell dismissed James Ashley, a Southwestern rate negotiator and close associate of Gravitt. Several years later, John Ryan, a former vice-president for Southern Bell in North Carolina, told the *Charlotte Observer* that before he had been forced to retire in 1973, he had made political contributions to candidates in exchange for favorable treatment. He got the money from kickbacks from subordinates and falsifying expense vouchers.

Although deButts had claimed that the Ashley-Gravitt case was isolated, the North Carolina incidents suggested that corruption in the Bell System may have been widespread.

Many more Bell people were dismissed during investigations of both matters. In 1976, Texas established a statewide regulatory agency taking power away from the municipalities which had formerly dealt with Bell on rate setting. The Texas legislature still considered Bell too powerful, and centralized its rate-setting procedures to keep it clear of Bell influence.

DeButts was a no-nonsense administrator who believed that AT&T did God's work on earth. It could not do anything wrong because the American people had given it a mandate to do whatever it wanted to do, and that was that. His belief in that omnipotence spread throughout AT&T, but instead of leading to *esprit de corps*, it led to arrogance. DeButts's beliefs may have driven some AT&T employees to skirt legalities in the name of profit and misplaced public service.

DeButts believed that the concept of "universal service," which brought reasonably priced phone service to all customers, would be ruined by having bits and pieces of the phone system taken over by other companies that could underprice AT&T on certain profitable routes yet not be obligated to serve the unprofitable areas. Universal service meant that AT&T might lose money on some calls, especially to rural areas, but make money on others. On a national scale, it would all even out. It's the same concept that the Postal Service uses: It loses money carrying a letter from New York to Honolulu but makes money when someone sends a letter crosstown.

Haakon I. Romnes, deButts's predecessor, understood the concept of universal service but didn't take it as one of the Ten Commandments. Romnes realized that AT&T existed in the real world and that the real world wanted competition. Right or wrong, times were changing. He welcomed competition as a way to inspire AT&T to work even harder and become even sharper. He believed that competition would be invigorating and lead to better telephone service. He was a humanist, believing that Bell should be bound by the public's rule because it was a public monopoly. He led AT&T through some of its worst years, including terrible service problems in the late 1960s. He advocated AT&T's responsibility to the public and instituted changes at AT&T for equal opportunity for minorities. He retired in March 1972, and John deButts took his place.

DeButts wanted no part of Romnes's liberal thinking and made it clear, publicly and privately, that AT&T wouldn't take easily to competition no matter who forced it upon them.

On May 8, he opened the conference in Key Largo. AT&T decided then to kill competition, even though the FCC and the courts said it was bound to accept it.

Alvin von Auw was an assistant to deButts. He had been Romnes's assistant, too. He took it upon himself to write down some of the proceedings, and they became the only record of AT&T's attitude toward competitors. Participants were told not to take notes, that they would be given notes with enough information to brief their associates back home. Part of a session went like this, according to von Auw's incomplete handwritten records:

Charles Brown, president of Illinois Bell, who would succeed deButts as chairman, asked, "How badly would we be hurt if we wait until we see the whites of their eyes?"

Thomas Nurnberger, president of Northwestern Bell: "I would meet 'em or beat 'em. You bastards are not going to take away my business."

Alfred Van Sinderen, president of Southern New England Telephone: "Shouldn't we act now rather than wait until they have going businesses which regulators might not permit us to dislodge? . . . if we're going to do this, we have to do it now."

Brown: "We must take [into] account [the] prospect of intrastate competition. Large amounts of revenues [are] vulnerable which we can preserve if we choke [them] off now. I think you have to hit the nail on the head."

McGowan continued to build Micom, not knowing that AT&T had already made its "decisions" on how to handle the upstart. Like everyone else, he knew that AT&T wouldn't welcome his company into the phone business, but he figured they would obey the law. He also figured that Micom would act as insulation for AT&T against more Justice Department attempts to break the company's monopoly. AT&T could, after all, now point to another long-distance company and say there was competition. AT&T didn't use MCI the way McGowan thought they would.

McGowan realized that in order to build a system that would really make money, it would have to serve the entire country, not just isolated point-to-point systems. They would have to merge all the little MCIs into one big one to achieve technical uniformity and economies of scale.

The person capable of doing that was already on board. His name was Stan Scheinman, and he agreed with McGowan.

Several years earlier, Scheinman had been vice-president of administration and leasing for Pepsico, and his boss was John Allison. When that division was phased out, Scheinman went to Revlon, and Allison left to go to Raytheon, where he oversaw the Chicago-to-St. Louis deal in which Raytheon totally financed the start-up and was the prime contractor for the microwave route.

One day, Allison called Scheinman and invited him to dinner at an Italian restaurant in midtown Manhattan to meet McGowan. As usual, McGowan laid out the plan and asked Scheinman to join as his financial guy. It wasn't until later that Scheinman realized that Allison had his own reasons for getting McGowan and Scheinman together. Allison knew that unless MCI had a nationwide network, it would fail, and if it failed, Raytheon would lose money. So what would be good for MCI would be good for Allison, and Scheinman may have been the best choice for putting the whole thing together.

Scheinman liked the idea. He liked that it was a proven market (the telephone business), proven technology (microwave radios), and that all you needed was some money, guts, and competence to make it work. He joined.

Scheinman began building a financial group at Micom, and one of his first jobs was to fold the regional companies into the entity. Most of them didn't want to join. They thought they had a great local business that would blossom like TV. They believed religiously in McGowan's original selling job. Scheinman was aggressive. He twisted their arms and threatened to build around them if they didn't sell out. Of course, years later, selling their companies for shares of stock was the right choice. Original MCI investors became very rich on stock they got as part of the buy.

His next job was to take the company public, selling stock in the open market to raise money for construction. Jim Fentress, one of the original MCI investors, introduced Scheinman to Jimmy Miller, chairman emeritus of Blyth Co., an old-line bond fund, which dealt mainly with paper company financing. They had never done a start-up company—they were too conservative—but like everyone else, it seemed, Miller fell in love with the MCI idea. He saw it as his last hurrah after a long career. Blyth underwrote MCI's first public offering.

In June 1972, Micom stock went public at $10 a share, selling 3.3 million shares, raising $33 million. Through the strength of the offering and Scheinman's creative financing, it also obtained bank credit of $64 million. Scheinman went to all the major suppliers from whom Micom would have to buy equipment to build its network. He told them Micom was going to buy $300 to $400 million worth of gear from them, and for every dollar it bought he wanted them to issue a loan guarantee at MCI's bank, the First National Bank of Chicago, for 50 cents. They all agreed except, ironically, Raytheon, which thought the plan was un-American. All the other companies raised their prices to MCI by 50 percent to protect their loan guarantees in case MCI failed, and they were liable for the loans. It fit nicely into Scheinman's business philosophy: *Create enough economic benefits to many people, and they will allow it to happen.*

Now Micom was in a position to build a national system.

Micom had the distinction of being the largest public offering ever for a company that had no product. Although other companies, especially small computer companies, raised lots of money based on some new gizmo they had created, at least they had something to show. All MCI had was a route from Chicago to St. Louis that had just begun service and was not making any money, and FCC approval to build a system from New York to Washington, D.C. The public seemed willing to invest in a dream.

Only one other developmental company—a company without a tangible product—raised more money than MCI, but it wasn't truly a public company. The government was behind it.

Communications Satellite Corporation—or Comsat—had raised $196 million in 1964 through a public stock offering to get it into the satellite communications business before it had any equipment working. Comsat was a quasi-government company that served as the United States's participant in a group called International Telecommunications Satellite Organization. Intelsat was a consortium of more than a hundred nations formed in 1964 to operate an international satellite communications network mostly for telephone service and TV, which would allow, for example, the Olympics to be broadcast all over the world. It would also handle international phone calls. Comsat satellites could not be used for domestic telephone service; the government wanted to stay clear of that business.

A few months before its public offering, Micom owned a part interest in something called MCI Satellite, Inc. Together with Lockheed Aircraft Corporation, they formed a company called MCI Lockheed Satellite Corporation, or MCIL. MCIL filed an application with the FCC to launch a domestic satellite communications system that would help MCI carry messages into areas where its microwave network didn't reach. Satellites were quite the thing in those days, and MCI hoped to capitalize on the fad. It gave the company a high-tech look.

Later, Comsat bought a third of MCIL and changed its name to CML, for Comsat, MCI, and Lockheed. In 1975, MCI would be forced to sell its share of CML for $1.5 million. The company desperately needed the money.

CML eventually became a company called Satellite Business Systems, a partnership of Comsat, Aetna Casualty & Life, and IBM. In 1982, it would become the first company to launch a satellite from the space shuttle.

Like Sprint, SBS would also become an MCI competitor.

McGowan had the foundation in place. The financing was set, the FCC licenses were forthcoming, and Micom had bought back most of the original little MCIs and merged them into one company now known as MCI Communications Corp., or just MCI.

Jack continued to lose interest in the company. He spent more time outside the office, even though he was the company president and was supposed to share responsibilities with McGowan, who was chairman. Jack's free spirit just didn't jibe with staying at the office. He was happier flying around or tending to the Chicago-to-St. Louis system that he had begun.

More and more, McGowan took charge and ran the company on a day-to-day basis. He made all the important decisions.

With Leming already building the network and Ken Cox taking care of the regulatory angle, McGowan set out to hire the other people to make the business work. His plan was to get people on board in new areas as they became important to MCI. Next on the list was sales.

McGowan's experience taught him that a company had to sell something to make money. Not a very original thought, but what MCI was prepared to sell, no one had ever sold before. This was a brand-new product in a brand-new business—low-cost long-distance service. AT&T had never had to sell it; people came to them because they were the only wheel in town. The last thing McGowan wanted to do was hire ex-AT&T people complete with fixed notions—most were too loyal to come over to the enemy anyway—so he set out to find people from other industries who would be willing to experiment, try new things, and not be afraid to make mistakes. The biggest problem would be to get customers to believe that MCI was for real, when all they had ever heard of was AT&T.

Carl Vorder Bruegge was used to selling services that no one had ever heard of. As director of marketing operations at IBM, Carl sold a lot of new computers and services that no one had sold before. Although he was close to the top of the pyramid at IBM, Carl realized after fourteen years that he wasn't having as much fun as he should. He didn't seem to be able to succeed or fail at anything. Major projects never ended, and he never really knew what he had accomplished. Carl also had a few run-ins with Tom Watson, Jr., who took over chairmanship of the company from his father. The two didn't get along, and they disagreed about the direction that IBM was taking. It was becoming too bureaucratic for Carl. In addition, unlike his father, the younger Watson relied more upon scientists and engineers to bring IBM into the increasingly competitive computer generation to the detriment of sales and marketing.

Carl decided to leave IBM after they had sent him to the advanced management program at Harvard in the fall of 1967. He was in a room with fifty other executives from other companies, and as he got to know them he became convinced that they were having a lot more fun and making a lot more money without a lot more talent. Carl began to look around for another job.

A former IBMer named Dan McCrackin was president of Leasco and worked under financier Saul Steinberg. He came at Carl with a big barrel of money, a bunch of stock, and a large challenge. Carl left IBM to become a vice-president of Leasco.

Saul Steinberg, a New York businessman, had begun Leasco to capitalize on the growing computer market. He was the first to realize that there was money in leasing computers instead of selling them. At age twenty-nine, Steinberg made a name for himself by making an unsuccessful run on Chemical Bank. Before his thirtieth birthday, he had made himself $50 million. In 1984, Steinberg and a group of investors bought 11 percent of Disney, which Mickey Mouse's owner was forced to buy back at a profit to Steinberg of $31 million. Wall Street saw the move by Steinberg as a ploy to hold Disney hostage— not really to buy the company, but to scare Disney into buying it all back to keep Steinberg from getting complete control. Steinberg was accused of a new pseudo-crime called greenmail.

Carl had several companies under his command. One was computer leasing begun by Steinberg. It was going great guns until Wall Street wrote it off as a dead duck less than a decade later. Leasco's timing stunk. It was a great idea but at the wrong time; computer technology was moving too fast, and swift obsolescence caught them by surprise. By 1968, Leasco had about $130 million in leases, making $25 million profit, but everyone was just waiting for the business to die.

Carl also handled another Leasco business: time-sharing. Time-sharing was a new idea. Instead of a company owning its own computer or leasing it, it connected its terminals to a remote computer run by someone else. Generally, a company paid only for the time it used the machines, and it could be used by many different companies at once, literally sharing time. The division was losing a million dollars a month when Carl took charge. He promoted Bert Roberts, who had spent ten years at Westinghouse merging a college co-op program into a full-time career once he had left school. He worked his way into a top technical position. Roberts was a calculating, brilliant manager who would later be called Doomsday because of his attitude that the worst could always happen. Roberts was as tenacious as a pit bull, and once entrenched in a project, he didn't let it go until it was completed. During his co-op program, Roberts worked sixty hours a week in contrast to most other students, who worked the required thirty-two. Carl and Bert Roberts almost killed themselves for two years bringing Leasco to a break-even point, at which time Steinberg sold it and moved into the insurance business.

Later, after Carl had moved to MCI, he brought Bert Roberts with him, who climbed until he became president of the MCI Telecommunications Company, the division responsible for MCI's long-distance business. To Bert Roberts, MCI was the computer business all over again. He had missed the beginning of that booming business by just a few years, catching a ride on the tail end. MCI would be different for him. He wasn't going to miss out this time.

Leasco taught Carl that it was just as easy to sell to large customers as it was to sell to small customers except that you got more money the first way. With MCI in the hole for $22 million, Carl knew that he had to get gobs of money quickly. Over Jack's objections, he went for the large telephone users who would be connected to the Chicago-to-St. Louis system, which began operating in January 1972.

Carl's first move was to hire ten teams of three men each—a salesman, a junior salesman, and a technician—to sell to specific industries. There was a banking team, insurance team, manufacturing team, aerospace team, transportation team, and so on. The technician was there to answer questions because there were no salespeople outside of AT&T who knew anything about communications. They just didn't exist.

Carl and his staff hired a personnel consultant to recruit college students who would soon be graduating. He explained private lines and all that but basically told them that MCI was out to get the phone company. Most students were signed, sealed, and delivered within days. Over the next six weeks, these people would be brought to Washington and taught how to dress, how to act, how to eat, and how to talk. At the end, these folks would become professional salespeople and customer service technicians.

Carl was laboring over how to sell MCI service when he decided to see a neighbor of his, Charlie Stauffacher, then president of Continental Can Company, to ask his advice. Charlie spent the day with Carl discussing the service and how he should go about selling MCI service to businesses. Charlie suggested that Carl stress two things: choice and competition. Most businessmen believe in competition, Charlie told him, and most businessmen want a choice. These are great American ideals that businessmen wanted to believe in.

Carl put together a canned slide presentation that teams could deliver almost by the numbers, no thinking involved. He obtained a list of AT&T's ten largest customers and set the teams loose. Even though the teams asked for large orders, it didn't work. Customers were reluctant to turn their entire telecommunications needs over to an unknown company all at once. Most of the time, teams received a small order, sort of a trial purchase, and if the customer liked it, the teams would return and ask for their entire communications business. That strategy seemed to work perfectly.

Carl took on one more job. He was responsible for making certain that the local Bell telephone companies connected MCI's private lines into the local phone network as necessary. Private lines were dedicated telephone circuits that connected predesignated points. Usually, a large corporation bought private lines to connect all its offices together because it was cheaper than direct long-distance dialing. Carl and others at MCI believed that the FCC was quite clear in its original order, the one that licensed MCI, and that the Bell companies had to supply interconnections except in cases where it wasn't technically feasible. He had recommended to McGowan that he hire Larry Harris, another Leasco refugee, to handle formal negotiations with AT&T, while he and his sales staff took care of the day-to-day connection crisis. AT&T balked at connecting MCI, often saying that what MCI wanted wasn't technically possible, even if it was.

The third sales call Carl made was to the Atlantic Richfield Company. He sold them a line between St. Louis and Chicago on the original MCI system, which didn't work. Carl flew to Chicago and learned that the line didn't work because AT&T's circuits called for nine leads and MCI's circuits "looked for" fourteen leads. "That's fine," Carl told the technician. "We can fix that. What's a lead?"

Carl and the technician went to St. Louis to see the Southwestern Bell people with a solution that the technician cooked up. They sat in a room about thirty feet by thirty feet filled with Southwestern Bell people, and Carl tried to convince them that ARCO was their customer as much as it was MCI's customer, and they ought to go out of their way to make the thing work. The technician explained his plan, and after lots of talk a Southwestern Bell engineer finally stood up and said, "These people are right. I think we ought to do it." The next week, they fixed the circuit with a minor adjustment.

Carl was convinced this was the way to go. No one at MCI would be permitted to blame the phone companies for their problems. It would make MCI look unprofessional and small-time.

Carl and his teams had great hopes that customers would buy their service, even though they had little to sell. Except for Chicago to St. Louis, which was up and running, they were selling systems stretching from Chicago to New York and Chicago to Dallas. The only trouble was they hadn't yet been built. All they could do was tell customers that it would be ready when they promised. If it wasn't, their credibility would be lost and MCI would go under.

It was time for Leming's cowboys to ride the microwave range and build some more things for Carl to sell.

Russ Smith and Art Roberts knew each other from Collins Radio, the same company that Leming had worked at. They didn't know then that they would become rivals in building what would become the nation's second largest telephone network.

Building radio towers took on the element of sport. Who could build the most sites, who could do it faster and at less cost? Because MCI didn't have very much money and was in a hurry, the two were forced to cut corners, do things out of the ordinary, and in some cases do it all just a hair inside the law.

In the fall of 1972, Leming handed both of them an obscene deadline. He wanted a route from Chicago to New York and Chicago to Dallas finished by early summer the following year. No one had ever built a network that quickly, and they were to be the first. Leming divided the job equally between them: Russ took Chicago going west, and Art had Chicago going east.

AT&T built its system in the 1940s strictly by the book. They would do a site survey, procure the area, call in construction crews to level the land, build an access road, construct the shelter to hold the radio equipment, calculate the height of the tower, and then build it. They placed huge antennas shaped like cornucopias on the towers. This was a high-class, first-rate, and very expensive way to do things.

Because the local Bell companies were public utilities, they had the

85

right of eminent domain. They could take any land they needed, at a fair price, and in many cases they were exempt from zoning restrictions. That was a big factor in cities that usually restricted or outlawed tall towers.

MCI had none of these advantages. It had to get land by any means possible and sometimes in unconventional ways. Jack's plan called for a site in Elkhart, Indiana, for the Chicago-to-St. Louis route. When they went to the place on the map where "X" marks the spot, they found a woman named Mrs. Drake who shooed them away. The lawyers tried to convince her without much luck either. Finally, Jack drove there with his son and explained to Mrs. Drake how important it was to him and his family that they build a tower exactly on this spot. It was a special spot that fit perfectly in line with the proposed route. She explained to Jack that it was a special spot for her, too. Someone important was buried nearby, and she didn't want the land desecrated.

Jack needed that exact site and offered Mrs. Drake a deal she found too good to pass up. Every Christmas, someone from MCI would come over and place colored lights on the guy wires holding up the tower. Every Christmas, they did just that until several years later when the lease was up. Leming pooh-poohed this light business, and he refused to do it. Mrs. Drake kicked them off the land, and it cost MCI about $700,000 to build a detour around it.

Russ wanted to work fast. Often, he would order a tower based on heights of terrain that he gleaned from topographic maps. If he guessed wrong, he could swap the tower with another one from a different site. Luckily, he was right most of the time. He was in such a rush that several sites were built before he had construction permits for them. One day, he got a note from Leming that read, "What's going on here? Is this site legal?" He responded, "Ask me that a week from now." He would take the attitude that if a tower wasn't finished, if the last bolt wasn't in place, it really wasn't considered to be legally built. It's sort of like the practice of leaving the front steps off a house so it's not considered finished and therefore taxable.

MCI's chief cost advantage over AT&T was that it built the shelters in a main fabricating plant in Richardson, Texas, and had them shipped to the sites for installation. Rather than install and trouble-shoot the equipment at the site, it would be done in Richardson, only a forklift ride away from Collins, where the electronic gear was being built. AT&T, on the other hand, would hire local contractors to build their shelters right on the site. Instead of hiring civil engineering crews to level the land and build access roads, Russ and Art would hire local farmers with graders and bulldozers to do the job. That would cost them a lot less than doing it the conventional way. It was McGowan's belief that towers could be built without the frills for a lot less money and still work properly.

He never forgot the lesson of the movie actors with their expensive jeans when the cheaper duds would have worked just as well.

The field crews were having a great time, rushing from site to site, seeing how fast they could build the towers. They worked in the cold and snow from dawn until way past 10 P.M. Only rain slowed them down. Not only couldn't they align the microwave dish antennas in rain but if a heavy truck got stuck in mud, it could take days to get it out. Building became a macho game. It was a way to "kill the snake."

The men on field crews acted like oil wildcatters. They were gruff, didn't want to waste time (they certainly wouldn't have strung up Christmas lights for Mrs. Drake), and wouldn't tolerate anyone who couldn't take sleeping in their cars or trucks while in the field. Driving through a cornfield in the middle of the night at ninety miles an hour was just good clean fun, and sleeping in the "Camaro Hotel" was good enough if the nearest hotel was more than fifteen minutes away from where you were going to be the next day.

Sometimes these roustabouts would get out of hand, and Russ would hear about it. He received a call from the new operations manager in Tulsa who was madder than hell about some steel cowboy who almost hit him with a sledgehammer. It seemed that after a site was finished, the crew chief stopped in to see him, just as a courtesy. The operations manager was the guy who made sure that the service was up and running after the sites were tested and the crews left. The crew chief was in a rush, had to get to the next site, but the operations manager insisted that a door be built between the office and the radio shed. "Where do you want the goddamned door?" the chief said, mad at himself for even stopping in. The operations manager held his hand against the cinder-block wall and said, "Right here," at which point the crew chief raised his sledgehammer and commenced to smash a hole in the wall. A week later, Smith saw the operations manager. The bruise had already begun to heal.

Field guys had little respect for paper, but they were big on concrete and steel. They did their jobs and left the carbon copies to others back at the home office. Again and again, Russ would hear about his bad boys. A crew chief named Elvin decided that he couldn't get between sites fast enough, so he appropriated an experimental aircraft. That would save him plenty of time and seemed like a pretty good idea except that Elvin only had one eye.

Even one-eyed pilots have to land, though, so he asked Bechtel Construction Company to cut him a little strip at one of the sites in the desert. Bechtel was used to building dams and twelve-lane highways in Saudi Arabia, but they didn't know how to scrape off a little topsoil for Elvin, so they just added it on to the rest of MCI's work request at a cost of $35,000. While the request made it back to MCI headquarters, Elvin had slipped a rancher a thousand bucks to flatten a 1200-foot strip for him and his aircraft.

Russ was in the field when Leming called him, furious: "What the fuck are you doing out there?"

Without waiting for a reply, he said, "I don't want to talk about it. You get your ass up here now!" It took Russ about a week to calm Leming down and explain what happened. He even squared things with Bechtel, but Elvin, alas, was grounded.

Despite the fact that these guys were having fun, they built a system that worked. They were breaking new ground, putting up a system that worked adequately—and for about 40 percent less money than AT&T. Sure, a site may have ended up a thousand feet away from where they leased the land, but what the hell: They were erecting sites at the rate of one every business day.

Sometimes when they worked late and were stuck in the middle of nowhere, they would call the MCI office on a special channel reserved for maintenance and talk to whoever answered. McGowan was not athletic enough to visit a site and climb a tower to see firsthand what it was all about, but he did talk to the boys quite a bit about the latest piece of iron they had put up just before midnight.

The construction techniques were new, but the technology wasn't; they were just combining the two without the bullshit.

Engineers learned a lot about microwave technology from radar during World War II. Instead of conventional radio waves of low frequencies, microwaves have a very high frequency range. That makes the wavelength, which is inversely proportional, very small, hence the name "*micro*waves." Microwaves were perfect for hip-hopping telephone messages because of their directionability. Unlike a conventional radio signal that usually goes out in many different directions, a microwave signal could be shot in a thin beam from site to site without interfering with other parallel microwave routes. That directional aspect of microwaves made it perfect for radar beams and telephone towers.

MCI erected three different types of sites. The first and simplest was the repeater station. It took a signal coming in from one side, amplified it, and sent it out the other side. The other was a junction site. This was like a repeater except it received a signal from more than one direction and sent it out in more than one direction. The third type was the terminal site, the end of the line. These were usually in cities. Most of the time, the antennas were placed on roofs and the equipment was in the basement. The field gypsies liked these best because it meant the route was finished. It also meant a good meal in a good restaurant.

Things were going well until mid-1973, when Russ and Art began to sense a problem back in Washington. Leming, who had told everyone to bust ass, was suddenly telling them to slow down. Bring in the contractors a little more slowly; take a little more time pouring the concrete; go back and fine-tune some sites already built. The two managers had built enough systems for Collins to know what was going on. MCI was in money trouble. They wouldn't realize how bad the situation was until construction would no longer dwindle but instead come to a complete halt.

THE FOURTH BUSINESS—

Litigation
1973—74

1

Around the time that Leming and his boys began building the
network, Larry Harris was starting negotiations with AT&T for
interconnection with the local phone companies. Under the FCC
ruling, AT&T had to supply these connections, but how much they
would cost and under what conditions they would be offered was still
unsettled. Naturally, AT&T didn't want to supply interconnections to
a company that would be its competitor, but Harris believed they
would bargain in good faith because the FCC had told them they
would have to.

Harris was perfect for the job. He was a lawyer with a technical
background. At Leasco, he had worked in the time-sharing business.
He was combative and liked a good fight.

He was ready for a change from Leasco, and Carl suggested that he
talk to McGowan about working at MCI. He told Carl he thought it
was a dumb idea, but he would talk to McGowan anyway. There was
something special about McGowan, Carl told him.

Harris was in Los Angeles when he received a call from McGowan's
secretary, Martha Hiney, who said McGowan would meet him at the
Admiral's Club in the L.A. airport around 7:30 P.M. that Friday.

As the time neared, Harris decided he wasn't going to wait around
for McGowan to arrive. All the planes from Chicago, where
McGowan was coming from, had been canceled because of bad

weather, and he had to catch a plane himself. He was just about to leave when McGowan walked in. Harris couldn't figure out how McGowan got there, and McGowan never offered to tell him, but Harris said to himself, "Maybe there *is* something to this guy. Maybe he *could* do it."

McGowan laid the whole thing out: how he was going to compete with the Bell System and how, if it worked, Harris could make some money and have some fun doing it. McGowan offered Harris $30,000 less than he was making at Leasco but with the promise of stock options that could be worth a lot more if they were successful. Harris was always looking for a challenge, but he told McGowan it was a little too crazy for him. He would call McGowan back on Sunday anyway. Over the weekend, Harris talked it over with his wife, and the more he told her, the more he sucked himself in. "You know, this could really be something. It could be an experience of a lifetime," he told her. Harris took the job.

For one of his earliest meetings with AT&T, Jack and he flew to New York to talk with Mark Garlinghouse, AT&T's general counsel. Garlinghouse was as straight as they came, totally of the AT&T mold, believing as did deButts that AT&T could do no wrong. It was Mom and apple pie wrapped snugly in Old Glory, and if Garlinghouse smiled at all, it was only to test his facial muscles. AT&T attorneys Charlie Jackson and Jack Wiley also attended the meeting.

Jack Goeken had already negotiated some agreements for the St. Louis-to-Chicago route, so he had some experience dealing with the AT&T folks. Jack and Harris met in Garlinghouse's office. Jack was an hour late—he had spent time picking up his clothes which were scattered near the Washington Monument after his suitcase fell off the back of his motorcycle on the way to National Airport.

Garlinghouse sat in an overstuffed chair behind a huge desk. Jackson and Wiley sat perpendicular to his desk on a couch. Harris and Jack sat opposite them in separate chairs.

Garlinghouse laid down the law immediately. He told Jack and Harris that MCI would have to buy facilities, not lease them, and that was the way it was going to be. Harris knew that wasn't possible because MCI didn't have the money. He also figured that might go against FCC regulations—it might violate the spirit although not the letter of the law. If AT&T made the price so high that MCI couldn't afford it, that might be the same as not supplying the circuits at all.

The meeting went downhill from there, and at one point, Jack said to Garlinghouse, "One of the reasons you may be angry with us is that you don't really know what we're trying to do."

Garlinghouse replied, "I understand what you're trying to do," and Jack, in his enthusiastic way, said, "I don't think you do," and he reached into his breast pocket and pulled out about six sheets of oversize easel paper with drawings and diagrams and started advancing on Garlinghouse. Garlinghouse tried to gesture Jack away, like shooing a mangy dog, but by now he was on the arm of his chair, inches from Garlinghouse's face. Jackson and Wiley wanted to laugh but couldn't. Harris was out of control. He couldn't stop laughing as Garlinghouse screamed at Jack to get out of his office. Finally, Harris contained himself enough to tell Jack, "We better go."

At the elevator, Harris thought, "This is the worst day of my life. This is a disaster. These guys are giving us a blueprint to put us out of business before we even build our towers."

Jack said, "You know, that was a good meeting. I think they know what we're trying to do."

"Okay, Jack, I guess so," Harris said, half laughing and half crying.

Negotiations over the next several months were getting nowhere. Harris had begun to think that AT&T was just wearing him down and had no intention of ever giving MCI the interconnections it needed. Harris knew he was in trouble when he would send proposal drafts to AT&T, and they would send back their own drafts without responding to the ones that Harris had sent. In the spring of 1973, Harris began sending copies of his correspondence to the Justice Department.

Still, negotiations continued.

In September, while in Jackson's office for a meeting, Harris got a phone call from his secretary. Jackson told him to use his phone, which was behind Jackson's desk on a credenza. Jackson got up and out of his way. Standing there talking on the phone, Harris read a memo upside down on Jackson's desk that said AT&T was prepared to file tariffs with the state commissions setting forth MCI's fees for interconnections. That meant MCI would have to negotiate with each local phone company and file a tariff with each state utility commission before serving customers in that state. Clearly, Harris knew it was an impossible task.

Harris was angry as hell. Here Jackson and he were negotiating about one thing—a nationwide plan for interconnection—while it appeared to Harris after reading the memo that AT&T knew months ago that it had no intention of following through on those negotiations. Tariffs take months to prepare, and all they were doing, Harris finally believed, was using up time until the tariffs were ready. It turned out later that AT&T had actually made the decision earlier that spring to file tariffs with individual states.

Harris told McGowan what he had seen on Jackson's desk. McGowan was furious. A short while later, Jackson called Harris to tell him about the new plan. Harris, of course, had already known. "Charlie," he said to Jackson, "this has got to be one of the most low-life things. Here you jerk us around for months when you had no intention of negotiating with us at all."

Jackson said, "We just decided to do it."

"Come on," Harris said, "it takes months to get tariffs ready. You knew months ago what was going on."

At that point, McGowan and the others knew MCI had entered a new business. It wasn't telephones; it was litigation. Like it or not, the next few years would belong to the lawyers.

Negotiations stopped dead. AT&T informed the FCC of its intention to file tariffs with the states instead of with them, but a month later, the FCC said they couldn't do that. The states didn't have jurisdiction, and AT&T better file with the FCC.

McGowan and the others realized they had to do something fast. If they didn't get interconnection, they would be out of business. So they filed for relief in the U.S. District Court in Philadelphia asking for an injunction against AT&T. There was a three-day hearing and Judge Clarence Newcomer told AT&T that they must connect MCI. The order came on New Year's Day 1974, two and a half months after they asked the court to issue the injunction.

Meanwhile, the FCC had asked AT&T to show cause why it should not stop its activities and connect MCI as it had originally ordered.

While all the legal mumbo jumbo went on, MCI was going under. It was forced to lay off 60 people in September and another 150 in December. Without the interconnections, they couldn't make any money.

AT&T lawyers appealed Newcomer's decision to the Third Circuit Court of Appeals. The court refused AT&T's request for a stay, and AT&T said it would comply with the court's order pending another appeal.

Meanwhile, McGowan knew he had no choice but to put the

ultimate legal pressure on AT&T. Although only a handful of people at MCI knew it, McGowan had had two private meetings with AT&T Chairman John deButts during the past two years. McGowan thought if he met face-to-face with deButts, they might work things out. He also wanted to let deButts know that if MCI didn't get relief from AT&T, they would be forced to sue. McGowan came away from the second meeting realizing that nothing short of a lawsuit would budge deButts. Now he was certain.

In March 1974, MCI filed a lawsuit against AT&T alleging that it violated the Sherman Antitrust Act on fifteen separate occasions by using its monopoly power to put MCI out of business. The suit would be expensive for MCI, but McGowan knew he had no other choice.

As the suit was filed, the Third Circuit heard AT&T's arguments on appeal of the injunction. It ruled that the FCC had jurisdiction in the case, but while the FCC was taking up the matter, AT&T struck its strongest blow against MCI.

During a management strategy meeting in Sterling Park, New Jersey, McGowan received a call from Jim Ferguson, Larry Harris's assistant, that AT&T had pulled circuits it had installed during the injunction period.

Bob Swezey, one of Jack's first employees, began getting calls from companies like Woodward & Lothrop, a Washington department store, telling him that they had no phone service.

Five days later, the FCC ordered AT&T to furnish MCI with all its interconnections within ten days. AT&T began to comply, slowly, but the damage had been done. MCI's credibility was zero. Although the number of companies that had circuits pulled was small, few companies wanted to do business with MCI knowing that at any moment their lines could be pulled. Salesmen found it difficult to sign up new customers, and old customers were afraid their lines would be cut again.

The banks were scared, too. MCI had spent more than $84 million on its microwave network, yet revenues from the system were less than $750,000. It had already borrowed $48 million of its $64 million line of credit, and money that was destined for construction was starting to go for everyday expenses. In May, MCI was forced to buy N-Triple-C, a company with a system in the Midwest and Southwest. MCI bought the company with stock instead of cash to keep it from going under. If N-Triple-C failed, McGowan reasoned, it might show that the concept of long distance supplied by anyone other than AT&T was a bust, and that might deter banks from lending MCI any more money.

MCI would have to do something dramatic if it was to survive. It did. It kept borrowing more money from the banks. McGowan figured if he could get in so deep with the banks that they wouldn't let him go under, but instead continue to lend him more money, he might be able to last until the revenue started flowing. McGowan knew the cliché was true: "If I owe you $100, that's my problem. If I owe you $1 million, that's your problem." The plan worked, so to speak. Within two years, MCI owed five banks $99 million.

McGowan had begun to isolate his staff from the banks. He believed that in order to maintain the presence that everything was okay, to keep morale up, he must act as a buffer between the two groups. For the most part, it worked, but as people came to him with their new projects and ideas, all McGowan could do was smile and say, "Let me think about it." He knew that they were doing the right things for their jobs and were only asking for the funds necessary to do them, but the coffers were empty. Although everyone at MCI knew the situation was bad, McGowan never let on how bad.

In mid-1974, Bert Roberts, now a vice-president, was in charge of new services and regulatory affairs. McGowan knew that any new services would be closely tied to the regulatory process, so to put them both under the control of one person made sense. Roberts's job was to start new services that exploited the small MCI network, cost no money, and needed little support.

Bert Roberts and his staff, John Montgomery and Stan Katz, found a device called a WATSBOX, manufactured by a small firm called Action. WATS stood for Wide Area Telecommunications Services and was an AT&T concept for bulk sales of telephone lines to large customers. A customer would lease a dedicated phone between two cities and make as many calls a month as he wanted for a single price.

It would be cheaper to call someone in a distant city over the WATS line than by direct dialing each time.

For a fee, MCI installed the WATSBOX at the customer's premise. On one side, they connected the customer's phone, and on the other side, they connected both AT&T's WATS lines and MCI's private lines. When a call was made, the box would decide if the call was going to a city on MCI's network or not. If it was, the call went over MCI's lines. If not, it went over AT&T's lines. Calls going over MCI's lines were cheaper than those going over AT&T's lines, so many customers saved money on their bills even though they paid a fee for the WATSBOX.

Later, the idea was expanded so the WATSBOX wasn't installed in the customer's office but on MCI's premises, and any customer, large or small, could use the WATSBOX by dialing a special local phone number and a customer billing number. Instead of paying a flat rate, calls were metered and customers would receive a bill based on how long they talked and where they called.

The service was called Execunet, short for Executive Network, MCI's answer to regular AT&T dial-up long-distance service. It would be perfect for customers who were not large enough to need their own private line.

Roberts convinced himself that Execunet was the future of MCI, and he sent scathing memos to McGowan and others telling them to get off their asses and get Execunet into gear. McGowan didn't have any money, and he was reluctant to give Roberts funding for more and larger WATSBOXES. Roberts continued to fight for the service, believing that it would save MCI. McGowan didn't know if it would save MCI or not. All he knew was that the banks were getting edgy, and he would have to justify every penny he spent. McGowan believed strongly that if you give someone the responsibility to do a job, then you must also give him the authority. In this case, however, only McGowan could authorize the purchase of WATSBOXES. What could he do? He couldn't tell everyone how bad the money situation was. No, he had to keep them sheltered for the good of the company. As a first step, however, McGowan authorized Roberts to file a tariff at the FCC for the new service.

Jerry Taylor was running sales and operations for the western United States out of Dallas. He was hot on Execunet, too. During Christmas of 1974, he went to Washington to try to convince McGowan to give him money for a WATSBOX that could turn private lines into dial-up service. Like Bert Roberts, he had trouble. Execunet had been tested in Washington, D.C., and it was a complete flop. It just didn't sell, and nobody knew exactly why. Carl thought it might be that customers didn't want to dial all the digits necessary to access the system. Others believed it was because the service was so different from private line that nobody at MCI knew how to present it to the customers.

Finally, McGowan gave in. By January, Jerry had begun formal marketing of Execunet within Texas.

Jack Goeken didn't like what was going on at MCI. He saw services such as Execunet taking MCI into an area he didn't want to explore. He felt it was dishonest, and his conscience couldn't handle it. He had told the FCC in his original application that he wanted to provide specialized services, something that Bell wasn't supplying. Now he found that McGowan and others were pushing MCI into services close to those already supplied by AT&T. He didn't want any part of it. He could have stayed and fought, but he didn't think it was wise. MCI was in a precarious financial situation, and any infighting, he believed, could only hurt the company. Besides, he thought that the company was so far along in the direction that McGowan wanted to go that it would be senseless for him to try to change it. It didn't hold his interest anymore, either, and he found himself keeping away from the office even more than before. Financially, he would do well. He left MCI with more than 1.5 million shares of stock that he could sell after a two-year moratorium.

On July 12, 1974, without any fanfare, Jack tendered his resignation to the board of directors in a letter and left MCI forever.

Jack tried to start a company with Bernie Strassberg, who had since left the FCC to become a consultant, and Tom Carter of Carterfone, but nothing came of the plan. Jack had other business ideas. He began a computer service that supported the FTD florists' network so people could send flowers by phone. That would keep him busy, and so would a small, specialized common carrier that he would build between Chicago and Milwaukee. It would be just like the one he wanted the original MCI to be.

Those two businesses plus his stock would be enough for Jack to launch another project. He wanted to be the first person to place pay phones on airplanes.

John Worthington made certain that the Justice Department's antitrust division knew what was going on. He had succeeded in piquing their interest to the point where they assigned one person to keep on eye on MCI and its dealings with AT&T. That person was Phil Verveer, who later became chief of the FCC's Common Carrier Bureau. Worthington met monthly, sometimes weekly, with Verveer and others at Justice, hoping that the government might institute a suit against AT&T. At the very least, he hoped that Justice's interest might deter AT&T from trying to crush MCI illegally.

After a while, Worthington began to doubt that AT&T realized what it was doing. He was beginning to understand the arrogance that everyone said AT&T possessed, but it had never really hit home to Worthington until one conversation he had with Mark Garlinghouse. He had been so pumped up by deButts's anticompetition speeches and rhetoric that he had lost sight of the antitrust laws.

Worthington said to Garlinghouse, "Mark, maybe if you had 25 percent of the market, and you were doing some of the things you were doing, you could get away with it. When you have 100 percent of the market, you just can't do these things. Why do you do them?"

Garlinghouse replied, "We're entitled to do them."

In November 1974, the Justice Department filed an antitrust suit against AT&T. Based on its own investigation, following up actions of

AT&T against MCI, Justice sought to break up, once and forever, the local phone companies and the long-distance company known collectively as the Bell System. The idea was to separate the locally regulated monopolies from the long-distance business, which was supposed to be open to competition. If that happened, it would loosen the stranglehold that AT&T held on MCI and others trying to compete in the long-distance market.

In addition, the Justice Department's suit also alleged that AT&T illegally stifled the telephone equipment market by coercing the local companies to buy all their equipment from Western Electric, AT&T's manufacturing arm. If AT&T and the local companies were separate, the local companies would be free to buy equipment anywhere and at lower prices, presumably getting better equipment as well.

That suit would accomplish its goal ten years later when AT&T, on January 1, 1984, divested itself of its local operating companies. Although Justice had tried to break up AT&T many times before, it was AT&T's blatant treatment of MCI and others that finally provided enough evidence to sustain the government's case. It was as if AT&T had brought it upon themselves.

THE FIFTH BUSINESS—

Survival
1974—78

1

Bert Roberts and Ken Cox believed they had been up front with the FCC about Execunet. They said it was a long-distance, metered, dial-up service different from the company's other offerings: private line, a dedicated circuit connecting offices in different cities, and FX, "Foreign eXchange," a term coined by AT&T. An FX circuit connected telephones in one city to the local phone network in a faraway city by way of a leased private line. With FX, a customer lifted his phone and was automatically connected to the local phone system in another city. For example, a caller in Houston would use his FX line to call Dallas numbers almost like he was dialing locally. FX was cheaper than direct-dialing long distance for companies that called many different phone numbers in a different city.

Execunet was operating only inside Texas, and that didn't require FCC approval. Now that Bert wanted to expand it to handle interstate traffic, MCI needed federal permission. Bert and Ken filed their tariff for Execunet after discussions and presentations with the staff of the FCC's Common Carrier Bureau. Staffers had asked for clarification of one point, and after that was straightened out, the tariff went into effect in October 1974, thirty-one days after it had been filed.

AT&T didn't oppose the Execunet filing during the usual thirty-day period, which had been extended an extra day for the clarification by MCI. Nobody at MCI knew why AT&T didn't oppose the tariff—MCI was ready if they did—but apparently AT&T was involved in tariff filings of its own and didn't want to split its attention.

In April, about three months after MCI had begun marketing Execunet, AT&T started going to the FCC commissioners telling them that it was illegal for MCI to offer the service. It was not within MCI's license authorization, they said. AT&T lawyers lobbied hard. To demonstrate the service to the commissioners, AT&T lawyers brought a tone generator to the FCC offices—to simulate the Touch-Tone phone necessary for Execunet to work—and dialed the Chicago weather report using an authorization code they had obtained from someone Ken Cox thought was a friend.

AT&T claimed that the FCC's original order limited MCI to private-line service only, and Execunet, they said, was just like MTS, or Measured Telecommunications Service, commonly referred to as direct-dial long-distance phone service.

In fact, the original FCC order said nothing about private-line service or MTS or anything else. All it said was that MCI could build and operate a microwave system and connect it to the local phone network, but AT&T disagreed on the interpretation.

While MCI and AT&T were exchanging letters on the matter, Ken Cox got a call from an FCC staffer who told him, "Hey, you guys better get worried; they've got this place covered like a blanket. The commissioners have been stampeded, and they're going to tell you to stop."

The commissioners believed that Execunet was such a radical product that the request to offer it should have been sent to them and not to the tariff division, which often handled routine rate requests. AT&T convinced the commissioners that MCI was using the tariff division to sneak Execunet through the FCC.

The following day, Ken was walking by the FCC and bumped into a commissioner who told him in a half-joking manner, "Oh, you sneaky people. The Execunet is really MTS."

"Now, wait a minute," Ken said. "You better sit down and read all the stuff we're filing. It's highly justifiable. It's a shared type of FX, and you've encouraged us to share our lines." Ken walked on, believing that AT&T had brainwashed all the commissioners.

The FCC issued an order telling MCI to stop offering Execunet within thirty days. MCI then went outside the FCC and asked the U.S. Court of Appeals to issue a stay of the FCC's order.

The FCC then asked the court to return the matter to them for review, claiming that it didn't follow the correct procedures and it needed to run it through again. The court was perfectly willing to do that, not wanting to work harder than it had to anyway. The FCC began formal proceedings on whether or not specialized common carriers such as MCI could offer long-distance metered service.

The matter began bouncing between the FCC and the courts. In the meantime, MCI could continue to sell Execunet service, knowing that right could be cut off at any moment.

Although everyone remained skeptical, Jerry and Bert felt that Execunet was a money-maker. By July, Jerry had signed more than two hundred customers, whose average monthly billings ranged from $85 to $1,800. He had three full-time salespeople who also sold private lines, so the cost of getting Execunet customers was low. He used college students to give the salespeople hot leads. If it went as planned, Jerry estimated that Execunet profit could top $18,000 a month, and if they reached full capacity of the WATSBOX, profit could be $60,000 per month. This was much more than private-line service could bring in. Not only that, Execunet could be supplied to the customer almost immediately (private lines took sixty days to install), and it took no maintenance to keep customers on the system. Moreover, it appealed to anyone with a phone whether he was a large or small user. One of the biggest problems Jerry had was trying to convince potential customers that this alternative to the Bell System was legal.

Slowly, Execunet was proving itself. It brought in lots of money for little work compared with private lines. In March 1974, MCI had sold only $728,000 worth of communications services, the *total* revenues since the company began. Only one year later, MCI racked up almost $7 million in sales, most of it because of Execunet. It looked like Bert and Jerry had MCI's salvation in their hands if they could continue to sell it.

While Ken Cox handled the courts, McGowan had his hands full with the banks. They were watching MCI more closely than ever. Five banks held notes on MCI: First National Bank of Chicago, First National Bank of Boston, Citibank, Continental, and Manufacturers Hanover. First Chicago, the name everyone gave the bank, was in the hole for $29 million, making it the lead bank. They assigned Bill Conway, a loan officer, to keep an eye on their money.

Conway had recently been transferred to the technology group at the bank and inherited what bankers like to call "difficult accounts." These are companies that the bank has loaned money to, but because they are shaky the bank doesn't know how it will get its money back. Basically, they're losers, and the banks kept close tabs on them. That's how Conway got to know MCI.

He became the junior person on the account and traveled to Washington at least once a month, sometimes more, to keep tight watch on the operation. When Conway took over the action, MCI was into the banks to the tune of $92 million. Eventually, it would reach $99 million.

Conway would travel to Washington and meet with McGowan, Bert Roberts, Tom Leming, or someone else who would fill him in on what was going on. He paid close attention to the little details like how many people had been hired or fired, what customers had been signed up, and so forth. Most of the time, he kept a careful account of the cash flow—what came in and what went out. Conway knew it was all too easy for failing companies to rejigger their books to show anything they wanted—not that he accused MCI of doing anything wrong—and he knew all the tricks. But cash didn't lie. How much a company spent and how much it took in were solid facts.

Often, Bert Roberts, who was operations manager, would tell him about the latest switches, or Tom Leming would regale him with how many more miles of microwave routes they had put in service, or McGowan would tell Conway about the latest regulatory happenings at the FCC. Conway dug deep and eventually became the senior man on the account. He probably knew more about MCI than any outsider.

On one of his first trips to Washington, Conway and his boss, Ran Sparling, had dinner with Bert Roberts and Tom Leming. Bert and Conway, being the younger two of the foursome, gravitated to each other, and Bert told him about a new product being tested in Texas: Execunet. He explained that anyone in Dallas with a push-button phone could call anyone else in one of five cities for much less than AT&T charged just by dialing about twenty extra digits. "It's a great product," Bert said. "It's going to catch on like wildfire."

Conway replied like any banker. "How much did you bring in last month on this?"

"Twenty-five hundred," Bert said.

Conway wasn't impressed. He thought, "This company is $99 million in the hole, and they brought in $2,500 on this new product. I don't know about this."

Conway knew there was nothing the banks could do to force MCI to pay its debt. He decided that his main job was to keep the other banks in check—keep them from doing anything rash like calling in the loans immediately—and rely on MCI's management to pull itself out. He thought that MCI's original revenue projections had been correct, and MCI would probably have been making some more money if the Bell companies had given them the private-line interconnections they were legally entitled to. Now with the court-ordered interconnections, MCI might have a chance.

In a sense, it almost didn't matter. The banks had no choice but to let the string play out. If the loans were called, the banks would get zip. They had nothing more to lose by letting it ride a little longer. Certainly, they wouldn't lend MCI any more than their original line of credit, but they could sign various amendments and waivers for payments and allow MCI to use its loans for everyday expenses instead of construction, as had been the target for much of the funds. By this time, MCI had stopped construction of its system anyway. Most important, the banks agreed to defer collection of interest payments for about six months. That was almost like a loan, but it didn't require anyone going into the till and actually handing over more money to MCI.

Some banks choose to replace management of companies that are going under, but Conway knew that would be a big mistake. If he did that, it would place First Chicago in a position of becoming the management and would then, according to banking rules, place them at the bottom of the creditors' list. If MCI did go bust, they would be the last to be paid and probably wouldn't see any money at all.

However, just before Conway arrived on the scene, MCI did lose one of its managers. Stan Scheinman, believing that his relationship with the banks and investment community had deteriorated to the point where he could no longer function, quit to work for FSC, a financial company in Pittsburgh. He didn't know if the banks had pressured McGowan to let him go or not. McGowan never said it, and Scheinman never asked. Scheinman, in his blind optimism about MCI, had promised great financial goals that never materialized. He felt it was best for him to leave before things got worse. MCI had been planning another public stock offering, and his presence might stand in the way.

McGowan, who was now acting as the chief financial officer in addition to chairman and chief executive officer, was forced by the banks to go public in November 1975 rather than wait for what he considered the "right moment." He was angry, but he didn't have any choice in the matter. The banks forced MCI to sell more stock to the public.

By McGowan's measure, the offering was a flop. The stock price was less than $2 a share. A company's worth is determined in large part by how many of its own shares it owns and how much that stock is worth. McGowan believed he was forced into selling too many shares for too little money. He thought he had given away the store.

MCI sold 9.6 million shares of stock—4.8 million common shares and 4.8 million in warrants—that brought in $8.5 million. A warrant is a right to buy shares of stock at a set price for a long period of time after it is issued. Warrants are a way to sweeten the pot when a company in poor financial shape sells stock. A buyer makes more money for almost the same risk as buying straight shares, with the additional chance of making even more money if the company turns around.

The bankers considered the offering a success. It may have hurt MCI to sell so much of itself, and higher-priced warrants might be costly to cover in future years, but it would keep MCI afloat a little while longer.

Even though MCI was broke, it still needed equipment to operate. It didn't have money to buy things so it leased almost everything, including copy machines, desks, chairs, and typewriters. It would have leased wall paint if someone could have figured out a way to affix the little colored tags showing to which leasing company it belonged.

MCI was so strapped for cash that they would lease a copy machine, for instance, and when they got too far behind in paying the monthly bills, the leasing company would take the machine away. MCI would then lease one from a different company, and when they got too far behind in *those* bills . . .

A favorite trick was to pay bills by check but not sign it. When the check came back and the "honest mistake" was apologized for, it was signed and mailed again. It was all done in the name of float. A delay of a week or two helped.

Major items had to be leased, too. Before Scheinman left MCI, he had negotiated some deals that would allow MCI to obtain expensive Execunet switches it needed for very little money. The deals hinged on a small company called Danray, begun by Jim Nolan.

Nolan was getting tired of counting Chiffon margarine and Seven Seas salad dressing bottles. As internal auditor of Anderson, Clayton in Houston, that's what his job boiled down to, and he was bored. He was only thirty-four, and after he got transferred to Dallas to be director of budget and profit sharing, he decided to take a chance and go into business with three other guys. Two of his partners were Dan and Ray, and it was their idea, so they called the company Danray.

Danray made private branch exchanges (PBXs) for offices. A PBX is a device that lets all the phones in an office seem like they're on their own little telephone company. To call another office down the hall, you just dial the last three or four digits of the phone number. For an outside line, you must dial a "9" to get out of the system. PBXs grew rapidly in the 1960s as companies erected huge office complexes and an easy way to call among offices became mandatory.

Danray also began a radio frequency coordinating company, called Compucon, that tracked microwave routes on a computer. If a company like MCI wanted to build a microwave route between two sites, the computer would digest the latitude and longitude and determine what other microwave route belonging to other companies might interfere. That way a company could change the sites or frequencies.

Nolan had met McGowan when he was in Texas trying to raise money for that area's local MCI company. Later, he met Jerry Taylor when he was just getting Execunet started in Dallas and Houston. Nolan believed that McGowan was on the right track. He had been following Jack Goeken's case at the FCC for several years and thought that alternative long-distance services might just make it. He knew that the Carterfone decision fostered the PBX business and maybe the MCI decision would do the same for long-distance phone service.

So the Danray company designed and built a switch that would accommodate new carriers like MCI. It was a big gamble but it sure beat salad dressing.

At that time, Jerry was using a WATSBOX with capacity for 108 lines, while the Danray product could accommodate 1,000. The Danray switch also allowed customers to call either way on the Execunet system, not just from Houston or Dallas outward. In a note to McGowan, Jerry outlined the advantages of the Danray switch. He wanted one. The only trouble was that MCI had no money, and the switches cost from $600,000 to $1 million apiece.

Danray had no money either. They were in worse shape than MCI. They had a product that their main customers couldn't afford to buy and that none of the other carriers, such as Southern Pacific, were far enough along in their networks to need.

Scheinman had introduced Nolan to Joel Mallon, a former

classmate of his at Columbia University. Mallon had created a new form of the "wraparound mortgage" that could be applied to equipment leasing. His plan relied on the all-American idea that companies should get tax breaks for investing in new equipment. It didn't matter if it was they who needed the equipment or if someone else needed it. That plan also held up to Scheinman's first rule of business: *Create enough economic benefits to many people, and they will allow it to happen.*

Mallon and Scheinman found companies that were taking in lots of money and needed tax deductions to reduce Uncle Sam's cut. One happened to be a vacuum bag maker in the Bronx, another a maker of fine ladies purses. The bag maker, for example, would have loved to buy the switch, lease it to MCI, and get tax deductions as the switch got older. That's known as depreciation. They system works fine if the bag maker is leasing equipment to General Motors, but it couldn't run the risk of MCI going bust and getting stuck with a switch that it didn't need.

Scheinman went to a bank and got a loan for the bag maker for about half the price of the switch. The bank is protected because if anything goes wrong, it takes custody of a million-dollar switch for a half million dollars.

Next step: Scheinman went to Nolan and agreed to give him an amount slightly higher than the cost of just building the switch. He made a teeny profit, but it allowed him to continue making switches and pay his employees. He accepted the money with the promise that he would get payments each month for about seven years until the switch's retail price was paid. In the meantime, his accountants allowed him to chalk up the full sale price of the switch on his books, and that made the company look good enough on paper so he could get credit elsewhere if he needed it.

Every month, MCI put money into a trust account from money it made because it had use of the switch. From that fund, Nolan got a monthly payment and so did the bank. The bag maker got his tax deduction and Mallon and Scheinman each got a cut for putting all the pieces together. By the end of seven years, Nolan had gotten the full price of his switch plus a little extra. The bag maker had paid off the bank loan and also had a little extra money. MCI could buy the switch it had been using all these years at a used rate if it wanted.

Danray and MCI were growing together. Each depended upon the other, and even though Nolan was paying exorbitant interest rates—by not getting paid up front for the full retail price of the switch—his only complaint was that he couldn't get enough of it. He believed that no interest payment was too high if you didn't have any money.

After three or four years of these leasing deals, MCI's credit became good enough that Nolan received much more up-front money for his switches.

Years later, in 1978, Nolan was forced to sell Danray to Northern Telecom, a Canadian PBX maker. Xerox and Bechtel owned about 50 percent of Danray by that time, and they wanted to sell it. The company was sold for $24 million, and Nolan, who was chairman, received about $2 million for his 10 percent share. That Danray purchase was the beginning of the rise of Northern Telecom, which went on to become one of the largest telephone equipment makers in the world, grabbing the lion's share of the market for PBXs, switches, and phones.

Three years later, Nolan got involved in a company called Digital Switch. The company's goal was to develop a totally electronic switch for local phone companies. The switches would be more efficient and cheaper to use than older electromechanical switches. By 1980, they still didn't have a product, but the new issues market was so hot that they took the company public and raised $8.5 million, even though they didn't even have a prototype. Still foundering, Nolan and James Donald, also of Danray, took control of the company's direction and turned it toward building a switch aimed at long-distance companies instead. By 1982, the company had introduced its first switch, and the product took off. The stock shot from around $10 a share in mid-1982 to more than $100 by late 1983, making a lot of people who knew about the company's chances for success very rich. MCI was Digital Switch's largest customer, and speculation arose that some MCI and DS employees made money on insider information. A Securities and Exchange Commission investigation was inconclusive.

As MCI was slowly growing, McGowan needed someone who could manage large numbers of people. He didn't want a lockstep manager to crack the whip, but he certainly needed someone who could bring some order to the chaos that he saw building around him. McGowan was good at starting companies and directing them, but he couldn't bring himself to handle the daily nitty-gritty matters. It just didn't interest him.

Through Dick Sayford, his Harvard Business School roommate and IBMer, McGowan met V. Orville Wright. Orville knew Sayford from their days at IBM. McGowan and Orville would run into each other for many years, mostly at Sayford's house. McGowan had asked Orville several times to join MCI, but Orville wasn't interested. He knew how to manage large companies with lots of people but he wasn't an entrepreneur and MCI was still an entrepreneurial company. Now things were different. Although MCI was still on shaky footing, it wasn't a start-up company. Orville decided to give it a try.

Orville worked at IBM for twenty years, during which he ran some of the firm's earliest computer projects. It was his first job out of the Navy—where he had wanted to be a bold, dashing pilot but instead got assigned to the supply corps. When he first heard about IBM, he was intrigued by the idea of a company actually building magical things called computers. He liked his first position there, working with customers, teaching them how to use the new machines. Later on, he moved to the management side and became an administrator. His career paralleled Carl's, which was on the sales side. The two of them never met, although they knew of each other by reputation.

Orville would have probably stayed longer at IBM, but in the 1960s the company changed. It was no longer feisty, innovative, and inventive. Bureaucracy crept in and people got lost amid the meetings and reports. Orville wasn't having fun anymore. It got to the point where he believed it didn't matter whether he came in or not. Without another job lined up, he quit IBM cold.

He wanted to join a smaller company, someplace where it mattered whether he came in or not. He didn't want public recognition, just a place where he knew he was making a difference.

Instead, he found himself at RCA, heading an entire computer systems group. It was something he had never done before. He would be developing new computers and systems, and he worked on a project to build the first IBM-compatible mainframe computer. Unfortunately, the project was quashed before it was completed because of a struggle between board chairman Bob Sarnoff, Jr., and the board over whether RCA should be in the computer business. The board won and forced Sarnoff to resign, and Orville was out of a job.

Orville went to work for Gene Amdahl, who began a computer company bearing his name in Sunnyvale, California. The two had known each other at IBM, where Gene was one of the main architects of their computer systems. He was a genius. Orville agreed to begin work at Amdahl after he helped RCA sell the assets of the defunct computer group. He believed that he had an obligation to RCA to do that much.

While he was still at RCA, Orville had second thoughts about his agreement with Gene. He and Gene really didn't get along all that well at IBM because Gene insisted that he knew how to run a business and Orville insisted that he should stick to what he did best: be an engineer. It didn't change at Amdahl, and it got so bad that Orville went to the board to complain about Gene. It became obvious that one of them had to go, so Orville decided to leave. Later, the board realized that Orville was right. They forced Gene to bring in a president to run the business while Gene concentrated on the technical side.

By that time, Orville had begun working at Xerox for Bill Glavin, who was head of the company's computer operations. Xerox had bought Scientific Data Systems, which manufactured a computer for heavy scientific use. It was a massive number cruncher for engineers. Orville headed Xerox's Office of Business Development in Xerox's quest to become the leader in the "office of the future," the paperless office. Xerox hoped that its excellent line of copying machines would be its entrée into the high-tech office.

Instead, Orville realized that SDS's computer didn't fit into the plan. It wasn't an office computer; it was much too sophisticated and powerful. Orville suggested they sell SDS. In fact, he suggested they forget about the office of the future and stick with the business they knew best, copy machines. He knew he was talking himself out of a job, but he had to do the right thing. Making SDS fit just wasn't right. After many presentations and meetings, Xerox abandoned the computer business and Orville decided to leave the company. He wasn't excited by copy machines.

After a few months at MCI, Orville became the president and chief operating officer, COO. With McGowan as chairman and chief executive officer, CEO, they became the perfect team to run the company. McGowan was the dreamer, and Orville was the detail man. McGowan knew where he wanted the company to go and Orville would do the proper day-to-day steps to get it there. McGowan never wanted to write any procedures while Orville wanted to write everything down. They compromised and wrote down only those things that were necessary. McCowan became the flamboyant company spokesman while Orville stayed home and minded the store.

Orville would help institute stock option plans and other minutiae necessary for a growing company. He would make sure the employees were well taken care of so that they believed management cared about them. McGowan was less paternalistic toward his employees, and that was taken by some to mean uncaring and cold.

While McGowan was off making flamboyant speeches about the new information age and MCI's role in it, employees would come to Orville with their problems, and he would sit thoughtfully, puffing on his pipe, and render a decision with warmth and charm although never forgetting that the company was in business to make money.

McGowan always believed that people should be allowed to do their jobs with virtually no direction from management. Orville believed that people should be given direction and counsel. The two compromised and decided to build a company that permitted diversity and free choice without anarchy. If one employee in New York wanted to do something one way and an employee in Los Angeles wanted to do it another way, and each believed his method worked best, each would be allowed to do it his way. If it didn't work, he would be expected to change it.

Both McGowan and Orville strongly agreed that people should be allowed to make mistakes without fear of getting fired or yelled at. They would both encourage experimentation even if it meant slight waste or duplication. It would be worth it in the long run if MCI was to remain a company where people could try new ideas and not be paralyzed by fear of making an error.

McGowan believed in the absolute right of transfer within the company. Any employee could ask for any other position without his present boss getting involved with the prospective boss. In other words, both bosses didn't have to agree on the move. McGowan believed that free movement was essential to keep a company *alive*. He didn't want to see the lazy, unmotivated people he had seen during his days with Shell Oil, who were victims of the oil industry's policy of not hiring from other oil companies. As a result, MCI employees would move around a lot. Although it looked like madness to those outside the company, it was a way of life and perfectly natural for those at MCI. Employees wouldn't feel stuck in jobs they no longer liked or work with people they didn't get along with. Orville was able to keep the policy going and get its full benefit while maintaining decorum.

McGowan and Orville would grow to respect one another because each would learn that he could never do the other's job. They were yin and yang, fire and water, the Odd Couple of corporations even down to their names.

Orville never connected himself to the younger of the brothers of flight. In fact, his first name was Verson, but he never knew that until he was in the Navy and somebody checked. He always thought it was Vernon. None of that mattered, though. To those in the company, Bill McGowan would be referred to as McGowan—often Bill—but Orville would *always* be Orville.

But to Orville, who looked more like a small-town banker ready to give you a loan for a new tractor than president of a large corporation, the younger McGowan would often be . . . "William."

McGowan needed someone to take care of the financial end of the business. With Stan Scheinman gone, McGowan hunted for a new money man.

Wayne English had been the chief financial officer for Hallmark Greeting Card Co. in Kansas City for almost five years when President Don Hall told him that it was the end of the line. Wayne heard him say that he just didn't fit in anymore, that he wasn't getting along with his co-workers. Wayne was hurt and he wracked his brain trying to figure out whom he had offended. He *could* figure it out, and finally decided that it was Hall who didn't get along with him.

Hall had brought Wayne to the firm to oversee a real estate subsidiary, Crown Center Redevelopment Corporation, which was in trouble. Nobody at Hallmark had the experience needed to turn a profit on the deal. Wayne did, but he paid a price. He had shaken up the family-owned company founded by Don Hall's father, Joyce, in 1909. Wayne had obviously stepped on some toes along the way.

The fault wasn't just with Hallmark, however. Wayne was a little frayed around the edges because of his own problems at home. His marriage was ending.

Wayne became depressed. His failing marriage and being fired at the age of fifty-three after what seemed like a job well done was too much to take. He broke away for three months and played golf, trying to sort things out in his mind, until he was ready to hit the bricks and look for a new job.

After talking with headhunters in New York City one day, Wayne was ready to go home to Kansas City. He had had some pleasant conversation, but it was Friday and time to go home when he got a call from Ray Foote of the Heidrick & Struggles agency, who told him to come over and talk.

Wayne told Foote that he wanted a company that was taking off, a place where he could apply his talents. A Hallmark psychologist, who was helping Wayne through this tough period, had him write down his best business skills. On top Wayne listed negotiating and financing. "If you know of a small company with outstanding growth prospects that could use my skills, I'd be very interested in something like that," Wayne said.

"I just happen to have one," said Foote, and he reached in the bottom right-hand drawer of his desk and took out a stack of papers and proceeded to tell Wayne about a company called MCI. They talked for about an hour, and Wayne was interested. It seemed like MCI needed his two best skills.

Foote set up a meeting between McGowan and Wayne for the following week in Washington. Wayne met McGowan and Orville and came away intrigued with what they were trying to do. McGowan liked what he saw, because a few days later he offered Wayne a job.

"I can't offer you much money," McGowan told Wayne, "but we can give you a large stock option." Wayne's children were grown, so his family responsibilities were small and he didn't need a lot of income. He was interested in the chance to make some money later on. They settled on a salary of $60,000 plus an option to buy 60,000 shares of stock. Wayne had been making more than $200,000 a year at Hallmark.

Before they shook on it, Wayne told McGowan, "I'm very much inclined to take this, but before I do I'd like to go to Chicago and talk to First Chicago." Wayne knew that the banks had the power of life and death over MCI, and he wanted to get the full story from the lead bank. McGowan said, "I think you should."

Wayne went to Chicago on his way back home to Kansas City and faced a room full of stony-faced bankers who assured Wayne that they wouldn't lend MCI any more money. But Wayne also came away with the impression that they wouldn't pull the plug on MCI, either. That was all Wayne wanted to know.

He went home and discussed the offer with his eldest son. He laid out the pros and cons. He could be out in six months if the company went bust, or in five years he could be a millionaire. His son told him to take it, and in February 1976 Wayne joined MCI.

Five years later, his son would telephone and say he figured his dad was indeed a millionaire—at least on paper.

In an exacting manner, Wayne set up a game plan for MCI's financial future:

1. He wanted MCI to be in an impregnable financial situation. He really didn't define what that meant except he knew they would have to be independent of the banks and boast a strong enough balance sheet to handle any crisis.

2. He wanted MCI to become a billion-dollar company—that is, have $1 billion in sales—by 1987.

3. He wanted to build a financial organization that could carry on after he left the company.

4. He wanted to get the price of the stock to $25 a share within five years. With the stock at $25 a share, he could then do the necessary financing. Obviously, he couldn't predict what the price of the stock would be in five years, but that didn't matter. The stock *had* to be $25 a share or the company would be lost. The price of the stock is a reflection of the success of a company, and unless it was at least $25 all would be for nothing. "It isn't a matter of predicting the price of the stock," Wayne told everyone. "It has to happen."

Wayne would work with Bill Conway of First Chicago and with the other banks, and would be able to meet all of his goals. He would be happily wrong on the second one; the company would reach $1 billion in May 1983, four years earlier than he hoped. The fourth goal would be off, too. It would take five years and four months instead of five years for the stock to hit $25.

By late 1975, MCI found its attention focused on Congress. An industry group known as the United States Independent Telephone Association, or USITA *(you-see-ta)*, representing 1,600 independent local telephone companies, introduced a bill that would, among other things, establish that monopoly, not competition, would be in the best interests of the nation.

The drafting of the bill was an open secret because of leaks through International Telephone & Telegraph Co. ITT had established a company called United States Transmission Systems (USTS) to compete in the long-distance business (nowhere close to the size of MCI or Southern Pacific) and also owned local phone companies in Puerto Rico and the U.S. Virgin Islands that were USITA members. Through them, USTS and the other long-distance companies knew about the bill before it was introduced.

An obscure congressman from Wyoming, Teno Roncalio, had the bill in his pocket after it had been given to him by some small phone companies. Not knowing that he was supposed to take the bill around and try to get cosponsors, Roncalio instead placed the bill in the "hopper." Once that happens, a bill is officially introduced and gets a title and a number. It's rare that such a wide-ranging bill would have only one sponsor, but it did.

Although USITA had gotten the bill off the ground, it was common knowledge that AT&T had been its principal drafter. AT&T and the independents had a cozy relationship in which the long-distance company kicked back to the independents a subsidy based on how much its local phone users spent on long-distance service. These arrangements were very lucrative to the independents as well as the local Bell companies, which AT&T owned. Any competition in long distance, AT&T believed, would not only hurt its business but also affect the local phone companies. Therefore, the bill was in the best interests of the independents, the Bell companies, and AT&T itself.

Realizing the impact of the bill, Gus Grant, president of Southern Pacific, called Glen Penniston, president of Datran, and they decided that something had to be done. Shortly after, Grant had lunch with John Guttenberg, who was doing PR work for Datran, and Bernie Strassberg, formerly the FCC common carrier chief and now a private consultant. The three agreed that the long-distance companies needed a lobby group, the first one to represent the new competitors.

In March 1976, when the Roncalio bill was introduced in the second congressional session, MCI, Satellite Business Systems, and USTS had been drawn into the process of building a group. SBS was not yet licensed, so it took a lesser role, but Datran, which was still trying to establish its long-distance network for high-speed data, Southern Pacific, MCI, and USTS all took an active role in a newly formed group known as the Ad Hoc Committee for Competitive Telecommunications, which had the strong acronym of ACCT. As the "Ad Hoc" part of the name implied, it was formed specifically to meet the challenge of AT&T's bill. Some smaller companies also joined ACCT as well.

ACCT's very first decision split the group into two camps. It was over who would head the lobby group. MCI and Datran favored Herb Jasper, a former congressional staffer, and SBS and Southern Pacific favored John Kenney, a Washington lawyer. If this was any indication of ACCT's future, it wasn't a good sign. After meetings with both candidates, USTS—which wasn't one of the search committee members—was brought in to cast the deciding vote, and they went for Jasper.

Jasper took office as ACCT's executive vice-president in July, and his first act was to take place in the Commodore Hotel on Capitol Hill. ACCT was one of the first lobby groups that had an office right next to both houses of Congress. Most lobby groups used their regular office in Washington or nearby Arlington, Virginia. The only exceptions were small, free-lance lobbyists who worked out of their Capitol Hill brownstone homes. Many had been ordered not to work out of their homes by the D.C. zoning board, which didn't allow businesses working out of homes. Starting around 1976, however, many lobbyists took up space in legitimate office buildings that have since been built on Capitol Hill.

Each of the big five in ACCT were to contribute $50,000 the first year. Some of the smaller companies contributed $5,000 to $10,000. Datran never gave a penny; by May it had gone bankrupt. All together, ACCT raised $235,000 to fight AT&T's bill. In the following years, ACCT also hustled some vendors of telecommunications equipment for about $175,000. These companies had a stake in keeping ACCT members going.

By this time, the bill had garnered 140 sponsors in the House and a handful of senators, and by year's end, it had more than 175 sponsors in the House and about 15 Senate backers. AT&T had changed the name of the bill to the Consumer Communications Reform Act, an ironic title considering not one consumer group had supported the legislation. Opponents of the bill, especially ACCT, took credit for successfully changing the bill's common, everyday name to "the Bell Bill," because of its blatantly pro-AT&T attitude.

A close reading of the bill revealed something that anyone, even a congressman, would question almost immediately. The bill would keep the Federal Trade Commission and the Department of Justice from determining antitrust violations as they concerned domestic communications common carriers. This would exempt AT&T from any antitrust violations.

Membership in ACCT didn't preclude any member from lobbying on its own. Southern Pacific hired Kenney to roam the halls of Congress, and at MCI Bob Swezey—who was now in investor relations—took it upon himself to spend the entire month of November 1976 visiting congressional offices. He started in those districts that MCI's network served.

Swezey learned an important lesson about Congress. He discovered that even though a congressman's name was on a bill as a sponsor, it didn't necessarily mean that he had read it. That's standard practice, Swezey found out, and in this case the Bell Bill seemed like a good bill for any Congressman to automatically cosponsor. Because of its official title, it sounded like it helped consumers with their phone bills. What congressman wouldn't want that? Moreover, since congressmen believed that AT&T wasn't out to screw the consumer, any bill to help AT&T would be okay.

As Swezey made the rounds, he asked congressional staffers to take a closer look at the bill to see what it really said. He finally curtailed his activities when ACCT got in high gear. By then Jasper had begun to implement his two-point strategy:

1. Slow growth in the number of cosponsors of the bill.

2. Lay the groundwork so that when the bill was reintroduced in the next Congress (often done automatically), it would show a decline in cosponsors.

Jasper couldn't visit all 535 offices himself, so he hired Sharon Coffey as a part-time lobbyist. Coffey had done some lobbying for the North American Telephone Association, a trade group representing about 350 suppliers of telephone equipment. Tom Carter, the inventor of Carterfone and the man who opened up the equipment business to competition, had begun the association after winning his battle against AT&T in the late 1960s.

Jasper and Coffey found that their main task was to debunk the credibility that AT&T enjoyed in Congress. They accomplished that by publishing their own propaganda to knock down the conventional wisdom that AT&T, which had served the United States so well, was misleading Congress about the harm of competition. Jasper had to walk a fine line of being outspoken without sounding like a crazy man He also had to juggle MCI, which preached competition, anti-AT&Tism, and was adamant about the evils of monopolies on one hand and Southern Pacific and SBS on the other hand, which were more reserved and owned by large companies that didn't believe in saying bad things about other large corporations.

Jasper put out a ninety-page history of telecommunications according to ACCT and several other position papers in order to educate Congress about ACCT's point of view. Unlike AT&T, which only had to say to congressmen, "Here, look at how well it works. This is a great phone system we gave you," Jasper had to be more like a lawyer, taking every opportunity—point by point—to show that AT&T's arguments were flawed. He had to use facts, figures, analysis, and statistics.

One of Jasper's most successful forays into purple prose was his "critique" of the "Telephone Industry's Analysis of the Bell Bill." Jasper had found a six-page analysis of the Consumer Communications Reform Act that didn't say on it where it came from or who wrote it. It had no date and didn't boast an affiliation, but it stated all the reasons why Congress should vote for the bill. Apparently, it was written by AT&T and its supporters, Jasper told House and Senate members in his critique, without mentioning AT&T by name. His critique expressed ACCT's indignation that the bill's supporters would have the audacity to lobby Congress with an anonymous piece. Moreover, the analysis contained inaccurate information and left out critical issues, he said. Jasper's critique won ACCT many friends on the Hill. More important, it showed congressmen that maybe AT&T wasn't always right and really didn't have the public's best interest as its own.

Lionel Van Deerlin, a California Democrat, had taken over for Torbert MacDonald as chairman of the House Communications Subcommittee upon MacDonald's illness and subsequent retirement. Van Deerlin held hearings on the Bell Bill, and from the testimony at those hearings Jasper culled damaging quotes, printing them in a pamphlet for distribution to the media and congressmen who hadn't attended the hearings. He had quotes from distinguished people like Alfred Kahn, a former consultant for AT&T who was now chairman of the New York State Public Service Commission. Kahn said, "It's a radical bill; it runs counter to our most inveterate traditions of free enterprise. . . . It would erect impregnable barriers to preserve a nationwide monopoly at the very heart of the American economy."

Jasper took quotes from Andrew Feinstein of Public Citizen Congress Watch and F. Graham Crawford, national manager of communications for Sears. Jasper figured everyone in America loved Sears. *They* wouldn't lie.

The hearings were a turning point for ACCT. The testimony was devastating for AT&T and the bill's proponents. During the next Congress, only 106 House members and 9 senators endorsed the bill. That was a substantial drop considering that most congressmen routinely placed their names on bills they had previously supported after the new session convenes. The following session, the bill only had one sponsor. He hadn't gotten the word that the bill was now out of favor.

Jasper's strategy worked. The bill was defeated, but he had done much more. He had brought the telephone industry to the attention of Congress. Lawmakers had never taken an in-depth look at AT&T and the national phone system. Certainly, few in either house *understood* the industry. By trying to solve its problems with competition and antitrust violations through the legislative arena, AT&T brought acute congressional attention upon itself, attention it could probably have done without.

ACCT's original philosophy was not to endorse any legislation. Its members liked things the way they were. On the whole, the FCC was moving in the direction of competition, albeit slowly, and they didn't want any complications. However, in 1977, ACCT found an unexpected ally in Tim Wirth, a Democrat from the Denver area whose interest was stirred by the Bell Bill. He and Van Deerlin sponsored the first resolution affirming that free enterprise and not monopoly should be the criterion for the telephone industry. A resolution is not a bill; it can't become a law, but it does show where Congress's beliefs lie. It's a statement. It showed that in Congress times were changing for AT&T. Gary Hart sponsored a version in the Senate.

Years later, Wirth would introduce a bill that would force AT&T to launch its largest congressional lobbying campaign ever. Bell would find itself on the defensive for the first time, fighting a bill that would strengthen its competitors and give them legitimacy beyond what they could receive at the FCC or in the courts.

Ken Cox kept Execunet alive in the courts and the FCC. During the litigation, MCI continued to sell the service, and the company was slowing increasing its revenue stream. In October 1976, the U.S. Court of Appeals modified its stay that had allowed MCI to market Execunet. The court now ordered MCI not to solicit any *new* Execunet customers after November 21, thirty days hence, but allowed it to maintain users currently in operation.

Carl and his sales staff worked day and night using every bit of the court's thirty-day time limit to sign up new customers. Several months before, New York City's second Execunet switch was installed and he placed great emphasis on that area.

MCI had already increased its private line rates by 10 percent. The reason was simple. Not only did McGowan want to bring in some money quickly, but he figured it would be a way to make private lines less attractive to customers who were potential Execunet subscribers. It was clear that the future of MCI was in Execunet and not private lines.

Carl visited American Express to explain why MCI was raising its private line rates. He ended up losing the account because their financial people had gotten into the bowels of MCI and reported back that the company was near bankruptcy and American Express should stop doing business with them altogether.

From that point on, MCI held on to most of its private line

customers but didn't expand the list. In fact, Carl was forced to lay off about sixty highly trained salesmen who were selling private line service as he kept hiring lower-priced salesmen to sell Execunet. Selling Execunet didn't require any formal training or even any knowledge of the business. All it required was someone who could pick up the phone and call prospective clients.

That same month, October, MCI had posted its first cash-positive month with a net income of $105,000. Two months later, MCI reported a net income for the year of $1.3 million on revenues of $16.8 million. If MCI could just hold on, it might pull itself out of its financial hole.

Orville and his wife went to church every Sunday and prayed for the company to survive. All he asked was for MCI to last another week.

Although the court said that MCI couldn't solicit any new customers, Carl interpreted that to mean that he could sell new service to old customers. He pitched service to subsidiaries of current corporate clients. It was within the letter of the law, even though it may have violated the spirit.

Wayne kept the banks at bay by negotiating an agreement to stretch out the loan payments from two and a half years to seven years. The banks, bolstered by the first positive month ever, were willing to give the company more time. Again, they really had no choice in the matter. If they had held MCI to the original timetable, it wouldn't have been able to pay. MCI continued to send out unsigned checks whenever it could.

That same month, Ken had argued the Execunet case before the Court of Appeals. It was the most important case of his life, and he was nervous. He had argued before the Third Circuit Court in 1974 and lost when the court overturned an appeal by MCI against AT&T. That loss allowed AT&T to disconnect MCI's private line customers.

Ken studied hard and rehearsed his presentation with the help of an outside lawyer/consultant to where he thought he could present the case in his sleep. Even so, with the memory of his only other oral argument before an appeals court, a loss, he was nervous.

The only advantage Ken had was that MCI was the appellant. It meant that Ken got to go first. He would be spared the tension of waiting. He took off his watch, placed it on the podium, and began. He gave his presentation before three judges, and only after he got going did the pressure begin to ease. After it was over, Ken let out a large sigh. Later that day, he got a call from the court clerk. Ken had been so eager for it to be over that he left his watch on the podium.

Ken was successful. A month later, the Court of Appeals said that MCI was entitled to offer Execunet but remanded the case to the FCC for further proceedings. Ken then flooded the FCC with dozens of motions. He and his staff worked around the clock.

In its petitions before the court, MCI had accused the FCC commissioners of illegal ex parte contacts with AT&T. According to regulations, commissioners must write in a log each time they discuss a pending issue with an outsider. MCI claimed that the commissioners hadn't followed the rules when AT&T lobbied them about Execunet. The Department of Justice, acting as counsel for the FCC, noted in one of its motions in the case that the FCC had indeed acted contrary to the rules. It would have been easy for the commissioners to have written down with whom they talked and what they talked about, but they hadn't done it in the case of AT&T and Execunet. MCI's accusations about the ex parte contacts and bringing it to the attention of the Department of Justice embarrassed the FCC and caused a rift between the FCC and MCI that lasted for many years afterward. Until then, the relationship had been cordial.

One result of the bad feelings was that the FCC threatened to revoke some of MCI's pending construction permits for its Chicago-to-Omaha network expansion unless MCI promised not to use the segment for Execunet. It was certainly within the FCC's right, but Ken couldn't help thinking it was done out of spite. MCI didn't agree to the restriction and continued to fight the FCC in court.

By August, the Court of Appeals granted the stay of Execunet sought by the FCC and AT&T pending review by the Supreme Court. The High Court in January 1978 declined to review the decision and MCI could once again market Execunet to new customers.

That same month, AT&T argued before the FCC that it didn't have to make available to MCI any *additional* interconnections for Execunet, and round two began.

Meanwhile, Carl was going nuts. He hired people then laid them off. He hired people again and then laid them off.

The following month, the FCC backed up AT&T's claim that they didn't have to supply MCI with any additional interconnections for Execunet. And Carl, once again, laid off about 150 people.

MCI appealed that FCC decision to the Court of Appeals, and in April the court ordered the FCC to tell AT&T that it had to supply the interconnections for Execunet expansion. Round two was over, and once again Carl began to sell Execunet despite AT&T's plans to appeal the case to the Supreme Court.

Without missing a beat, AT&T filed tariffs with the FCC outlining its rates for the interconnections that the court ordered it must give MCI. The proposal would triple the current rates that MCI was paying. MCI argued that the rates were excessive and that AT&T was once again wielding its monopoly power of the local phone companies to put MCI out of business.

Larry Harris, who had had little contact with AT&T since negotiations broke off four years earlier, got involved once again with the interconnection issue. This time talks were held under the auspices of the FCC and the National Telecommunications and Information Administration, an arm of the Commerce Department. Within several months all the common carriers (MCI, Southern Pacific, USTS) and those representing local phone interests (GT&E, Bell, and USITA) agreed on a complicated system of interim interconnection fees called Network Facilities for Interstate Access, or ENFIA.

In November 1978, the Supreme Court declined to review the case. AT&T exhausted its appeals and had to provide *all* interconnections to MCI for Execunet.

For the first time, MCI's future was clear. It had established an absolute legal right to sell and expand its Execunet service, and the government was overseeing the interconnection agreements, meaning that AT&T had to bargain in good faith.

McGowan and everyone else at MCI knew that with the court case over, MCI was free to grow. The company was about to enter a new business.

THE SIXTH BUSINESS—

Grow Like Mad
1978–82

1

MCI now had the right to market any service it could devise in any part of the country it wished. It had won the right to grow, and McGowan's plan was to push the company to grow as fast as possible and to bring in as much money as it could by concentrating on the Execunet business. It wasn't the time to sit back and watch the money roll in easily, because it wouldn't, nor was it time to seek new wars. It was a time to build on the established base.

Telecommunications was a capital-intensive business, and it would take millions of dollars for MCI to expand its network, but the more it expanded, the more money it could generate. McGowan believed that in this stage of MCI's life, revenues were more important than profits. If MCI could continue to raise money, build its network, sell services, and produce revenue and continue the cycle for several years, profits would automatically follow.

With the court case behind them, MCI was now prepared to obtain capital to pay back some debts and put the company on a more solid financial footing. McGowan and Wayne English had agreed that the best way to do that was the public market. They were going to sell stock.

Wayne had been negotiating with the banks and underwriters since May in order to put together an offering that would be suitable to creditors such as Bechtel, which had done most of the microwave tower construction, and to the banks.

In December, MCI had sold 1.229 million shares of convertible preferred at $25 a share, raising $28.6 million after expenses. The banks took most of the money, but the move got MCI known in the public market and paved the way for other offerings. More important, it placed MCI into a positive equity position of about $10 million. Until then, the stockholders equity had been wiped out, and the company had been living totally on borrowed money.

Wayne had made certain that the public offering would go smoothly by buying out the interests of First of Boston, one of the five banks that had loaned money to MCI. During all the meetings with the banks, the only bank that was difficult was First of Boston. McGowan believed they were purposely acting uncooperative and disagreeable so all the other banks would buy them out just to get rid of them. Both Wayne and McGowan decided that something had to be done about First of Boston before they wrecked the pending public offering.

While he was putting together the offering, Wayne had lunch with Marty Silverman, president of the North American Corporation in New York City. Marty's company had done equipment-leasing deals with MCI since the early seventies and had always liked the people at the company. He truly believed that MCI would be successful.

Wayne said, "Marty, we're trying to get things ready to do a public financing. I think we're going to make it but nothing is certain. In the event that we can't put this thing together, would you be interested in an issue of convertible preferred stock from us? We'll structure the terms to make it attractive for you."

Marty waited for an amount to be mentioned. Wayne had no idea what the right figure was, so he took a deep breath and said, "Somewhere between five and ten million dollars."

Marty said, "I couldn't do that much, but I can do three million."

Wayne said, "Thank you very much, Marty, I'll remember that."

During a meeting with the banks at MCI headquarters on 17th Street N.W. in Washington, Wayne had pulled aside the representative from First of Boston and asked if the bank would be willing to sell out its position in MCI. He said he would find out from his superiors.

A couple of days later, the answer came back. Yes, First Boston would be willing to sell out its position.

One day, all the banks were gathered, and Wayne, seeing that First of Boston's representative wouldn't agree on anything at all that day, asked if he would excuse himself from the meeting. He left, and Wayne asked the remaining bankers, "If I can find someone to buy out the position of First of Boston, would the rest of you go along with it?" Without hesitation they all said they would.

Wayne then excused himself from the meeting and walked to the Washington Hilton Hotel, a few blocks away, which was holding a business equipment show. He made his way through the crowd and found Marty Silverman, who he knew would be attending the showing. He said, "Marty, come with me," and the two went into a corridor and sat on a bench. Wayne took out an old envelope from his pocket and said, "Marty, do you remember that three million dollars that you were willing to invest?" and Marty said, "Yes, I remember."

Wayne said, "Do you think you could borrow another eight or ten million to go with that?" and Marty said he thought so, to which Wayne said, "Marty, how would you like to be a banker?"

Marty smiled and said, "I would love to." And they worked out the deal on the back of the envelope.

Marty bought out First of Boston for about $12 million, and on August 30—one day before First of Boston's deadline for any buyout—Marty had his check in hand for $3 million and a check from Continental Bank for another $9 million that he had borrowed. He turned the checks over to First of Boston, which was now out of the picture.

But that was only step one. MCI still had an interest payment due in October on its loans and Wayne wasn't sure that the company had enough money. So he went to the Riggs Bank across from the U.S. Treasury Building and saw the bank president, Dan Callahan. Wayne said he wanted to set up a line of credit to tide the company over until the public offering. Callahan said he would love to help MCI, but its balance sheet didn't justify it.

Wayne told him, "Suppose I came up with a guarantor acceptable to you?"

Callahan said, "Sure, that would be fine."

Wayne went back to Marty and asked if he would be willing to back a line of credit at Riggs. Marty said he would, and Riggs looked at Marty's books and okayed the line of credit based on its strength.

Everything was set for the offering, but Wayne wanted to get more equity out of the deal, so he called Marty and asked if he would be willing to trade his $3 million in loans for $3 million worth of the convertible preferred stock. Marty said, "If it would help MCI, I'll do it."

Wayne did the same with Bechtel. They turned in $3 million in notes for stock as well.

Then, just before the offering in October, the stock market fell sharply. MCI's stock, which had been trading at around $5 a share, had dropped to less than $3. Wayne had no choice but to go public anyway, and with the help of Allen & Co., MCI made the offering on December 9 of convertible preferred for $2.64. Really, there were three offerings: the public offering and two private offerings—Marty's and Bechtel's—all done simultaneously.

Marty was well paid for his risks. Over the following years, he made more than $20 million when he sold MCI stock. With the money, he built a Jewish chapel at West Point. When people asked him why he built a synagogue for so few Jewish cadets, he would say jokingly, "It's a neighborhood that's not going to change very much." But McGowan and everyone else at MCI believed there was another reason. Building a Jewish chapel was a way for Marty, a New York Jew, to tweak the Waspy bastards at First of Boston who had given his friends at MCI such a hard time.

By March 1979, the end of MCI's fiscal year, the company had racked up $95 million in revenue, compared with $74 million for the same period the year before. Net income was $7 million, compared with $5 million the year before. The company's microwave network, which had cost more than $200 million to build, ran coast to coast and served more than fifty cities. More important, those cities accounted for more than half of all business telephones. The network carried more than a million intercity calls daily for more than 18,000 customers, including 34 percent of the Fortune 500, 26 percent of the fifty largest commercial banks, 40 percent of the biggest transportation companies, and 41 percent of the members of the New York Stock Exchange. On the over-the-counter market, MCI's stock was the ninth most traded issue.

The long-distance market stood at $12 billion and was growing at a rate of 15 percent a year. New installations were being added at the rate of a thousand a month, and Carl's sales force was ready to expand once again. To McGowan, it seemed like there was no limit to how far MCI could penetrate the market.

But there were limits. Although Orville had tried to keep the company growing in an orderly manner, the operation was getting out of hand. Employees didn't have enough working space, billings were going haywire, and the company couldn't handle all the new customers who had to receive authorization codes for Execunet service once they signed up.

So far, MCI had enjoyed a good reputation to the outside world, but Execunet started to change that.

Private-line salespeople were generally well trained and professional. They were able to convince clients that despite AT&T's shenanigans, MCI would still be around. Clients liked working with them, and many stayed loyal even during the interconnection crisis.

Now with Execunet, Carl and his staff hired loads of people to sell the service. Few were professional salespeople. Many were drifters, bums, part-timers who didn't care, and con artists looking for a quick buck. They sold Execunet over the phone, often making promises they couldn't keep. In many instances, they promised customers services in areas where the MCI network didn't reach. They were paid on commission based on how many customers they signed up, and they would pad the accounts with fictitious names and take their money and split.

Because of this, Carl was forced to pay commissions based on the first month of a customer's bill, instead of when the order was signed. He soon discovered that salespeople would call each other from outside pay phones, order service under a phony name, use the service for a month, then split the commission check. Then they would reapply the following month under a different name. Finally, Carl changed the commission plan and pegged it to the third month's usage. That helped.

Carl was appalled at the level of salespeople he was forced to hire, but he needed warm bodies and plenty of them. He felt he had no choice, but it still got him sick to walk through the MCI office in New York City and see what he had created. One day, he went through the sea of desks and telephones when a great big German shepherd barked at him and snapped at his leg. He turned and said to the salesman by his desk, "What the hell is this dog doing here?"

The salesman answered, "He's protecting my leads."

He had brought the dog in to discourage others from grabbing his prospect list off his desk. There was no territory; no one doled out leads. Salespeople called companies listed in the Yellow Pages. It was anything goes; every man for himself.

During the following five years, MCI went through almost five thousand telephone salespeople who worked on straight commission. Many worked a month or so and were never heard from again.

Carl believed he was doing the job McGowan hired him to do: bring in money quickly. And it wasn't until a decade later that Carl would take the blame for doing what he thought was best.

During the Execunet sales rush, many of MCI's best-trained salespeople either left voluntarily or were let go. These were high-class people who knew how to walk into a large corporation and close a high-priced deal. But MCI didn't need them anymore.

Neither Carl nor McGowan knew then that MCI would be caught ten years later without salespeople who could walk into a company like General Motors or Boeing and walk away with a million-dollar contract. That kind of person had to be nurtured, and MCI didn't have any. They left when Execunet arrived.

Carl took the blame for something else. As MCI grew rapidly, it couldn't service all its customers. There were problems with too little capacity, and callers often got busy signals or poor-quality circuits. Carl couldn't do anything about it; the company was growing too fast to control.

McGowan believed it was an unfortunate but necessary trade-off if MCI was to keep growing, and Carl took the attitude that if a customer didn't like his service, there were others who would take his place. Hell, anyone with a telephone was a possible Execunet customer. He couldn't run out of potential users. Churn rates topped 20 percent in some months, but as long as there was someone new to sign up, nobody worried.

That practice, like the loss of strong salespeople, would come back to haunt MCI as competition in the phone industry grew in the early 1980s and customers began to demand low price *and* high quality. MCI had a reputation for low quality and poor service that was difficult to change.

While Carl was out there selling like crazy, back home the place was a mess. It, too, was suffering from too-fast growth.

By November 1979, Orville had all the line organizations reporting to him, and in addition there was planning and administration. In that group were six divisions: corporate planning, distribution, purchasing, human resources, corporate services, and MIS, or management information services, commonly referred to as the computer guys.

Orville was looking for someone to take over the divisions, and Charlie Skibo seemed perfect for the job. Charlie was a slow-talking, methodical worker. Like Orville, he presented a calm, well-mannered demeanor, but when it came to being tough where it counted, Charlie could be as ruthless as a prison warden. He had worked at Exxon for nineteen years, most of the time in charge of procuring sites for service stations and dealerships in the mid-Atlantic region.

Charlie was ambitious and decided that he wanted a senior management position. To do that, he would have to find a smaller company. After studying different industries, he saw that telecommunications was coming into its own. He liked what he saw at MCI in particular. He wrote McGowan a letter, and McGowan passed it to Orville. Orville called Charlie and said that the company was going through some reorganization and that this wasn't really the time. Charlie told him, "I'm in no rush. I want to do the right thing."

Orville and he decided to get in touch in about six months. Six months later, Charlie came to Washington from Houston, where he was working, for an interview. He was impressed with Orville. McGowan was out of town, but about two weeks later, Charlie returned to talk with him.

Charlie was awed by both McGowan and Orville. He felt the immediate rapport between the two. They knew where they were going and how they were going to accomplish it. He was touched by the respect they had for each other and was amazed that two different personalities could work together so well. Orville offered Charlie a job as senior vice-president, and he accepted.

When Charlie arrived, MIS was in the worst shape of all the divisions. He discovered about sixty people reporting to one director, and they had about ten times more projects than they had the ability to handle. Charlie wasn't surprised. With the great rate of growth of MCI, turning a profit only about two years before, it was no wonder that MIS had gotten squeezed by people who wanted their projects done yesterday.

Charlie went around to all other divisions asking them to list in priority order what projects they wanted the computer guys to handle. He hoped it would narrow down the number of jobs or at least place them in order of critical importance to the company as a whole. Then he sat down with Orville and asked for enough money to double the number of MIS employees. A year later, he would double it once again.

MCI was within two or three days of running out of authorization codes for new customers. By throwing more people and money at the project, he was able to get ahead of that problem. Charlie added another MIS facility in Rockville, Maryland, just north of Washington, to help do that project. He also opened up another building in Sacramento, California.

Charlie didn't know anything about MIS, but he did know how to manage and plan. He planned ahead, something that had never been done before at MCI as far as MCI was concerned. Certainly, the fires had to be put out, but he was going to get ahead of problems as well.

By not knowing how MIS worked, Charlie was able to get it working better. He was able to go to the Rockville facility and watch how information came in one end, was processed, and left at the other end. He found that it was disjointed. Projects jumped around from group to group without a smooth flow. Just by bringing in a fresh viewpoint, someone who didn't know anything about MIS but did know how to organize, he was able to cut down wasted time and effort.

One example was billing. When he arrived at MCI, it took twenty days to get bills out after a specified time period. He got it down to five days by better organization, and later he began cycle billing. Instead of customers all receiving their bills the same time each month, it was staggered. This not only prevented huge spikes of work at the billing centers but assured that MCI's income flow would be smoother as well. This helped prevent spikes of work for the customer service people, too, who got loads of calls and complaints shortly after bills were received by customers.

Like any growing company, MCI was purchasing large numbers of items that it had only bought in small numbers as they were needed: desks, chairs, paper clips, hard hats, first-aid kits, "Keep Out" signs, and so on. There was no organized way to buy these things until Skibo arrived. He organized a distribution center on the West Coast and expanded distribution centers in Chicago and New York. A new facility in Richardson, Texas, was bought and expanded as well. He also set up an automated purchasing system to keep track of who bought what and where it went. This was the first time that anyone knew where everything was.

Charlie then turned his attention to Human Resources. It was basically a record-keeping group noting how many employees were working, what each one did, how much they were paid, and what their benefits were. Charlie wanted to get Human Resources out of the record-keeping business and address the issues of stock options and geographic pay scales. He brought people in to take surveys to make certain that management was addressing the problems of employees who were outside the sight of headquarters. Charlie and his staff also developed ten management training programs that managers were encouraged to take, although they weren't mandatory. The only mandatory training program was one about unions.

If there was anything approaching a religion at MCI, it was unions. In June 1980, McGowan read a piece in *The Wall Street Journal* about how the Communications Workers of America was thinking about organizing the common carriers other than AT&T. McGowan went wild. Although he had come from a union family (his father had spent about one year as a union delegate), he was antiunion. He believed that unions damaged more companies than they helped and that they should, if anything, focus on companies that hurt their workers, such as chemical and mining companies. As a youngster working on the railroad, he saw a distinct and destructive "them and us" attitude perpetrated by the unions. If MCI became unionized, it would destroy it, McGowan believed. It would only slow things down, and in a highly competitive industry, unions were the kiss of death. He didn't blame the unions entirely, though. He saw unionization as a failure on the part of management to relate to its workers.

After the article appeared, McGowan brought in a consultant to teach union avoidance to his senior managers. Charlie pulled together a training program based on what the consultant had to say and gave a yearly lecture to managers thereafter, giving the corporate philosophy about unions.

In a sideways way, that antiunion philosophy led to one of MCI's most obvious characteristics. It became one of the most open companies in America. Employees were kept aware through publications, video presentations, and visits to the field by senior officials who answered their questions and made them feel like part of the management process. At the same time, the antiunion rhetoric was preached. It wasn't done in a threatening way. McGowan just wanted to make sure that everyone knew that employees didn't need a third party to speak for them.

In addition, Charlie and his staff undertook an examination of employee benefits to make certain the company didn't give employees any reason to feel they needed a union. MCI hired a consultant to run a survey which revealed that despite their best efforts, employees didn't feel that the company was doing an adequate job of internal communications. It was probably because things were moving so fast and all the information couldn't get disseminated quickly enough. Because of that survey, MCI began *Management Notes*, a newsletter aimed at managers and giving them the latest company news. All corporate managers met frequently with field managers to discuss what was going on at headquarters.

Orville began visiting all offices at least once a year and established an annual award known as "Excellence in Service," given to employees who had contributed a little extra to MCI. Until the company grew too large, he would try to meet every employee on his visits. "We have to show them that we love them," Orville would say with a smile. "Because they don't always think that we do."

Despite all the safeguards, nobody could foresee that the company that was so antiunion would be embroiled in one of the meanest strikes in telecommunications history just a few years later.

Although MCI's customers were generally pleased with the 5 to 50 percent price differential between MCI and AT&T, businessmen began to complain that unlike AT&T, MCI didn't have a discount for calling after 5 P.M. Many businesses, especially those on the East Coast, waited until after five to call the West Coast. During those times, some calls going by AT&T would be competitive with those going over MCI. In some cases, AT&T was even cheaper. Carl was forced to offer a discount to the almost forty thousand business customers after 5 P.M., and it became MCI's strategy to *always* be cheaper than AT&T.

Still later, because of competitive threats from Southern Pacific, which had begun to call its service "Sprint," Carl was again forced to offer another feature: credit cards. He never intended for credit cards to be a big item. It was just another tool for his salesmen to take with them when they made a sales call. Sprint already had that feature, and it allowed businessmen to give their authorization numbers to their sons and daughters so they could call home from college. Unlike an MCI authorization code, a Sprint code could be used in any city it served. Although this allowed more fraud, it also gave Sprint customers more leeway when they traveled. Even with a ten-dollar fee, MCI sold about twenty thousand cards almost immediately.

The gimmicks just kept on coming. McGowan was having a ball

152

with Execunet and all the strange things he could do with it. The beauty of owning and operating your own network was that if the network was not filled to capacity, it didn't cost anything to give away free time. You didn't lose anything because you weren't keeping paying customers off. On the other hand, you weren't making as much money as you could.

So in December, MCI became the first long-distance company to give its customers free calls on Christmas Day. It was great publicity and showed the public that there was nothing sacred about the phone system and AT&T could have done the same if it wanted to. Actually, AT&T couldn't do the same because it was highly regulated by the FCC, which wouldn't have given permission for such a frivolous stunt. For the first time, MCI was getting noticed in the newspapers and on TV. MCI was gaining a reputation as an offbeat company—people still didn't understand what it was they really did—and McGowan reveled in all the attention.

McGowan had some more ideas about what he could do with Execunet. He telephoned Jerry Taylor, who was still working in Texas selling Execunet, and asked him to come to Washington for the weekend. McGowan had decided that filling the network to capacity was crucial. If it wasn't being used at night, for example, they weren't losing money but they weren't making money, either. Filling the network's capacity became an obsession with McGowan. He told Taylor that if MCI could sell to the residential customer, not only would they fill the network, and make more money, but they would begin to build a national presence. McGowan had gotten a taste of being interviewed on television and seeing his name in the newspaper, and he liked it.

Selling the service to the consumer would be different from selling to the commercial user. Salesmen just couldn't call on each of the 80 million home phone customers. It would require a different approach. So McGowan and Taylor flew around the country visiting companies that knew how to sell to the residential customer. They tried to persuade Sears, MasterCharge, and others to sell the service, but they soon realized that even though they knew the retail customer, they weren't really set up to sell MCI service. They didn't have the billing or collection facilities. More important, they weren't prepared mentally to sell something as outlandish as phone service.

That's when Taylor hit on television advertising. How else could

MCI reach such large numbers of people? Besides, as he learned later, being on TV gave a company instant credibility. It became legitimate.

MCI had never advertised on TV before. In fact, the only major, national buy was a full-page ad in *The Wall Street Journal* in 1975 at a cost of around $40,000. It was for private lines. Teams in every MCI city were sitting by phones, ready to handle all the incoming calls, but the day that it ran nothing happened. It was a disaster. No calls. McGowan of course discounted the adventure saying it really wasn't for selling, it was to raise market awareness of MCI.

Several months earlier in late summer, McGowan had received a letter from an old Harvard Business School chum who had just begun working for Ally & Gargano, a New York advertising firm, and was trying to bring new business to the company. He suggested to McGowan that perhaps the company that had done such a good job of advertising for Federal Express might also do some work for MCI. After all, he pointed out, the two firms had similar traits. They were both feisty and went against the conventional wisdom.

As it turned out, McGowan knew Carl Ally from the mid-1960s when McGowan was involved with another one of his crazy companies. This one was called Servicator, and its main product was a gizmo attached to machinery that ejected little cards, about the size of calling cards, stating that it was time for maintenance. The device could be used on cars, for example, and would pop out a card that reminded you to "change the oil" or "rotate the tires." McGowan had tried to sell the product to Toyota while he was visiting Japan on his around-the-world trip, but they told him they had other mechanisms to do the same thing. Ally was supposed to do an ad, but Servicator never got off the ground, so the deal was scrapped.

McGowan decided to give Ally some ad hoc contracts to handle research about residential customers. The union between Ally and MCI would make Madison Avenue history.

One other element had to be in place before Ally began its work. That was public relations. Until McGowan decided that MCI should get into the residential business, there was little need for a public relations department. Bob Swezey had handled the stray call from the occasional reporter, McGowan was always available to chat, but it wasn't until the company saw the enormous change from courting the business customer to wooing the consumer that a public relations strategy became necessary. Once MCI was in the consumer arena, they would be getting lots of phone calls from people wanting to know more. The search for that person, like most of MCI's personnel searches, came by way of chance and serendipity.

Gary Tobin dropped out of the University of San Francisco after competing for a five-year law scholarship and getting it. He couldn't handle the rigid structure of a Jesuit education, so he left and enrolled in San Francisco State, where he got a degree in history. His minor subject was journalism. While in school, he got a job as a copy boy at the *San Francisco Chronicle*, and within three months he was offered a summer job as a junior reporter. It wasn't until someone read the guild contract and realized there was no such thing as a junior reporter that Tobin got offered a job as a regular reporter. When the summer ended, Tobin wanted a full-time position. The *Chronicle* didn't have any openings, so his editor found him a job on the *Palo Alto Times*, where

Tobin told them about all the things he had done, even things he hadn't done, and they put him in charge of production for the sports section.

Tobin had never done production before, never laid out a page or measured a story. He came in at 2 A.M., six hours before he was expected to arrive. By 7 A.M., when everyone else came to work, it looked like Tobin had everything under control. He never told anyone that it took him six hours to do what they had expected him to do in one hour. He did this for a month before he was able to come in at a regular time.

During his six-month tenure at the Palo Alto paper, the *Chronicle* suffered a fifty-day strike, during which many reporters got fed up and left to work at other papers. One was a sports reporter who went to a Seattle newspaper. After the strike was over, Tobin got a call from his former editor asking him if he wanted a job as sports reporter. He said he did and worked for the next five years covering baseball games.

Around that time, a part-time reporter at the *Chronicle* had used Tobin as a reference on an application for a PR job. After Tobin gave the prospective employer a good recommendation, the guy decided he wanted to stay in newspapers after all. Tobin called back the job agency, which was prospecting for Heublein, and said he might be interested in the job himself. It fit with the three things he did best: edit, write, and drink wine. While everyone at the paper was drinking beer, Tobin drank wine. He didn't just drink it, he studied and collected it as a hobby. He and two co-workers would eat cheese and sip newly discovered wines on their lunch hour in the back of the newsroom. Wine was a way of life in California. Candlestick Park, the home of the Giants, was the first stadium to sell wine by the glass.

Tobin took the job at Heublein, and he handled all the western states PR for the Connecticut-based company that owned Kentucky Fried Chicken, Smirnoff vodka, Hamm's beer, A-1 steak sauce, Inglenook, Italian Swiss Colony wine, and more. Tobin did a lot of sports promotions, including the first Annie Green Springs national hang-gliding championship and bicycle races in the wine country called the Italian Swiss Colony 150.

Tobin got to run his own shop when he was promoted to public affairs director of United Vintners, a subsidiary of Heublein that owned Inglenook and Italian Swiss Colony. He had to do his own budgets, plan projects, and hire people. He got his first real taste of business, and he liked it.

After seven years at Heublein, though, Tobin was due for a change. He had just gotten divorced and was eager to leave California and his troubles behind and go East. He telephoned agencies, contacted trade associations, and wrote companies that he thought might need a PR man. On one of his trips East, he saw an ad for MCI. He wasn't sure what MCI was, but he sent in a résumé. He got invited to an interview with a staffer, but nothing ever came of it. When he got home, he wrote McGowan a one-page letter saying that the trouble with high-tech companies, or companies perceived as high tech, is that they don't know how to talk to the public in easy-to-understand language. A week later, he telephoned McGowan. Tobin was taken aback when he answered his own phone. McGowan said that he had passed the letter on to Orville Wright, and he transferred Tobin's call.

Orville said that MCI wasn't in a position to fly him out, but if he was ever in Washington he should come over for a chat. Tobin made himself appear in Washington in a very short while and talked to Orville for more than an hour. Orville hinted that they were at a decision point, and if it went one way, they would need someone like Tobin. Tobin didn't know that the decision was about whether or not MCI was going to enter the residential market.

A short time later, Tobin got a call from someone he didn't know named Carl Vorder Bruegge, who said he was in San Diego but would be in San Francisco the next day and could they meet? Carl and Tobin met the following day while Carl was still upset at having been mugged the night before in San Diego. As they chatted, Carl drew concentric circles on a piece of paper trying to show Tobin how MCI was run, and even though Tobin had a hard time understanding what he was trying to say, he must have impressed Carl enough that the next day he got a call from Jerry Taylor, who was vice-president of marketing.

Tobin flew to New York City to have breakfast with Taylor, and he offered him a job. Tobin knew he wasn't supposed to accept a job without saying he would think about it, but it was what he wanted, and he accepted it right there.

Jerry said, "Good, because we're shooting our first commercial today and we've never done it before. Can you come to work?" Tobin said, "When?" and Taylor said, "Right now." Tobin, puzzled at this loose way of doing business, said, "I guess I can." He went to the first commercial shoot, and the next day flew back to San Francisco and resigned from his old job.

The ad that Tobin saw being shot was the brainchild of Tom Messner, a letter carrier turned ad agency copywriter at Ally & Gargano. At first, he was skeptical. Tom had never heard of MCI. He had no idea that there was any competition in the telephone industry. He had heard something about equipment—somehow he knew that you could own your own phone—but he knew nothing about alternative service. He didn't think it would be a big account for Ally & Gargano. In fact, he thought the product might be better suited for cheaper, direct mail instead of expensive TV ads. He didn't see the mass appeal. But he changed his mind rather quickly after he began reading about the field. He found himself caught in that inexplicable phenomenon of learning a word then seeing it every time you pick up a magazine or newspaper. It happened with MCI. Every time he got an article about the telephone industry the name MCI popped up. Had he never noticed it before, or was it all just coming out?

He went from totally skeptical to totally optimistic. He said to himself: "You're selling the same thing as somebody else, but you're selling it for up to 50 percent less. How could I miss?" Then he realized it wasn't *exactly* the same. You had to dial all the extra digits. Moreover, MCI couldn't be used from everywhere, and the network didn't reach everywhere. Then Tom realized: Neither did Federal Express when it first started. They only went to sixteen cities at first.

He thought: "If we tell people that we're limited, they'll assume they can't use us, and they won't call us for service. Let's not mention anything. Then, when they do call us for service, we'll tell them whether we can give them service or not." He remembered that's what Federal did.

Much of Tom's knowledge about consumers came from focus groups. Focus-group research involves taking a sampling of people and asking them questions about your product, how much they are willing to pay, and so on. Usually, the questions are worded such that the people don't know what company is being represented. This is to prevent their prejudices from creeping in. In the case of food products or household cleansers, focus-group participants actually try the goods and give their comments. The client, in this case MCI, usually hides in the audience or views the proceedings from behind a one-way mirror.

The thrust of the focus groups was to answer the following: How do you present a palatable product to the public, how much do you charge them, what are they willing to pay, what kind of billing are they interested in, and so on. AT&T never had to do such focus groups. There was no competition, and so marketing studies were irrelevant. Certainly, AT&T tested its ads for customer likability, but it didn't have to do much more. There was nothing written about consumer habits on telephone usage the way marketing pundits wrote about consumers' buying habits concerning cars and stereos. When it came to telephone service, MCI had to start from scratch.

Jerry Taylor and Tom learned together about what focus groups had to say about telephone service. Taylor wasn't a market guy; he was a technical guy and he thought that this focus-group and market research stuff was a bunch of bullshit but he went along with it. He already had the pricing figured out and the program planned. He didn't need the groups.

The more he observed the groups, however, the more he realized that everything he had done was wrong. He discovered that although they bordered on the cute, he could learn a lot from focus groups.

Jerry had planned on selling residential service with a minimun usage fee, the same as Execunet. Business users paid a $75-a-month minimum usage fee. If a customer didn't spend $75, he had to pay it anyway. That was Carl's creation and he did it for two reasons. He didn't want his salesmen chasing small accounts. Second, Carl didn't believe that customers would actually dial all the extra digits to use

Execunet unless they had something hanging over their heads to force them to dial. Seventy-five dollars did the trick.

Jerry learned from the focus groups that people wouldn't pay a monthly minimum of $75, or any amount for that matter. So he changed his plan to a flat fee of $10 a month. Because most long-distance users spent that much anyway, it kept out the too-small customer yet didn't scare away the larger residential user. When residential service was launched, Carl was compelled to change his business rates to come in line with the residential rates. Business customers could choose either the $75 minimum or the $10 flat monthly fee.

Jerry was just as surprised by the other things he discovered. He found that people didn't blame the phone company for their high bills. They blamed themselves for talking too long. That led to MCI's advertising motto: "You're not talking too much, just spending too much."

He also found that older people made prearranged phone calls based on convenience of the person on the other end. For example, a mother might call her son every Sunday at 10 A.M. and would continue to do so even if rates for that time slot were raised. Younger people were more careful with their money and allotted a certain amount each month for telephone calls; if they paid less for service, they would simply talk longer.

The most important lesson learned from the focus groups was that consumers trusted the fact that businesses used MCI. Although MCI wasn't mentioned by name, focus-group participants were asked to evaluate services that were endorsed by big businesses and others that were not. Despite an innate distrust of big business, the groups showed that people truly believed that something must be okay if big businesses used it. The bottom line was that good businessmen make good judgments.

That point was crucial to MCI's first TV commercial titled "Big Business," which showed that MCI was legitimate because it was used by more than forty thousand companies.

Tom decided that "direct response" would be the strategy of the ads. Direct-response ads tell someone to call a number or write to an address for a product or service. He couldn't sell MCI service any other way because of the company's distribution network. It wasn't like cookies where the ad said, "Look for it on your grocer's shelves." There were no shelves, no way the consumer could go and find MCI service.

The ads had to be the distribution point. MCI's thirty-second direct-response ad would make Madison Avenue history as the first of its kind. There were 60s and 120s but never 30s. They tested 10s but they were too short. Sixties were too expensive. Although 30s went against the conventional wisdom, Tom bet on them.

The ads themselves had to do two things. They had to be competitive with the market leader, AT&T. There was no way to walk away from that fact. MCI had to define itself through AT&T, so people would instantly know what the ad was saying. It would show immediately what was being sold. The second strategy was to show that although it may seem new, it wasn't new at all. Again, from the focus groups, Tom and Jerry both learned that consumers liked to buy something that businesses had chosen for themselves and that had been used for some length of time.

During the first week of January 1980, Tom presented his proposal to McGowan, Orville, Wayne English, and Carl Vorder Bruegge. Jerry presented his plans for dealing with the incoming calls. Messner showed four ads in still-life form called "storyboards." Tom recommended that two of them be produced, and ultimately they were. To McGowan and the others, the proposals made sense. The ads showed MCI just as McGowan had pictured it in his own mind. The company was legitimate, feisty, and the service was just as good as AT&T, only cheaper.

The first ad was titled "Big Business," and it showed people in offices using the telephone. The announcer said: "Last year we saved big automakers almost $2 million . . . We saved a bank $750,000, an oil company $1 million, a computer company $600,000. All told, forty thousand companies used us to cut their long-distance bills up to 50 percent." Then the announcer began showing people in their homes. "And starting now, you can begin saving on long distance with your own home phone. This year, MCI will save Nancy Bryant, who calls her son a lot, $400. We'll save Mr. and Mrs. Sadler, whose son's in college, $500." It ends with a baby on the phone and the mother saying, "Say hello to Gramma. Come on, say hello to Gramma." The last few seconds showed a blank screen with the MCI logo and the phrase "The nation's long-distance phone company," followed by a local phone number.

Jerry kept getting surprised. He thought the phrase "The nation's long-distance phone company" was the most presumptuous idea he had ever heard. He shied away at first but realized later that it was the only way that MCI could preempt other competitors. Part of the MCI advertising strategy as Tom saw it was to make it seem that AT&T was MCI's only competition and that the others, like Sprint, didn't really exist. Despite Jerry's initial snickering, it worked.

"Big Business" came in two versions, sixty- and thirty-second spots. The sixty was to run for two weeks in Denver, the first city in which MCI offered residential service. Then the thirties were run. Tom was surprised because the commercials were aimed at home users, but for every four residential customers who signed, they signed one business user, too.

Tom's other commercial was the essense of simplicity. The question he posed to himself was: How do you show the same phone call, at the same time but with a different cost, for MCI and AT&T? The solution was a commercial that ran along with "Big Business" called "Comparison." It showed a split screen with the same person on each side talking on the phone. Under each caller was a meter that ticked off money, like a gas station pump. One was labeled Bell, the other MCI. By the end of thirty seconds, the Bell charge was $6.05 and the MCI meter showed $3.07. Throughout the commercial, the announcer described MCI service saying that the same phone call placed at the same time doesn't have to cost the same. It ends with the same MCI logo and phone number as "Big Business" but says, "You haven't been talking too much, you've just been paying too much."

The commercial was MCI's biggest success and it has been used ever since. Unlike other commercials, it rarely needed to be "freshened up." It never had to be changed because it was becoming stale to TV viewers. "Comparison" was so simple and so pure it just kept working effectively no matter how many times people saw it. Over the years, a man was substituted for a woman and the announcer's copy changed slightly but the idea itself never changed. "Comparison" became so popular that it started becoming 100 percent of some advertising buys in certain areas to the exclusion of all other ads.

The TV ads broke on a Monday. Print ads ran on Thursday. Tom figured the public relations thrust would hit on the Tuesday or Wednesday in between. Tom got word in New York City that the phone banks were flooded by people wanting MCI service. In fact, MCI was too successful in Denver. Studying the early records of calls, there was great fear that residential customers might change their calling habits and use the network during the day instead of at night when the network was relatively empty. If customers did that, it would overload the network and calls wouldn't get through and people would be unhappy. The early returns indicated it might just happen. So, rather than risk that, MCI pulled the ads after about two weeks until things settled down. When they did that, the calls for service stopped immediately. That taught Jerry and everyone else a very important lesson: They could easily control the market with TV advertising. It was almost like a switch.

But advertising was only half of the blitz. The other was PR, which was given an unexpected boost when MCI's service didn't work and MCI blamed it on AT&T.

7

Tobin had sent press releases and "media kits" describing MCI to reporters the week before the advertising broke in Denver. He didn't know how big a news story it would be, so that week he was in Washington watching from a distance. He had set up phone interviews with Jerry Taylor and some with McGowan, but that was the extent of his work. On Wednesday, when MCI service didn't work as expected, Tobin realized he had an excellent news peg to wave the story before the media again. Whether Mountain Bell intentionally cut MCI's lines or not didn't even matter. The fact was that Bell, which had tried to keep MCI out of business before, was now doing it again, and this time it was blatant. Tobin began calling the media in Denver again, telling them about what had happened. He gave them numbers to call themselves so they could hear that the lines were "temporarily out of order." He also had them call the information operator and ask for MCI. He knew what would happen because he called them before himself. The operator gave out the wrong number or said that MCI didn't exist.

This was great stuff and got even better when MCI employees found two Mountain Bell people wandering around their terminal site and had to kick them out. Who knows if they were just curious or what? It didn't matter a bit when Tobin told the media about the "snooping" Bell "spies."

Tobin couldn't wait any longer. He told McGowan that they better fly to Denver and do more interviews and talk more about what they were trying to do. The momentum was strong enough now, but he couldn't count on its lasting forever.

This was the first time the two had ever flown together, and Tobin was startled by McGowan's reading habits. He would take a stack of papers and magazines along with him to read and when he finished an article he would pass it along to Tobin, who sat on the other side of the aisle. He learned that McGowan would read anything from *The Wall Street Journal* to the *National Enquirer* and digest the information like he was storing it in a computer memory. Tobin also found out that when McGowan traveled, he took two suitcases, one for his clothes and one for his reading material.

With the help of PR contacts in Denver, Tobin got McGowan booked on TV and radio shows. The strategy was simple: Just tell the story, keep away from the technical stuff, and whenever possible have fun even if it meant self-effacing humor. McGowan was a natural for TV. He was well spoken, and he knew how to give concise answers. They both played up the David versus Goliath routine, especially after Mountain Bell had called a press conference to announce they had accidentally cut MCI's lines. McGowan never said that Bell intentionally cut the lines; he let the audience make up their own minds. Besides, with TV time so short, Tobin instructed McGowan that it was best spent telling the MCI story in a positive light rather than using the time in a pissing match with AT&T.

McGowan was a trouper. He did show after show after show with very little time for sleep or rest. Despite the rigorous schedule, he loved every minute of it. TV and radio show hosts seemed to like it, too. It's not often they got to talk with the chairman of a $150-million company. Usually, they got just the vice-presidents or the highly paid PR men. It didn't become vogue for company chairmen to be on talk shows until the early 1980s.

On one radio show, McGowan fielded a call from someone who seemed to know a lot about the telephone industry. Not only that, the caller asked just the right questions for MCI to tell its story the way it wanted. After a while, McGowan knew who it was and he winked at Tobin when the camera wasn't looking. Tom Messner was holed up in a hotel room, drinking beer and talking on the phone to some guy on radio named McGowan.

The test marketing was supposed to take twenty-four weeks. Eight weeks in Denver, eight weeks in Cincinnati, and eight weeks in Kansas City. After five weeks in Denver, McGowan scrapped the whole plan. It was all going so well. MCI was luckier than most companies. It had the mechanism to move quickly, mainly because it didn't have much machinery in place. Things were done when McGowan and others wanted them done without any reports or studies.

Tobin began to cultivate other spokesmen at MCI. He found that Carl worked well because he used his sales charm to look a reporter right in the eye and answer the questions with great sincerity. Orville also worked well because of his calm and precise answers. Tobin purposely kept away from the techies like Leming who might confuse people with how the microwave towers worked instead of how much money they could save.

Within a few weeks of Denver, MCI began service in Cincinnati and the response was excellent. Tobin found that unlike Denver, which had more of a frontier spirit and tended to embrace entrepreneurial spirit, Cincinnati was old-line conservative, and the reporters were much more skeptical. They wanted to know what effect MCI would have on rates, and they often raised the issue of cream skimming. In Indianapolis, the response was much the same except that this time it happened because AT&T had briefed reporters before MCI's arrival.

Through a friend who worked in radio, Tobin got a copy of a four-page briefing paper that Indiana Bell had prepared and sent to reporters. It outlined questions that they should ask MCI, like why MCI doesn't go everywhere, its quality of service, and, of course, the cream-skimming issue. This was a smart move by Bell, not because it showed MCI in a poor light—Tobin prepped everyone on what to say to these questions—but because it detracted from the opportunity to tell the MCI story and placed attention back on AT&T.

By the spring of 1980, MCI had opened residential service in dozens of cities, and once again Tobin found himself with a built-in news peg. MCI had won the largest antitrust settlement in history: $1.8 billion.

In February, a month before MCI had entered the residential market, John Worthington was completing work with his old law firm of Jenner & Block preparing MCI's lawsuit against AT&T.

Both sides had completed "discovery" about twenty months before. When someone sues someone else, he is permitted to ask for and receive certain documents, private and public, from the person he is suing. The defendant is permitted the same right. That procedure is called discovery. If you ask for something, the other side is required under penalty of contempt of court to supply it. You may, in some cases, declare documents privileged and off limits upon appeal to the court citing national security or other reasons. Judges are inclined not to allow many instances of that. AT&T's strategy was to ask for *everything*. MCI's attorneys had decided not to request privilege on any of Larry Harris's documents, mostly to make things easier on themselves. AT&T responded by microfilming every piece of paper in Harris's office, including the books on his shelves, most of which were engineering books which could be purchased anywhere. Discovery took more than five years.

MCI was well prepared for the trial. Even before they filed suit, they had tested public opinion about the case. They hired an outside firm to do a public survey about competition in the telephone industry and their beliefs about AT&T and, because the trial was to be held in

Chicago, Illinois Bell. They discovered that people liked the idea of competition and generally distrusted large businesses. Those polled believed that if a large company was faced with competition from a small company, it would step on it any way it could, including by illegal means.

MCI's litigation department under direction from Jenner & Block established one of the first computerized law data bases. This allowed them to easily retrieve documents that had been brought out during discovery, which in turn permitted the lawyers to quickly cross-check material that may have been in many different documents. During the trial, it made it easy to see if someone's testimony jibed with a document or his deposition—statements made under oath during discovery.

About six months before the actual trial, MCI held a mock trial. Although that's standard procedure now, it was not all that common when MCI did it. Twelve people were selected, much the way a jury is chosen, and they got a short version of the case presented to them. Then MCI's attorneys would listen to the jurors discuss the issues among themselves. There was one aspect of the case that Jenner & Block thought they might have trouble with: Why should AT&T be required to have its operating companies give facilities to MCI so it could compete with the parent company, AT&T? On the face of it, they believed most Americans would answer, "No reason at all," so they were surprised when the mock jurors didn't have trouble accepting that idea when it was applied to antitrust law.

Worthington worked night and day for months, and he began to show signs of fatigue. During dinner, he would fall asleep in the middle of a conversation, and his concentration was starting to fail. Whenever he worked, he did so feverishly. He was "Type A," keeping his frustration bottled up, rarely letting it out through channels like exercise or extended rest. Although he wouldn't try the case himself, he was the point man at MCI through whom Jenner & Block worked, and he took his task seriously. He had coordinated the discovery procedures years earlier, and as the time neared for the trial, the tension had built up inside him to the point where McGowan and everyone else would tell him to slow down. But Worthington couldn't help it. That was the way he was.

With the usual delays and legal protocol taken care of, the trial was set for February 5, 1980, in the U.S. District Court for the Northern District of Illinois in Chicago. On the afternoon of February 4, before the biggest day of his life, Worthington suffered a heart attack. After a few days in the hospital, he was able to keep up by reading transcripts of the day's proceedings. A month later, convalescing at home, he suffered another heart attack.

The trial opened with MCI's attorney, Bob Hanley, giving the opening arguments. He laid out the case in simple, easy-to-understand language. The telephone industry was so full of jargon that unless he scaled down his talk to plain English he would lose the jury's attention quickly. He described how the FCC authorized MCI to be in business and how AT&T had tried to stop them at every turn. He described the negotiations for interconnections and how AT&T had pulled the circuits after those talks had broken down. He told the jury not to be afraid of all the complex ideas involved, and he reassured them that he would explain everything.

George Saunders, from the law firm of Sidley & Austin, was AT&T's attorney. It was a mystery why they had picked him. Although Saunders was brilliant, he was an appellate attorney. He was used to trying cases before learned judges and not juries. In fact, this was the first time he had worked before a jury. Either AT&T figured the case was so locked in that it didn't matter who represented them, or they just figured that Saunders could do something that he had never done before.

Saunders got off on the wrong foot with the jury when he began to paint a picture of MCI as a company that was out to destroy the nation's phone system and when they began to realize they couldn't do it sued AT&T to hide their failure. He said they needed someone to blame it on. He also described a conspiracy between the FCC and MCI in which the two worked together to destroy AT&T. Almost from that point on, the jury didn't buy anything he said. Interviews with jurors after the trial ended showed that they didn't believe either of these arguments, not even a little bit.

Moreover, the jury didn't like the way Saunders presented himself. They found his manner abrasive. Saunders's style was confrontational, and he appeared to try to rile the MCI witnesses. He would say things like: "Isn't it a fact!" and before the person could answer he would add, "And isn't it also a fact that blah, blah, blah." To the jurors, it seemed like *his* testimony and not that of the witnesses. Saunders also presented a technical approach to the case, using a lot of buzzwords and jargon. He brought many engineers to testify, which may have caused a chasm between him and the jury.

AT&T witnesses were rather formal, stuffy. MCI's witnesses seemed like they were enjoying themselves.

McGowan was a most credible witness, presenting the side of one who was wronged by the big bad company AT&T. The jury was impressed by his answers, which were focused and concise. They also liked the way he handled abrasive questioning by Saunders; McGowan remained unflappable.

When Ken Cox took the stand under cross-examination, Saunders was trying to show that there was a conspiracy among Cox, who was once at the FCC, and Bernie Strassberg, who was also at the FCC, and others. Saunders was trying to compare the conspirators in the movie *Casablanca* with an alleged conspiracy at the FCC. He asked Cox, "Did you see *Casablanca*, where in the last scene everyone shows up at the airport?" Ken replied softly, "The line was, 'Round up the usual suspects.'" The courtroom howled.

Then Saunders said seriously, "That indeed was the last line, wasn't it? I have no further questions."

Ken said, *"That's* what Claude Raines said at the end of the movie."

The jury continued to be amused by MCI's sassy demeanor and AT&T's stuffy approach.

On June 13, the jury found AT&T guilty of violating the antitrust laws and awarded MCI damages of $600 million. Under antitrust laws, that award was trebled to $1.8 billion, which AT&T appealed all the way to the Supreme Court. Although the courts upheld AT&T's culpability—they had broken the antitrust laws—it would eventually throw out the amount of the award. A new jury wouldn't decide until 1985 the exact amount of the settlement.

At a victory party and dinner at the Madison Hotel, people watched the airport scene from the movie *Casablanca*, and someone ran around with a coat that had written on the back: "THE USUAL SUSPECTS."

The antitrust trial award came at an excellent time for MCI. Because of news coverage of the event, it placed the name before many consumers who would soon try the company's residential service. They had heard about this small company that just won a case against The Phone Company and here they were offering phone service. Even though many consumers mistakenly tied the two incidents together— MCI beat AT&T in court, so now it can offer phone service—that misconception worked to the company's advantage because MCI came out the good guy and AT&T was the big baddie. And consumers, as Avis car rental knew, loved to do business with the underdog.

Tobin found himself getting calls from reporters who had experienced the same thing as Tom Messner. They never heard the name MCI before, and now they were seeing it all the time.

After the award, MCI started getting calls from reporters, not the other way around. Although the trade press had been plugged into MCI for a while, now the general press and even the TV media were interested in this company that really had beaten AT&T.

When the news came that the jury found AT&T guilty, Tobin was in Washington. He had just flown back from Chicago after watching the closing arguments. It was Friday and he figured there was no way the jury would reach a verdict that day. He thought they would take the weekend. He was getting ready to go to sleep when he got a call from *Washington Star* reporter Caroline Mayer, who wanted a comment for her story about the suit. She said, "What's the reaction?"

Tobin said, "What's the reaction to what?"

"Don't you know?"

"No, I don't know," said Tobin.

"The jury came in about 8:30 and they got [Judge] Grady down from where he lives way outside of Chicago and the jury awarded MCI $600 million, trebled to one-point-eight."

Tobin said, "Gee, I didn't know that," and hung up the phone and called McGowan in Chicago. They chatted about PR when McGowan said, "Just a minute. I have to talk to Worthington," and he put the phone down with Tobin hanging on.

He never came back. Tobin waited for an hour before somebody— he didn't know who—walked by and put the phone back on the cradle. McGowan just plain forgot.

The next day, Saturday, Tobin arranged interviews for McGowan, who had been up the whole night high on the court win. A TV station did an interview with McGowan that morning, but only from the neck up. McGowan was still in his underwear. That afternoon he flew back to Washington and met with *Time, Business Week,* and other magazines. McGowan worked the entire weekend talking with reporters and doing interviews. It was grueling for him, but he knew it had to be done. Unlike other companies, McGowan wanted to show that a chairman and CEO was accessible to the news media. He knew that the biggest gripe of reporters is when they got a PR guy or some lower-level executive when they really wanted to talk to the top guy. He also knew that AT&T's chairman wouldn't have done it, and it always looked good on TV or in print when McGowan told the MCI story while some flak from AT&T told their story. It perpetrated the friendly MCI image versus the cold AT&T image, and McGowan rode that for all it was worth.

All the attention turned MCI into a different company. The media was now doing what a sales force had done before: provide visibility.

It became clear to McGowan and Carl that MCI didn't need its large sales force anymore. All it needed were TV and newspaper ads and people to answer the phone. The salesmen knew it, too, and rumors about layoffs were floating around the company.

They would forever call the first Tuesday in June Black Tuesday. On that day, the company let go about 80 percent of its commercial-sales people. The company was now fully committed to TV, radio, and newspaper advertising for both its residential and business customers and didn't need salesmen knocking on the doors of corporate America anymore.

On that day, salesmen from the New York City office were to report extra early, before 9 A.M. MCI had bought a full-page ad in *The Wall Street Journal*, and the leads generated by those who called in were to be divided up among the crew. One of those was Robert Pons, who had been with the company a little over a year.

Pons was the quintessential MCI salesman and indeed the *perfect* MCI employee. He was likable, competitive, ambitious, and he wanted to make lots of money. He had some friends living in Manhattan who were working in sales and buying nice things. He was envious. So he dropped out of law school, moved from New Jersey to New York, and got a job working for Kraft Foods selling Sealtest ice cream. His job was to visit the frozen-food managers at supermarkets and get more shelf space. Mostly, that meant rearranging the freezer displays to show off his company's products. The managers were perfectly willing to let him do it because stocking ice cream was a cold, messy job, and as long as the displays looked nice they didn't care what the salesmen did. Pons would then take a Polaroid picture to show his boss what a good job he had done. He was making $12,750.

One of his friends saw an ad for a "telecommunications seminar" which was really a recruitment ad for MCI. Pons struck a deal with his friend that he would go to the morning session and if it was worthwhile, he would tell his friend, who would then go to the afternoon session. About fifty people showed up and Pons felt uncomfortable because everyone was at least ten years older and asked technical questions that he didn't understand. When the applications were passed out, Pons didn't know what to put down for an expected salary. Those around him were putting $35,000, but to Pons that seemed like a fortune. He was making less than $13,000, so he wrote $15,000. Pons was so competitive that later he told his friend, "It was okay, but I wouldn't waste my time with it." He thought he had found the right thing, and he didn't want anyone else competing for his job.

Pons knocked on company doors selling Execunet service in the two World Trade Towers and buildings on Battery Park Place in lower Manhattan. He did nothing but knock on doors. Cold sales calls. His trick was to go into an office and say, "I'm from the phone company," because if he had said he was MCI, he wouldn't have gotten in the door. Few had heard of MCI. He loved the job, and whenever he made a sale he would call his dad and tell him. The quota was twelve for the month. His base salary was $12,000 plus $100 a sale plus 120 percent of the customer's third-month phone bill. Unlike the Execunet salesmen who sold over the phone, Pons and his colleagues were the classy ones and were trusted with up-front money. This lasted until June and Black Tuesday.

The day of the full-page ad in *The Wall Street Journal*, Pons got stuck on a crowded bus and arrived late, about five minutes past nine. Paul Keeler, regional manager, was standing by the door with a clipboard when Pons came in, sweating.

Pons apologized for being late.

"Sit down," Keeler said sternly.

Rumors about pending layoffs were all over MCI, and Pons thought he knew what Keeler was going to tell him. By his harsh businesslike look, Pons figured he was going to go.

Keeler told Pons that they didn't need salesmen knocking on doors anymore, that the ads would provide the leads and they were running out of capacity anyway. MCI was going to lay off about 80 percent of the sales force.

"But," Keeler said as he started to smile, "we're happy with you, but we feel bad that we have to take you off the commission plan." Pons was offered a salary of $24,000, and he went nuts. He had just left Kraft at $12,750, and he didn't have the pressures of a quota anymore. He had hit the jackpot.

For the next five months, there wasn't much for Pons and other salesmen to do except service the commercial accounts. Because of the increase in customers, the quality of the service was poor. Too many calls were greeted by "blocking," a condition in which calls don't get through because the network is 100 percent busy. This was McGowan's dream, to fill the network to capacity, but it also made for some pretty sore customers. Eventually, more capacity was put in, and Pons and others could once again sell to commercial customers.

Pons was invited to a sales meeting in Key West and told to bring a spouse or date or anyone else. He was going to call up an old girlfriend when his father suggested that he not bring anyone. He said that since he was only twenty-four years old, he wasn't expected to bring a wife, and if he went by himself, he would have more opportunity to mingle.

He followed his father's advice, and Saturday night at a cocktail party Paul Keeler asked Pons what he was doing on Sunday. Pons said nothing, and Keeler invited him to go deep-sea fishing with him and a vice-president of the ad agency they did business with. Pons used the time alone with Keeler to talk about his future at MCI. He said he would like to leave selling for a managerial job. Keeler said, "Give me two weeks."

Sure enough, two weeks later Pons got a call from an MCI manager who said he understood that Pons was ambitious, looking for a challenge, and that MCI was always looking for that kind of person and would he be interested in building the Boston office—which had about five people—into a full-fledged business? This was Pon's big break, and he took it, even though he had never done anything like it before. He was just a salesman, but MCI gave him complete control of the project.

Over the next seven months, he procured the real estate, designed the offices, hired people. He had stepped on some toes of MCI's real estate people in New York City who wanted Pons to use some space that MCI had available in Boston, but they were moving too slowly for Pons. He was told by a friend in Washington that he better move quickly on the project. Pons got a call from a real estate guy in New York who said, "Pons, what the hell are you doing?" Pons got angry and said, "Fuck you. You guys haven't helped me at all here. I'm not waiting for you anymore." They cursed each other some more, and the conversation ended. Pons had made the other guy look bad for his slow movement; Pons was a man in a hurry and this real estate guy was dragging his feet. He was shaken by his first confrontation with management, but he later learned that this kind of behavior was acceptable at MCI if it was done for the good of the company. It was okay not to follow all the procedures and get caught in the red tape if it meant moving a project swiftly so the company could make more money. Pons learned he could do almost anything as long as it worked and it was in the interests of the company.

Pons invited Orville to the grand opening. Pons continued to get great exposure in Boston. He was the first to contract for outside telemarketing, and at one time the office had more residential customers than New York City. He was getting a good reputation at headquarters.

But he still wanted to move further in the company, and he realized that he would have to work in Washington. Pons was a good friend of Tony Abell, who had been assistant to the president, Orville, then later put in charge of investor relations. Orville created the position for people like Abell and Pons who were young and ambitious but needed some exposure working in the corporate offices. They needed to be smoothed out, the rough edges taken off. Abell told Pons he should apply for the job, and Pons wrote Orville a letter.

Other people in the running for the job had been granted interviews with Orville, but Pons hadn't. Two weeks later, Orville telephoned and said, "You don't have to come to Washington for an interview. We can do it on the phone if you don't mind." What could Pons say but "certainly," even though he was in the middle of something and not mentally psyched up for an interview. Pons didn't think he would get the job. He figured it was a token telephone call because Orville was a nice guy and that was that. To his surprise, he got a call from a friend in Washington who told him that Orville had chosen him and that he should expect a call. The next day, Pons got a call from Orville, and he was in Washington a week later.

As assistant to the president, Pons became Orville's right-hand man. He would handle complaints from customers and others that were directed to Orville. He followed Orville most everywhere. He became his confidant, and Orville became his mentor.

Like everyone else, Pons was caught up in the "MCI hype." It was a feeling—no, it was almost a religious belief—that the company could do anything. It had beaten AT&T in the courts. It had shown that once and forever AT&T was the bad guy. MCI lawyers had shown they could work the FCC like a carnival barker taking money from a rube. McGowan had shown that he could use the regulatory process as a business discipline. Unlike other entrepreneurs, McGowan built a business by manipulating the regulators, not by inventing and selling a new high-tech doodad.

McGowan could manipulate people, too. He treated his employees as if they could do anything, as if they could accomplish the unthinkable. He gave his workers incredible leeway in their jobs and how they did them. He knew that once people were given lots of responsibility, they would rarely fail him. Some did, but most succeeded because they didn't want to disappoint him. He was the kind of person who believed so much in you that you didn't want to prove him wrong. If he said you could walk through a brick wall, you would believe it.

On the outside, in the newspapers and on Wall Street, McGowan was getting a reputation as the man who made it all happen. He was pictured as a CEO who didn't play by the rules. He didn't dress in $500 suits or vacation on the Riviera. He didn't act pleasant and smile when reporters asked him questions. He answered them straight on with that crooked smile of his and a twinkle in his eyes that seemed to say, "I could be putting you on, you know." And then he began to rant about the future of the telecommunications industry and the information age. Sometimes he would call reporters who covered the industry just to chat and see what they were thinking. He loved the intellectual challenge of conversation.

He shunned the usual night life of Washington—the banquets, the balls, the important parties—for dinner with friends and business acquaintances.

Around this time, Wayne English had negotiated to lease a new office. The company was growing, and the old offices on 17th Street just didn't fit anymore. Not only that, but it was about time that MCI had headquarters more fitting the big company that it was fast becoming. McGowan liked the fact that the new building was within a block of the FCC, and he was fond of telling visitors: "I don't trust them any further away."

But an unexpected thing happened when MCI moved to the new building. All of a sudden, they got THE TWELFTH FLOOR. This was the top floor and housed the company's executives. For the first time, the vice-presidents and other senior officials weren't among the other employees. It was a sure sign that MCI was no longer a small, entrepreneurial company.

THE TWELFTH FLOOR cut down on McGowan's "management by walking around." He and others made many of their decisions by walking around, talking to people and seeing what they were doing. Often, someone would get an idea at a meeting and start pulling people from their offices. Now, with THE TWELFTH FLOOR, the decision makers were cut off. McGowan tried to get back in the flow by always leaving his office open and working behind a large round desk instead of his regular desk. This way, he could see people passing by and tell them to come in, or people who were just walking past might see him and walk in and talk. He continued to answer his own phone and encouraged anyone in the company to call him directly.

Unlike Orville, who had an assistant president, McGowan didn't have an assistant chairman. He preferred that no one run interference for him. He did have a secretary who he insisted be promotable to another job in the company at least every two years.

A change was coming to his private life, too. Now that MCI was large, people at the company began to fear for McGowan's safety. He never worried about it, but they did, and the company instituted picture badges that everyone had to wear in the building. Someone also had the bright idea to place a button under McGowan's desk that would immediately snap the door shut and protect him from intruders. McGowan acquiesced, but his biggest fear was that he or someone else would get his fingers caught by accident.

People at MCI also didn't like the fact that McGowan walked home late at night. It just wasn't something that a chairman of a major company did. McGowan walked the few blocks to an apartment that he kept in a hotel. It wasn't that he was cheap; he just didn't think having a home was important. He felt the same way about clothes. Although he could afford expensive suits, he bought the first thing that came off the rack, usually some polyester number. It simply wasn't important.

Martha Hiney, Jack's first secretary, had become close to McGowan over the years. Their families got together often. She and others interested McGowan in a house in Georgetown, which he eventually bought, mostly as a project that he could occupy himself with rather than as a house to live in. He was on the road so much anyway.

He hired a houseboy named Conrad to oversee the place. Conrad was married, and his wife would live in the house, too.

McGowan had fun with his new house, fixing it up to his liking with such things as a waterfall and fake rocks, like the kind at the polar bear pool in the zoo, and his favorite piece—a bas-relief bell in a concrete keystone, very much like the AT&T logo, cracked down the middle and set in an archway.

The house overlooked the Potomac River and was in keeping with the chairman of a major company.

The new office building had a lunchroom where executives could eat such things as chili dogs and bacon, lettuce, and tomato sandwiches. The fare resembled a good luncheonette except when visitors came to talk business. Now that other company executives came to visit MCI, they needed a place to eat without distraction. It also filled another role. The dining room got McGowan to eat properly. Often, he worked without eating and people worried about him. They didn't want to lose the man who had brought them this far. And they loved him like a friend.

By now, MCI was doing better than anyone expected. In October

1980, MCI reported second-quarter profits of more than $4 million, *triple* its profits for the same period a year earlier. Revenues were $52.7 million, up from $33.4 million, much of it attributable to residential service. MCI had more than 100,000 residential customers and 70,000 business customers.

During that period, annual meetings were really pep rallies. Everyone—investors, employees, news media—was caught up in the MCI hype. The company, it seemed, did everything right and could do nothing wrong. Unlike other corporations, MCI wasn't a gray little company run by gray little men. It had a *style*, and it was headed by a charismatic leader who also had style. He was still the kid from Scranton, but boy was he smart.

At the 1980 annual meeting, only a month after MCI won its lawsuit against AT&T, a shareholder asked McGowan what MCI meant. He responded, "Money Coming In!" The crowd loved it.

Others were taking notice of MCI as well. Not only was it changing the face of telecommunications, it was, quite simply, one of the few major companies actually located in the District of Columbia. For those who lived in the Washington area, MCI was a big fish in a little pond and was highly visible because of it.

Tim Wirth, a Democratic congressman from Denver, had noticed MCI shortly after he joined Congress in 1975. Just like the character played by Dustin Hoffman in the movie *The Graduate*, who was told "Plastics," Wirth had been advised: "Telecommunications."

Wirth represented an area of the country that felt comfortable with information technology. The cable TV industry had grown up in Denver. Because of the mountains, it was the only way for people there to enjoy many channels of clear reception. As a result, Wirth's district included some of the country's largest cable and communications companies.

Wirth became chairman of the House Subcommittee on Telecommunications, Consumer Protection and Finance after Chairman Lionel Van Deerlin of San Diego was defeated. Van Deerlin had the distinction of being the first congressman to be unseated by AT&T supporters. Van Deerlin had taken the lead in Congress by introducing the first procompetitive bill several years earlier. When he came up for reelection, his opponent had door hangers placed on voters' homes telling them that Van Deerlin was going to double or triple their phone rates and to call Van Deerlin's office for an explanation. Days before the election, Van Deerlin's office was flooded with irate callers who disrupted his staff's routine. Van Deerlin, who had been the candidate to beat going into the race, lost by a close margin. The door hangers bore the AT&T bell logo.

One of the claims leveled against Van Deerlin was that his legislation lacked facts and figures to back up his belief that competition was good. Wirth wouldn't make that same mistake. During the spring and summer of 1981, the subcommittee held weeks and weeks of hearings with academics, economists, industry officials, and anyone else who wanted to speak. The only criterion, it seemed, was that they be long-winded or boring. The hearings never seemed to end, but when they finally did, Wirth and his staff produced the definitive congressional work on the U.S. telephone industry. It was 435 pages.

The report, released in November, came to several conclusions. First, certain areas were competitive, such as the equipment business, and that was going rather well. Second, long distance was on its way to being competitive and had good potential. Third, local service was a natural monopoly and should stay that way. It was crazy to have more than one phone company serving a city. Wirth's underlying belief was that you regulate an industry with an eye toward deregulating it when the time was right.

The report was well received by competitors like MCI and Sprint. AT&T, naturally, opposed the findings.

The following month, Wirth introduced a bill to rewrite the Communications Act of 1934, the industry's holy Koran. The bill's number was HR-5158, known affectionately as "fifty-one-fifty-eight."

Fifty-one-fifty-eight was introduced as a working draft. It wasn't meant to be perfect, but Wirth believed it went in the right direction.

ACCT members had always opposed any type of legislation. They believed that the FCC and the courts would take care of the situation, albeit slowly, and that Congress's meddling would only complicate matters. The only problem was that Herb Jasper and the ACCT members knew they couldn't rebuff Wirth if he introduced a bill that would strengthen their side. It pays to have friends in Congress, and if you say no now, he may not help you when you really need help. Reluctantly, MCI and the other members of ACCT supported the basic idea of the bill.

AT&T opposed the bill but didn't think it would go very far. Many of the reasons for the bill's existence were now moot because of what was happening in a courtroom less than a mile from the Congress. The Justice Department's antitrust suit against AT&T had been under way for several months, and it looked like the drama that had been playing out since March was reaching a climax.

In 1981, AT&T had the largest corporate law staff in the United States, almost 930 attorneys. It was more of a necessity than a luxury. At the time the Justice Department suit against AT&T was under way in Washington, the Bell System was in the midst of defending itself against forty different lawsuits. This case would be the granddaddy of them all. Justice had planned to call 110 witnesses in 55 days. AT&T, which had planned to call 900 witnesses, whittled that down to about 400 and was going to present its case in 250 days. Justice had already spent $10 million and used a handful of lawyers preparing for the case; AT&T said it spent more than $250 million and used more than 50 attorneys.

It would take a very special judge to handle the case. His name was Harold Greene, and he was widely known for drafting the 1964 Civil Rights Act for Attorney General Robert Kennedy.

Both sides had great respect for Greene, and they knew that if any judge could get this monster moving it would be him. Gerald Connell, a methodical, low-key, well-prepared attorney, was the lead counsel for the government. He delivered his opening remarks like a college professor outlining the course on the first day of class. He stood at the lectern and mostly read from his notes, beginning his three-hour opening remarks with: "This case is about regulation that didn't work

. . . about refusal to interconnect competitive equipment . . . and about how Bell fought off each new wave of competition."

He called the Bell System a slow-thinking elephant that couldn't figure out the message of its masters—the regulators. Paraphrasing AT&T's advertising slogan "Reach out and touch someone," Connell said, "From time to time, this elephant might reach out and crush someone."

Connell added, "AT&T seemed to be saying that being big means never having to say you're sorry."

The government's case went beyond the long-distance market and how AT&T tried illegally to stifle competitors such as MCI. It dealt with the phone and equipment market and the procurement policies of the Bell System, especially the local Bell companies.

The government was going to show how AT&T forced the Bell companies to buy only from its manufacturing arm, Western Electric, and how it prevented small companies from selling equipment such as telephone answering machines and PBXs because AT&T insisted on "protective connection arrangements" or PCAs, which were expensive and unnecessary devices. Not only that, only AT&T could supply them.

Connell worked with a rotating team of three to five young attorneys.

George Saunders, who had lost the MCI antitrust cast for AT&T, led Bell's defense. Saunders was his usual flamboyant, striding, brilliant, pompous, colorful self. Unlike Connell, Saunders sparingly referred to his notes. He strode around the room, believing that the government's case was weak, that the MCI decision was a fluke, and that Judge Greene wouldn't believe that this group of guys was nothing less than cream skimmers out to wreck the best phone system in the world.

For the next six hours, Saunders made his opening statement. He said that AT&T was only doing what the FCC had told them to do and that on many occasions Bell had asked the FCC for clarification of its regulations so as not to run afoul of the law. He emphasized that AT&T's pricing polices were not predatory—that is, not purposely priced below actual costs (the main argument in any antitrust case)—but that in order for AT&T to provide universal phone service, as called for in the Communications Act of 1934, Bell had to use national rate averaging on all products and services.

Shortly after the trial began, both sides asked Greene for a postponement. They said they might be able to reach a settlement.

Reluctantly, Greene agreed but said the trial would begin March 4 if a settlement wasn't reached. Despite rumors that the two sides had reached an agreement, and despite their requests to Greene for an extension, on March 4, the trial began.

The Justice Department began by bringing on equipment makers who testifed how AT&T had tried to force them out of business with its illegal actions.

One of the most damaging was Lowell Hoxie, former vice-president of Litton Industries. Litton had its own antitrust suit against AT&T in New York claiming that Bell kept it out of the PBX business by insisting that its equipment first be connected to a PCA for systems with fewer than five lines. Without the PCAs, Bell told Litton, the nation's telephone network would be damaged. The PCAs added extra costs to the equipment and were not always available. Those two obstacles were enough to kill off much of Litton's business. Documents obtained by the government showed that Bell later offered the same gear without a PCA.

Officials for another company called Phonemate claimed they were damaged when South Central Bell filed an injunction against the company that prohibited them from connecting their answering machines to the telephone network without PCAs. The government showed the court an internal AT&T report stating that the Phonemate device caused no harm at all.

The witnesses kept coming with similar stories of how Bell said one thing about connecting equipment to the network yet did another.

Saunders could not refute the integrity or the accuracy of the witnesses. All he could do was wait until he could bring on his own witnesses, especially the ones from Bell Labs who would say that anything not approved by AT&T could not be connected to the system without causing damage to it.

Around this time, William Baxter became head of the Justice Department's antitrust division. Speculation arose that because he was Ronald "big business is not always bad" Reagan's appointee, perhaps the government would withdraw its case. No go. Baxter was his own man and said that the government had a perfectly sound case and would pursue it. He said, "We'll litigate it to the eyeballs."

The Justice Department's attorneys produced AT&T internal memos showing how AT&T tried to cover its tracks. It brought up an AT&T memo that was dated March 15, 1973—less than two weeks after McGowan and deButts had one of their talks. It read: "We have been moving towards reviewing and cleaning out our files. Several things have been done . . . a shredder is available and in use."

Also introduced was an AT&T video titled "What's in Our Files." The video described how employees should handle sensitive documents and even portrayed a Bell competitor using AT&T memos in its antitrust case.

Saunders confronted McGowan with the same conspiracy theory that he used in the MCI case. He claimed that MCI had worked surreptitiously with the FCC, mostly with then chief of the Common Carrier Bureau Bernie Strassberg, to go around the usual procedures. In his dramatic way, Saunders began several rounds of questioning with his "And isn't it true . . ."

Saunders tried to show that when MCI stopped construction of its network, it was really because of poor weather conditions and lack of financial planning, not because AT&T had kept it from getting its local interconnections. He introduced MCI memos that said of the company's condition, "Our problems are our own," meaning that AT&T wasn't to blame for MCI's money problems. McGowan said that he lied to his employees about weather being the cause of the construction stoppages to boost morale. It was the same line of questioning Saunders used at the MCI trial.

Larry Harris testified about his problems negotiating with AT&T for the vital interconnections. He described how negotiations broke down after he discovered that AT&T wasn't really bargaining in good faith but just clocking time until it could file its tariffs in each state rather than on a national scale. Harris told the court how he wanted the same agreements that Western Union had made with Bell for its domestic Telex machines. Western Union paid ten dollars for a four-wire connection, but Bell wanted to charge MCI thirty dollars for it. Saunders couldn't shake Harris's testimony.

At this time, the Justice Department introduced one of the most controversial documents in the trial. It was a deposition from a woman named Leigh Tripoli who worked in AT&T's research department in Chicago. The deposition had been introduced during an appeal of the MCI case but not during the original trial. Tripoli's statement said that she "was instructed by Edward Lowry [a regulatory research supervisor] to go through my files and discard any documents that might be embarrassing to the Bell companies on interconnections, specialized common carriers and competitors and to discard copies of drafts of speeches I had written."

Tripoli's deposition described how she saw six or seven wastebaskets in the halls leading to paper shredders. She also outlined a scheme in which AT&T executives would mail documents to each other so they would officially and legally not be in anyone's possession if they were called for by the suing party.

Saunders fought to keep the damaging deposition out but lost.

A strong witness for the government was Barry Hallamore, chairman of SAN/BAR Corp., a company that manufactured line cards. Line cards control the action of multiline phones such as ringing and call holding. None of the Bell companies would buy his company's product, even though AT&T's own reports showed that their failure was 2 percent compared to 6.8 percent for a similar Western Electric product. Saunders was able to thwart Hallamore by showing that the SAN/BAR product cost nine dollars more than the WE product. However it didn't look good for AT&T when Hallamore testified that during a WE strike that began August 5, 1974, he immediately sold $5 million worth of his products to the Bell Operating Companies but only delivered $3 million worth because the strike ended on September 3.

Justice Department struck another strong blow when Datran officials took the stand. The now defunct data transmission company went bust because Bell wouldn't give them interconnections, the company said. AT&T documents showed that Bell didn't even think of developing its own system for transmitting data until Datran filed for its license in the early 1960s. AT&T's actions slowed Datran's growth because of its tremendous market presence. Customers wanted to see what AT&T had to offer, even though it was more than four years behind Datran. Documents also showed that AT&T priced its proposed data service much lower than Datran, in fact, below AT&T's costs.

Datran never really had a chance to see if it could succeed anyway, because it couldn't get the local interconnections from the Bell companies—just like MCI.

Wyly Corp., the owners, finally gave up and sold Datran's facilities to Southern Pacific for $4.9 million only two years after it began service in 1974. In exchange for dropping its suit, AT&T paid Datran $50 million in an out-of-court settlement in 1980.

One of the important elements in antitrust violations is to show that the alleged offender is actually pricing its products or service below actual costs in an effort to thwart competition. When it's done internationally, it's called dumping, and it's against the law. The Justice Department knew that it couldn't prove that AT&T engaged in below-cost pricing because nobody knew what AT&T's costs were. So it took a novel approach. It tried to show that AT&T priced its services and product *without regard to cost at all*. That, they figured, would establish at least that AT&T wasn't doing what all other businesses do. They didn't figure the cost and then add on a profit margin. They tried to show that products and services were priced to maximize market share and exclude competition and not to maximize company profits.

This unprecedented pricing theory was backed by economists and other witnesses for the government, even though they were easily challenged by Saunders, who knew that when it came to the nitty-gritty, nobody could actually prove that AT&T priced its products and services below cost because nobody knew what AT&T's costs really were.

In fact, several FCC officials testified that they didn't know AT&T's cost, even though they were supposed to regulate the company's prices. They said AT&T was too big and the FCC was too small. They just did the best they could based on what AT&T told them.

The Justice Department rested its case after four months, ninety-three witnesses, sixty-one days of actual courtroom work, two thousand exhibits, and 11,500 pages of transcript.

This was half time, and AT&T was prepared to deliver its defense. As is usual, the defendant asked for dismissal, and during a five-hour oral argument, Saunders told the court that the government's case was weak. "I think we're entitled to have the whole damn thing thrown out." Saunders was fond of acting like a bumpkin, reminding the court that he was just a poor boy from the South. His southern accent did indeed come out when he got agitated. During one of these self-effacing routines, Greene said, not looking at Saunders, "This country boy routine may work elsewhere but not in this court." Even Saunders had to laugh.

Greene told Saunders that if he wanted to, he could present the court with a written argument for dismissal, and the court would respond in writing. Saunders said he would.

That may have been Saunders's biggest mistake, a tactical error that will be talked about in legal books and at lawyers' luncheons forever. Saunders was convinced that AT&T was winning despite all the contrary testimony, and he was hoping that there would be something in Greene's response that would help AT&T in the MCI appeals trial.

So instead of Judge Greene hitting the gavel and saying, "Motion for dismissal denied, let's get on with the trial," Saunders's request for a written answer to his motion caused Greene to say for the first time in public that AT&T appeared to be guilty.

In response to Saunders's 550-page motion for dismissal, Greene responded with a 74-page document which countered: "The testimony and documents . . . demonstrate that the Bell System has violated the antitrust laws in a number of ways over a lengthy period of time."

Wham.

AT&T was going to lose and everyone knew it. Speculation got even stronger that AT&T and the government would settle the case on the government's terms.

The reporters who covered the trial smelled blood. Moreover, they were eager to see Saunders in action with his own witnesses. Paul Travis, who worked for the newsletter *Communications Daily*, and Marilyn Richter of *Electronic News* newspaper covered nearly every day of the trial. They used to take bets on how long it would take Judge Greene to cut off one of Saunders's long-winded speeches. They watched Greene closely, seeing who would be the first to spot the subtle changes in his eyes and mouth that telegraphed his move to tell Saunders to get on with it. Greene's impatience didn't fall only on Saunders and the AT&T attorneys. Connell got his share of the judge's wrath, too, but Saunders's flair for the dramatic seemed to irritate Greene more.

All the reporters were impressed by Greene's hold on the court. He was like a quality control inspector in a factory, making certain that everything that left was exactly as it should be. Reporters like Travis and Richter knew the complicated telephone industry like few others, and they were amazed at Greene's grasp of complicated issues such as pricing and tariffs. Greene had obviously done his homework, and witnesses were unable to put anything past him. He was able to cut off long lines of questioning when he knew it wouldn't add anything. When he didn't understand something, he would question the witnesses himself in a manner that said, "I know what I'm talking about."

Greene continued to be tough when both sides asked for a postponement for eleven months so the Congress could tackle the question of AT&T and its future by way of legislation. Bills were moving through the House and Senate that would answer some of the problems that the Justice Department had with AT&T. Greene wouldn't hear of it, saying that what happened in Congress had nothing to do with what the court was doing. The trial would continue no matter what else was going on.

Saunders opened his defense with former AT&T chairman John deButts. The courtroom was packed. Saunders asked deButts open-ended questions that would allow deButts to talk as long as he wanted. He used phrases like being "raised in the system" and "growing up in the system" and told of how AT&T had an obligation to the public to fight competition. He talked about the proud history of the Bell System and how it had served the country so well all these years. He painted a sad picture of a man who couldn't adjust to a new age that was out to get his "family." It was almost as if AT&T was a benign dictator that did what it had to do to give Americans the best telephone system in the world and how the ungrateful subjects were revolting.

After deButts, Saunders started to bring on all the Bell company chief executives. Greene put a stop to it, complaining that they were all saying the same thing and that he wasn't impressed with who they were or their status. The reporters were surprised that Saunders continued to try to impress Greene when he gave the court a calendar of upcoming witnesses that included Secretary of State Alexander Haig, Defense Secretary Caspar Weinberger, and Commerce Secretary Malcolm Baldrige. Saunders was trying to show that the breakup of the Bell System would hurt national defense, but Greene saw it as just some more of his theatrics, and he said so: "This court is not impressed by big names." Whether they would have taken the stand was in doubt, anyway. There were rumors they would invoke executive privilege when the time came.

Saunders's case began to break down. He had little evidence to refute the Justice Department's case. All he had was glamour and glitz, so that's what he went with. Saunders did have one document, however, that he wanted submitted as evidence to show that the Bell System should not be broken up because of national security. AT&T and the government had always been tightly linked. AT&T supplied all the communications for the military and the federal government, and some of the deals were considered dirty.

One of these deals went back to the early 1950s when the government began to press a twenty-year-old antitrust suit against AT&T. It was prompted by several states that were having trouble setting telephone rates because they couldn't figure out the true costs of equipment bought from Western Electric. The whole thing was so intertwined that the only answer was to separate WE from the rest of the Bell System, and the U.S. attorney general agreed.

At the same time, an unrelated event took place. The University of California told the Atomic Energy Commission that it was not going to run the government's Sandia Atomic Laboratory anymore, a task it had performed for several years. Sandia manufactured atomic weapons, and the official reason for the university bowing out was that it was inappropriate for a school to engage in such work. The more likely reason was that Sandia Labs had become very political and bureaucratic. Little work was getting done, and it just wasn't worth it anymore.

Whatever the real reason, the AEC had to get another contractor to run Sandia, and they approached Bell Labs. Bell officials refused, saying they couldn't engage in defense work. Their rules limited defense work to less than 20 percent of their budget. AEC officials suggested that something could be worked out, perhaps a scheme in which Bell Labs merely lent its management skill to Sandia but didn't do the actual work.

Finally, after lengthy negotiations, President Truman wrote to Leroy Wilson, AT&T president, asking that Bell take over Sandia in the national interest. Wilson responded, saying that Bell would accept the task for the sake of the country. He pointed out that the government had this antitrust case, you see, and they were trying to break up the very system that you, Mr. President, said was so vital to this country. Hint, hint, hint.

In a letter to AEC Chairman David Lilienthal, Wilson came right out with it. "We are concerned that the antitrust suit seeks to terminate the Western Electric/Bell Labs relationship which gives our organization the unique qualifications to which you refer." He continued: "The effectiveness of [our] work would depend upon their close connections." The suit was quashed, put on hold until 1956, when the government and AT&T signed a "consent decree" that said AT&T had to stick with regulated businesses like telephones and couldn't get into unregulated business like computers. The hope was that the government could at least stop AT&T from getting its guaranteed, regulated rate of return at the public's expense and use it to compete with others in unregulated, competitive businesses.

The government/AT&T connection surfaced once again during Saunders's presentation when he tried to introduce a Department of Defense report showing that national security would suffer if AT&T

was broken up. The Justice Department was in the strange position of calling to task its own client, the Department of Defense, after it was shown that DOD got its facts and figures for the report from AT&T, and that AT&T had a major role in checking the report before it was finished. Greene was angry that Saunders tried to introduce this as evidence of an independent opinion. He held special hearings on it and found that it would be accepted as evidence but that it would carry less weight than other pieces of evidence.

Things were looking bad for AT&T, and by late December rumors once again were flying around Washington that a settlement was near. Then on December 31, William Baxter announced that negotiations were under way and neither side would say any more.

On Friday, January 8, reporters covering the trial knew that something was happening. At 10 A.M., when the stock exchanges opened, AT&T and IBM asked the New York Stock Exchange to stop trading in their companies pending an announcement. Requests to halt trading aren't uncommon when a momentous event, such as a takeover offer, is near. Companies ask for the halt to keep the stock from moving wildly up or down, and the exchange usually grants the request because they want an orderly market, too. Although no reason for the request was made public, everyone knew why. This was Justice Department antitrust cleaning day. Not only was it going to settle the AT&T matter but it was going to dismiss a pending antitrust case against IBM that had been bogged down for thirteen years. The IBM case almost went unnoticed, however, compared to what AT&T was going to do.

Jack Goeken, MCI's founder, had big plans for the company's earliest vehicles. He wrote on the back of the photo: "I plan to install indoor-outdoor carpet on the floor after we get the radios." *(Courtesy Jack Goeken)*

Jack Goeken (left) and Larry Harris at a party celebrating the first year of operation of the original Chicago to St. Louis system, 1973. *(Photo by Dane Gazlun, Courtesy Jack Goeken)*

Bill McGowan (left) and Jack Goeken before the filing papers for regional company MCI-New York West Inc. in the fall of 1968. Several years later, McGowan would take control of MCI from Jack. *(Courtesy Bill McGowan)*

Bill McGowan getting his makeup for the big press conference announcing MCI Mail in Washington. He would be seen via satellite in New York, Chicago and Los Angeles. *(Photo by Ron Solomon Photography, Courtesy MCI)*

Publicly and privately AT&T Chairman John deButts vowed to fight competition in long distance telephone service. He was chairman from 1972 to 1979 serving during one of AT&T's most difficult periods. *(Photo by Superior Fototech, Inc., Courtesy AT&T)*

(Left) The first repeater container on its way to Portage, Indiana, 1973. *(Courtesy Art Roberts)* (Right) Rather than wait for the walls of a repeater site in Bridgewater, Michigan, to be built before installing the microwave radio gear, MCI engineers covered the equipment with a tent which permitted them to install and test the radios until the structure was completed. The ploy saved them 60 days during the summer of 1973. *(Courtesy Art Roberts)*

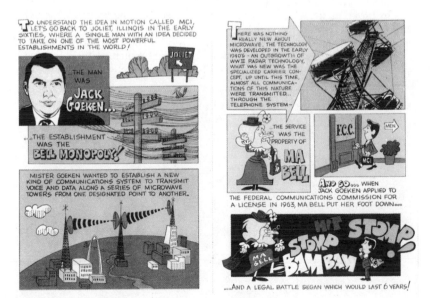

Excerpt from a comic book titled "The Fifth Freedom" published by MCI in 1973 to explain how the company started and what it was trying to accomplish. *(Courtesy Mike Bader)*

Jerry Taylor (left) was successful in offering MCI's Execunet program in Dallas in 1975 using this Danray switch that filled an entire room. Dan Dennis, regional director of operations, now works with Taylor as the West Division's vice president of operations and administration. *(Courtesy Jerry Taylor)*

(Bottom left) Tom Leming, responsible for building MCI's microwave network, made it a point to visit all sites at least once a year. This installation is on Slide Mountain, south of Reno, Nevada. *(Courtesy Art Roberts)* (Bottom center) As traffic on MCI's network increased, it was forced to change from the thin, low capacity towers on the left to the larger capacity, free-standing towers on the right. This site is in Waynesville, Ohio. *(Courtesy Art Roberts)* (Bottom right) During the first years of construction in 1972–73, Art Roberts was in charge of building the MCI network eastward from Chicago. This picture shows the newer type of microwave "cornucopias" used at the site near Butcher Knife, Wyoming. *(Courtesy Art Roberts)*

Orville Wright (left) and Bill McGowan after the 1980 annual meeting in Washington where the company announced a whopping 89 percent increase in net profit from the year before and an increase in customers from 16,000 to 41,000. *(Copyright* Washington Post; *Reprinted by permission of the D.C. Public Library)*

(Right) AT&T Chairman Charles Brown (left) and Assistant Attorney General William Baxter after a news conference January 8, 1982, announcing that AT&T would divest itself of its local phone companies if the government would drop its antitrust suit Months earlier, confronted by speculation that the government might drop the case, Baxter had promised: "We'll litigate it to the eyeballs." *(Photo by Reni, Courtesy AT&T)* (Below) MCI corporate attorney John Worthington introduced Jack Goeken to Bill McGowan. He suffered a heart attack on February 4, 1980, a day before the company's monumental lawsuit against AT&T began. *(Courtesy MCI)*

Seth Blumenfeld, a former Green Beret, used his cunning to secure agreements with overseas telephone administrations that permitted MCI to expand its network internationally. Here he is (checked shirt) relaxing with a group of French telecommunications specialists during a meeting in Geneva, Switzerland. *(Courtesy Seth Blumenfeld)*

Nate Kantor, president of MCI International (left); Bill McGowan (center); Ed Gallagher, president and chairman of Western Union International, after MCI's purchase of the international carrier was approved by the Federal Communications Commission in 1982. *(Photo by Mark Haven, Courtesy MCI)*

Bill McGowan testified before a Senate subcommittee investigating antitrust in July 1973. Here he is talking with Michigan Senator Phillip A. Hart. Ken Cox is next to him. *(Photo by Del Ankers Photographers, Courtesy Bill McGowan)*

Electronically transmitted MCI Mail messages were delivered to reporters at the end of the press conference, but nobody there knew how close MCI was to blowing the entire event. Just a few minutes after the messages were sent, the system went kaput. Foreground left to right: Bryan Wilkins, *MIS Week*; Bill McGowan, MCI chairman; Bob Harcharik, president of MCI Digital Information Services; Larry Kahaner, *Business Week*; Norm Black, Associated Press; Paul Travis, *Communications Daily*. *(Photo by Ron Solomon Photography, Courtesy MCI)*

Ally & Gargano, Inc.

Client:	MCI
Product:	TELECOMMUNICATIONS
Title:	"PARENTS REV. 2"
Commercial No.:	DMMC 4854
Date Approved:	5/14/84

1. (MUSIC UNDER THROUGH-OUT) MAN: Have you been talking to our son long distance again? WOMAN: (NODS AND WHIMPERS)

2. MAN: Did he tell you how much he loves you? WOMAN: (NODS AND WHIMPERS)

3. MAN: Did he tell you how well he's doing in school? WOMAN: (NODS AND WHIMPERS AND CRIES)

4. MAN: All those things are wonderful.

5. What on earth are you crying for?

6. WOMAN: Have you seen our long distance bill?

7. ANNCR: (VO) If your long distance bills are too much, call MCI.

8. Sure, reach out and touch someone. Just do it for up to 30, 40, even 50% less.

MCI
The nation's long distance phone company
1-800-624-2222

This commercial spoofed one of AT&T's most famous and popular commercials. Admaker Ally & Gargano exactly matched the camera angles and the set, and many viewers didn't realize it was an MCI commercial until the end. *(Courtesy Ally & Gargano)*

As MCI grew in stature it could afford celebrities in its commercials. Ads produced by Ally & Gargano under the hand of copy chief Tom Messner featured Merv Griffin, Burt Lancaster, and Joan Rivers. The Griffin commercials bombed but Lancaster and Rivers were effective. Left to right: George Euringer, art director; Tom Messner; Burt Lancaster on location. *(Courtesy Tom Messner)*

As part of his aggressive campaign to put MCI before the public, Ron Spears, (right) president of the Midwest division, has pledged $1 million to the "Heart of America Challenge" to try to wrest yachting's America's Cup from the Australians in Perth in 1987. If the HAC is successful, the 1991 races will be held in Lake Michigan. Buddy Melges (left) is the skipper of the Heart of America. *(Courtesy MCI)*

On June 25, 1985, Bill McGowan (on left) and IBM Vice Chairman Paul Rizzo announced that MCI would trade 16 percent of its stock worth $360 million to IBM for the computer maker's ailing long distance company, Satellite Business Systems. The move combined IBM and MCI against AT&T for control of the computer/communications industry. *(Courtesy Bill McGowan)*

Even while he was at MCI, Jack Goeken had the idea for an air-to-ground public telephone system. Dubbed "Airfone" the system had run into technical and financial troubles and Jack was forced to sell half of it to Western Union Co. *(Courtesy Airfone)*

AT&T public relations people called the news media to invite them to a briefing at the National Press Building in Washington. At one time, almost all newspapers had their Washington bureaus in that building. It was strategically located, two blocks from the White House and the Treasury and two blocks from an area called Federal Triangle, home to most of the federal bureaucracies. With the advent of better telecommunications, however, news organizations no longer had to cluster together, and many had left the building to seek other quarters around town.

William Baxter, Justice's top attorney, announced that an agreement had been reached with AT&T. The settlement called for AT&T to divest itself of its twenty-two local phone companies, but it could retain Western Electric and Bell Labs. It was everything the government had sought.

The Bell Operating Companies, or BOCs, were estimated to be worth $80 billion, about two-thirds of AT&T's assets. The agreement called for AT&T to spin off the BOCs either as one cohesive group or individually, whatever AT&T wished, within eighteen months. Stockholders would receive shares in both AT&T and the BOCs.

For many reporters, it was the first time they had seen AT&T Chairman Charles Brown. He was sharp, demure, and didn't look like all those old-fashioned AT&T types they had always heard about. For those who knew his predecessor, John deButts, Brown was a vast change. Although he, too, was "raised in the system," he looked beyond his emotions. Sure, he loved AT&T and the glory and the tradition, but he also knew that it was a business and times were changing. AT&T had better change, too.

Brown told the reporters: "In agreeing to this consent order we are influenced by our belief that consensus has largely been reached on a framework for new national policy with respect to telecommunications." The policy, Brown said, included dependable phone service, more competition, more free enterprise, and less government regulation. Then he said something that deButts would never have said: "In the end, we realize, of course, that our obligation is to conform to national policy, not make it."

In the following weeks, Brown submitted to hundreds of interviews with news media who were trying to make sense of one of the largest corporate divestitures ever. Over and over, he employed his favorite phrase: "Divestiture wasn't our idea." He wanted to make it clear that AT&T didn't want to break itself up into little pieces but didn't have any choice.

Except for a few knowledgeable folks, most reporters bought the argument. Actually, AT&T had another choice. It could have continued the trial to its conclusion. Who knows? Maybe it would have won. Even if it didn't, no one knows what Judge Greene would have decided to do with AT&T. He may not have wanted to go down in history as the judge that broke up the best phone company in the world. He may have decided on other solutions such as keeping different types of records or divestiture of just Western Electric.

Brown enjoyed telling the American public that AT&T was beaten, its nose bloodied. Actually, the divestiture was the best thing that could ever have happened to AT&T, and AT&T's top brass knew it. It was a way to get rid of the stodgy, unsexy part of AT&T, Plain Old Telephone Service, without having to do it themselves. They had wanted to get rid of POTS (as people in the industry called it) for years. It was labor-intensive and not very exciting. It was hanging from poles and stringing wires. It was crawling through rat-infested sewers and pulling cables. Not only that, but local service was deteriorating in most of the country. It had been on the downswing since those days in New York City during the early 1970s when business callers held on for twenty minutes or more to get a dial tone, and it took weeks to order a new phone line.

AT&T didn't want that anymore. It wanted to be part of the new age, unencumbered by anything that wasn't high technology. In return for divestiture, the Justice Department would allow AT&T to enter formerly restricted businesses, such as computers. Under the 1956 Consent Decree, AT&T couldn't enter any competitive markets. With this settlement, it could do so as long as it set up a separate subsidiary, a simple thing to do. AT&T wanted to build computers and go head-to-head with IBM for the "office of the future."

The antitrust trial provided that excuse. And if anything went wrong with local phone service, they could blame it on the Justice Department. It wasn't our fault, they could say. Divestiture wasn't our idea.

AT&T officials also changed their minds about what would happen to local service. For years, even at the trial, AT&T officials swore that if AT&T was ever separated from the BOCs, the BOCs would wither and die because they wouldn't get their long-distance subsidies. Now they were saying just the opposite. The BOCs would be okay. They would make it, Brown told everyone. The matter of subsidization of local service was never clear. Although AT&T said that thirty-four cents of every long-distance dollar was kicked back to local companies, they couldn't prove it. On the other hand, those who didn't believe it couldn't prove otherwise. It was a stalemate, and either side could spend forever trying to prove its case and never do it.

Another crucial argument fell, too. AT&T had fought against divestiture for reasons of national security. Now they said it wouldn't be any problem. Few people noticed these inconsistencies. They were too busy figuring out what they had to do to get phone service once the giant was dismembered. And reporters, most of whom were writing about flower shows the day before and got the assignment because no one else wanted it, were overwhelmed by the complexity of the material.

During the following year, whenever consumers got confused or complained about all the changes, AT&T blamed it on the Justice Department, and the Justice Department never fought back, never refuted it. It was almost like there was an unspoken agreement between the two: AT&T could say what it wanted, and Justice wouldn't disagree.

For consumers, it was a time of confusion. Who will own my telephones? Where do I get service?

For companies like MCI, it meant something else. With the BOCs no longer sharing the same concerns as AT&T, the long-distance competitors would now get from the BOCs something called "equal access." No longer could a local phone company play favorites with AT&T. Any long-distance company would now enjoy the same quality connections as AT&T. No longer would MCI customers get stuck with dialing all the extra digits. If AT&T customers didn't have to, their customers didn't have to.

McGowan believed, however, that AT&T made an error in keeping Western Electric. His belief, one that is pivotal to the company's philosophy, is that MCI will never own any manufacturing facilities. In an age where technology moves quickly, McGowan thinks that owning a manufacturing plant is an albatross around a company's neck. It keeps the company wedded to a technology, even though it may not be the best technology. By not having a stake in any one product, a company is free to flit around, try different devices from various competitors, without having to worry about whether it will become obsolete. If it gets outmoded, buy it from someone else. Manufacturers have an interest in getting more customers, and that means building the latest device or going out of business. So there will always be a pool of people ready to supply the best products at competitive prices.

Then a strange thing happened. Judge Greene refused to bang his gavel and declare the trial dismissed after AT&T agreed to Justice's terms, and they, in turn, withdrew their complaint. Both sides knew that Greene might give them trouble, so they tried to go around him by giving the settlement a different name. They called it a modified final judgment, saying that it was really a modification of the 1956 Consent Decree. They filed the appropriate agreement papers in a New Jersey court where the previous antitrust case had been settled. Greene didn't buy any of it. He invoked the Tunney Act, a law that requires hearings before a court can approve an antitrust settlement. Greene was angry and told both sides: "Calling documents a stipulation of dismissal instead of a consent decree and filing in an old case in New Jersey instead of here won't make what has been done other than what it is. . . . I don't believe the purpose of Congress [passage of the Tunney Act] can be defeated by such legaling."

He continued: "Whatever the New Jersey Court may do, it would seem to me this court must make certain that the Tunney Act is applied, and I expect to do just that." Greene was tough, and both litigants knew he could make it stick.

Besides believing he had the law on his side, Greene thought the issue was too important not to have public input. He wanted to know what all sides thought about the settlement. He wanted to hear from the BOCs. He wanted to know about dividing the long-distance service (what AT&T, MCI, and others could serve) and local service (the areas that the BOCs could serve) so the lines could be drawn fairly. He wanted to make sure that AT&T didn't bleed the BOCs of their best assets or leave them with unreasonable debts. He wanted to make sure that companies like MCI really got their equal access connection in an orderly manner without undue financial burden on the BOCs. There were other questions. Who would get the Bell logo? How would AT&T's 3 million shareholders get their new shares?

In the following months, Greene received more than a thousand comments. Most were from consumers who blamed *him* for breaking up the phone system that worked so well. "If it worked, why fix it?" became the most common comment. He and his staff read them all, and Greene was put in the odd position of setting telecommunications policy, something that was supposed to be up to the lawmakers in Congress. He took great criticism for it, but did it anyway. He had little choice but to see the entire divestiture through, even though it would mean several more years of work and decisions that would shape the future of the information age.

Congressman Tim Wirth and his staff had mixed feelings about the AT&T settlement. They were relieved that it was over—maybe they could get back to normal hours again. During that cold winter in Washington, they had joked about taking some time off and heading south for some rest and warm sun now that the pressure was off. On the other hand, they were sorry to see such a good issue leave their realm.

Wirth, however, didn't want to let it go. He liked being in the limelight, and he wasn't about to give it up. After looking over the settlement, he decided that it still left some issues unresolved. His bill, fifty-one-fifty-eight, was rewritten and introduced about two months later.

The bill was going to make sure that the Bell Operating Companies remained financially healthy. It prohibited AT&T from providing any services that bypassed the local companies for at least five years. It required AT&T to license patents that were funded by rate payer funds, pass along some of its tax benefits to the spun-off companies, and keep the Yellow Pages and its huge revenues with the local companies.

AT&T went berserk. Chairman Charles Brown called the bill premature and unnecessary and said it was ridiculous for Congress to deal with a bill while Judge Greene was still considering the matter.

Wirth ramrodded the bill through his subcommittee by a 15–0 vote in record time, only three days after it was introduced. The actual vote took only an hour and a half, another record. That same day, AT&T Vice-Chairman James Olson called a news conference where he made the most angry speech AT&T had ever issued. He said that Wirth had railroaded the bill through the subcommittee. He charged that Wirth had used the issue for his own political gains. Olson said that AT&T would begin an unprecedented campaign to stop the bill from going any further.

The plan called for AT&T to send its 1 million employees information about the bill and urge them to call their congressmen. It also planned to let its 3 million shareholders know that the bill could jeopardize their investments. AT&T was also planning to spend more than $1 million on ads and another $900,000 for letters to shareholders.

Olson was true to his word. The AT&T lobbying machine began its work. The following week, AT&T bought ads in twenty newspapers, and its labor union, the Communications Workers of America, sent more than a thousand members to lobby Congress to kill the bill. Union Vice-President John Carroll told CWA members that the bill would cost them jobs. The letters began rolling into congressional offices, with some lawmakers reporting more than five thousand letters in a week, the most pieces ever received on a single issue in so short a time.

The local companies began to lobby, too. New Jersey Bell President Rocco Marano sent a letter to employees that showed five sample letters they could send to their representatives. New Jersey Congressman James Florio found his office swamped with more than four thousand letters.

To many congressmen, this campaign was another indication of Bell's great lobbying power, and one that couldn't be ignored. AT&T always had the largest lobbying presence on Capitol Hill, using a system of "shepherds," as they have been called. Every congressional member had his very own shepherd who worked for the local Bell company in his home district. Shepherds follow their representatives around, attending every meeting that has anything to do with their company or AT&T. They don't use a high-pressure approach, often sitting quietly in the front of the room and staring directly at the congressmen they're assigned to. The shepherd is tending his flock, and is a constant reminder to his congressman that he is there. On a busy day, a shepherd may take sandwiches and coffee to congressional aides who haven't been able to take a break.

Although lobbyists are required by law to register, AT&T's shepherds never did. Because they spent most of their time with staff members or engaging in the "stare-downs," AT&T didn't consider them lobbyists according to the definition of a lobbyist.

In Wirth's home district of Denver, Mountain Bell placed inserts in phone bills calling on customers to rally against the bill. They claimed the bill would raise phone rates and destroy pensions for phone company employees. Wirth's office got hundreds of phone calls from loyal Bell employees asking why they were destroying Bell. "I've worked there forty years and you're jeopardizing my pension." Wirth's staffers tried to explain that AT&T had lied to them about the bill, but the callers didn't believe it.

Wirth was particularly disturbed at what he saw as a campaign by AT&T of fear and deception to Bell Lab employees. He was especially disturbed by a letter-writing campaign from Bell Lab employees that expressed fear that the bill would destroy Bell Labs. AT&T had told lab personnel the bill would decimate that research facility. Wirth tried to assure them that the bill said nothing like that.

Wirth was forced to hold special meetings for other House members to explain what the bill said and what AT&T said the bill said.

At the AT&T annual meeting in April, Brown told shareholders to keep up the pressure. He said that shareholders and employees had sent at least 135,000 letters to Congress. At the meeting, shareholders received sample letters to Congress that they could sign and drop off in a box before leaving the meeting. AT&T would mail them.

Finally, in May, Wirth met with AT&T's board in New York. He had hoped to change their minds about the intent of HR-5158, but when the ninety-minute meeting was over, neither side gave an inch, and the fight continued.

Actually, Wirth relished the battle. He enjoyed being in the spotlight of the biggest issue of the day—the breakup of AT&T. He was under siege, and it was exhilarating. What kept him going was that the bill enjoyed support from most newspaper editorials and that it had support on the telecommunications subcommittee. He had the votes for passage.

By late June, however, AT&T had gotten to Tom Corcoran from Illinois and Don Ritter of Pennsylvania, members of the full committee. They were heavily briefed by AT&T on procedural matters and used them to slow down the bill's movement. For example, they insisted that the full bill be read aloud instead of having the reading dispensed with, as is done with most pieces of legislation. The bill's supporters were angry with the tactics. Marc Marks of Pennsylvania said the reason given by opponents for the reading of the bill—that they needed to understand it better—was a bunch of baloney. "You know damn well what's in this bill," he told Corcoran. Marks then held up one of AT&T's newspaper ads and yelled, "This company thinks it's more powerful than the country itself. What we have here is obstructionism."

Still, the delaying tactics continued.

The following month, Wirth stunned everyone by suddenly withdrawing the bill. At a committee meeting, Chairman John Dingell called the meeting to order, and Wirth read his statement. The two had only decided that morning that Wirth would withdraw the bill. Wirth said that AT&T's delaying tactics had made it impossible to pass the bill in the time left for the congressional session. He had simply run out of time. He said: "The AT&T victory is a major setback for the American people. The kind of bill AT&T would find acceptable is a bill that only serves their interests and no others." He continued: "I have seen nothing like this campaign of fear and distortion that AT&T has waged to fight this bill in my eight years in Congress."

And then he walked out of the room.

Many reporters who were covering telephone issues missed Wirth's speech. They were attending MCI's annual meeting a few miles away. McGowan received word about what had happened from MCI's lobbyist, who had taken a cab from the Hill to tell him. McGowan, who never missed a chance to have fun with the press, and certainly wouldn't pass up the opportunity to show how awesome AT&T's power was, said to the reporters at the meeting, "I shouldn't be telling you this, but Wirth withdrew his bill." A few reporters got up and headed for the pay phones.

Although Wirth and Judge Greene were the two most powerful people in America shaping policy on telecommunications, they had never met until December 1983, days before AT&T's divestiture.

They met in line in a phone store while buying their own telephones.

THE SEVENTH BUSINESS—

Positioning
1982–83

As the AT&T divestiture drama was playing out, McGowan and Orville knew that MCI had reached a sort of "critical mass." The company was in solid financial standing. "Money Coming In" was no longer just a quip; it was real. The last quarter, September through December 1981, saw revenues increase almost 130 percent over the same period a year before, from $61.6 million to $140.6 million.

Wayne English had hired Bill Conway away from First Chicago to work on his financial team. And months before, he had negotiated a deal with the lending banks to pay them off. Now Wayne could do all his financing in the public markets by floating bonds and selling stock. That would be cheaper than borrowing more money from banks.

The stock market was cooperating, too. Wayne's dream of having the stock reach $25 a share had happened a few months earlier, and Wall Street buyers couldn't get enough of it. In 1981, the stock whose symbol was MCIC became the most actively traded company on the Over-The-Counter market—64 million shares. The year before, it was fifth. In January 1980, it had sold for 5¾ a share, a year later it doubled, and by the end of 1981, it had reached 35⅞. What attracted investors was the company itself, the management, and the network, not the hope of dividends. Unlike other company chairmen, who viewed paying dividends as a show of corporate strength, McGowan believed just the opposite. He thought it was smarter for a company not to pay dividends, but to reinvest the money in the company. Only when a company stopped growing and couldn't attract any more investors would he even consider paying stock dividends. So investor confidence in MCI had to be rooted in the company and not in dividend checks. McGowan would defend that belief at annual meetings every year, saying, "Telecommunications is a capital-intensive business. We must not give out dividends. We must reinvest the money in ourselves."

With its rosy future, especially the possibility that it could win $1.8 billion cash from its antitrust award (despite numerous appeals by AT&T), MCI was starting to become a prime takeover candidate. Someone could buy the company, keep the cash award, dismember the organization, and sell off its greatest asset, the network. McGowan sensed that he might be in trouble, so at the 1981 annual meeting, shareholders were asked to vote on some "shark repellent," the name given to corporate bylaws that keep away unfriendly takeover bids. Put simply, the new bylaws would prevent anyone who owned more than 15 percent of outstanding shares from engaging in "significant corporate transactions" (read "takeover") without the approval of 80 percent of voting shares or approval of MCI's board of directors. That would make a hostile takeover difficult because the raiding company would have to court the board or at least 80 percent of the voting shares. McGowan also counted on MCI's litigious reputation to keep away unsuitable suitors.

MCI was now in a position to do something it had never done before: long-term planning. This was the perfect time to think about where the company was going and what it was trying to accomplish. How could it position itself for the future?

Two years earlier, Orville and McGowan were sitting around on a Saturday afternoon when the subject of international phone service came up. Would it be possible and profitable for MCI to offer international service to its customers? Nobody knew much about it, so they asked Nate Kantor, who was then vice-president of eastern operations, to look into the matter. Nate had been with MCI since 1972, when he was hired as director of procurement. The department consisted of Nate Kantor.

Nate was a West Point graduate, not the kind of credentials that a Jewish kid from Brooklyn normally had. It was all because of TV. As a child, one of his favorite programs was *The West Point Story*. He was a product of the tube, and all he wanted to do was join the Army. Once he graduated West Point, he took part in a special program that permitted Point graduates to work in other military branches. That was a good thing because the Army didn't have anything that excited Nate. He really wanted to be in the Air Force and fly the F-4 jet. He couldn't do that, but he was interested in something else just as new. He was offered a job at the National Aeronautics and Space Administration, NASA, and he worked on the Gemini and Apollo programs maintaining the radar tracking sites.

Nate found military life too constricting, so he left and joined Sperry Rand. There he negotiated and managed commercial contracts for computer equipment. After three years, however, the company became too confining for him as well. Everything was planned— where he would be in so and so years and what his title would be, what his office would look like. He wanted some excitement. Moreover, he wanted control of his future, and at a company like Sperry, he couldn't.

One day, he saw an ad in the newspaper for director of procurement. He called the agency that had placed the ad, and that night he met with Stan Scheinman and a few others. The next day at 7 A.M. he met with McGowan in New York, and bingo, he was hired. He moved to Washington.

When McGowan asked Nate to do the study on international telecommunications, Nate didn't realize how different things were outside of the United States. During the following months, though, he learned that foreign telephone systems were all run by their governments. There was no competition in equipment or services, and for the most part, the same group that ran the post office ran the telephones. Generically, they were called PTTs, for Post, Telephone, and Telegraph.

Only AT&T had agreements with these PTTs for voice lines to their countries. There was a complicated system of dividing the price of the call between the PTT and AT&T that would take Nate months to figure out. In fact, just like the cozy relationship between the Bell Operating Companies and AT&T, there was no reason for either side to change the way it was doing business in order to accommodate new competitors such as MCI.

Telex was another matter. Just like telephones are a way of life in the United States, in Europe, Asia, and the rest of the world a system of typewriterlike devices known as Telex is commonplace. Each Telex machine has its own unique number, and to send a message to any

Telex machine, you only need to know the country it's in and the machine number. Telexes are so prevalent in the world that Telex-printed messages are considered binding contracts. If a company in the United States sends an order via Telex to a Swiss company for ten thousand watches, that's regarded as a legal agreement to buy the watches. Telex was a natural for most of the world. The technology was sound and simple; it worked in the worst of climates. It overcame language barriers because a printed message could be taken to a translator, and it got around time difference. A message sent during the day in one part of the world would be read when the recipient got to work the next day, even though it was transmitted while he slept.

When it came to Telex, about a half-dozen companies, known as International Record Carriers, or IRCs, were the only authorized participants. Only they could send and receive Telexes between the United States and foreign countries. The tight group included RCA, ITT, Western Union International (WUI), FTC Communications, TRT Communications, and Cable & Wireless, Ltd. ITT, RCA, and WUI were far and away the largest of them all, accounting for more than 90 percent of all Telex traffic. The others were smaller and had been making modest profits living off their agreements with PTTs that had been worked out years before. The IRCs were an elite international club, and membership was now closed by order of the PTTs.

Kantor's report took several months to complete, and it came to one important conclusion: In order for MCI to enter the international market, it would have to acquire an IRC. Kantor discovered there was no way that MCI could negotiate all the agreements it needed with the PTTs. They would have to buy those agreements by buying a company that already had them.

A likely candidate was TRT Communications, a company owned by United Brands. United Brands owned United Fruit, which had banana plantations in Central America, and they built Tropical Radio & Telegraph so they could communicate with their foreign offices. United Fruit conspired with the CIA in 1954 to overthrow the government of Guatemala, and the TRT network proved invaluable for carrying covert communications between corporate offices in Boston and United Fruit officials in Guatemala. TRT had a small number of agreements with overseas PTTs, too, and Nate was impressed by their aggressive pricing approaches and nonunion work force. Most important, it looked like MCI might be able to afford to buy TRT.

Unfortunately, TRT wanted too much money, well over $100 million. To McGowan and Nate, that was far too expensive for a company like TRT. So the idea of acquiring an IRC was put aside and didn't reappear until mid-1981, when Orville read about his old company Xerox and the trouble they were having establishing a worldwide computer network.

Orville was in California when he read that Xerox was disbanding its XTEN system. XTEN stood for Xerox Telecommunications Network, an ingenious system that allowed local distribution of high-speed data without going through the local phone company. The system worked like this: Each office in a building would have its computers and word processors connected to the building's main cable system. The information would flow to the roof, where it was transmitted over microwaves to a large dish in a central location, usually atop the largest building in the city. In some cases, several large dishes would be used. From there, the information was transmitted to a satellite that relayed it back to earth to another large dish in another city. The information flowed back to the receiving office by way of its city's XTEN system.

This method even had a fancy name, digital termination systems, or DTS, and it was ideally suited for sending and receiving massive amounts of high-speed data.

Xerox wasn't just thinking nationally. In 1979, it had purchased Western Union International, an IRC, so it could extend its XTEN system around the world. Xerox was still hot on its "office of the future" kick, and this kind of end-to-end service fit in.

Although WUI fit well into Xerox's grand scheme, there were rumors that something else was going on below the surface. Western

Union International was once owned by Western Union Telegraph Co., but it was forced to divest itself of the overseas arm in 1963. From 1963 to 1979, it was an independent company, and because of its IRC status and because it was making money, it became a likely takeover candidate. Edward Gallagher, president and chairman of WUI, was getting offers from Continental Telephone, the third largest independent telephone company in the United States—the same company that had hired Tom Leming to build a domestic long-distance network using cables instead of microwave towers. As the story goes, Gallagher didn't want to be bought by ConTel, so he went to Xerox, hoping they would be his white knight and buy the company. Gallagher knew Peter McColough, Xerox's chairman, and the two struck a deal. Xerox would buy WUI. The fact that the purchase fit into Xerox's end-to-end scenario may have been secondary.

After receiving experimental authorization from the FCC to test its XTEN system and pouring millions of dollars into the project, Xerox decided to call it quits. They didn't believe that it would be economically feasible, and in some cases, the technology was a little too quirky to work consistently. In April 1981, Xerox announced it was quitting the DTS business.

When Orville read about Xerox's abandonment of XTEN, he knew they would have no use for the international part of the plan, Western Union International. It made no sense to keep it. Orville called McGowan and told him that Xerox might want to sell WUI and MCI should try to buy it.

Xerox did want to sell WUI, and Orville got a prospectus on the company. Orville believed that other companies might be interested in it as well. He wasn't sure, but he thought that GTE might also make a bid. Over the following months, Orville went to Xerox headquarters to negotiate the purchase. It helped that he knew many of the officials from his days at the company.

Orville couldn't have asked for better timing. Not only did MCI have the money necessary to make a reasonable bid, but Brian Thompson had just been hired to head MCI's new corporate planning department, and he would help Orville handle WUI. Aside from McGowan, Brian was the only Harvard Business School graduate in the upper echelons of MCI. As a rule, MCI shunned hiring MBAs from Harvard or anywhere else, but Brian was different. He had more than book knowledge. He had a strong, varied business background, and his experience seemed to lead him straight to this new job.

His first job after getting a chemical engineering degree was with the Kendall Company, a textile manufacturer that made Curity diapers and Curad bandages. His job was in the new area of nonwoven fiber products, researching new products and seeing them through marketing, production, and sales. This start-to-finish responsibility fit perfectly with his own psychological makeup, although he didn't realize why until years later when a psychologist told him that he had an overwhelming desire to succeed and control his existence at all times. Ego.

While dating a woman whose businessman father was so rich he couldn't see straight, Brian decided that business was the way to go. After the Navy, he enrolled in the Harvard Business School and afterward got a job working for McKinsey & Company, the business think-tank group. Brian could control companies by giving them advice. His clients included Comsat, Intelsat, and even AT&T. He stayed for nine years and loved it, but left when he wasn't elected a full partner. He believed he deserved it.

Brian entered the pay-TV business by joining Subscription Television of America in Rockville, Maryland, just outside Washington, D.C. While there, he learned about the world of high finance and deal making. He and the owners didn't get along, though. Brian would buy stations and the owners would sell them and make lots of money. Brian got discouraged and, more important, didn't get rich on the deals. He did, however, learn a lot about buying and selling businesses.

Brian was a mixture of Orville and McGowan. He was a dreamer like McGowan, with unending verve and optimism, but he also possessed a good business sense, like Orville, which allowed him to temper his enthusiasm with economic considerations. By the time he joined MCI, the company was in the midst of its purchase of WUI. Brian helped coordinate the deal with Orville. Nate Kantor, meanwhile, was evaluating WUI's capability. What was MCI actually buying?

His report said that MCI shouldn't buy WUI. It had old technology and equipment. Its operation was inefficient, and it was out of capacity. It also had bad union problems. Despite Nate's negative assessment, McGowan knew MCI had no choice but to buy WUI if it was to enter the international market. It might never get another shot at joining the closed club of international carriers.

So in December, MCI would pay Xerox $185 million for WUI, subject to FCC approval. And who better to be in charge of it than Nate Kantor, the man who said not to buy it?

By the end of June 1982, the FCC had approved MCI's purchase of WUI. At that time, the international voice business was about $3 billion and growing at a rate of 20 to 25 percent a year. Americans were beginning to feel comfortable calling overseas, just as they had become comfortable calling "long distance" within the United States about a decade earlier.

AT&T had the entire overseas market locked up. They were the only carrier allowed by the PTTs to send and receive voice traffic to and from the United States. McGowan wanted to challenge that position, but unlike MCI's domestic business, which had to get FCC approval, MCI had to deal with the PTTs. Kantor knew it wouldn't be easy because the PTTs had absolutely no incentive to deal with MCI. They had enjoyed a smooth and lucrative arrangement with AT&T, and there was no reason for them to change.

That's not what Brian thought, though. He was pumped by the MCI hype and his own ego and believed that all he had to do was show the PTTs that MCI was here, it was active and aggressive, ready to inject good old Yankee competition into the staid overseas market, and boom! it would all work out. MCI was on a roll domestically, and he thought all he had to do was introduce himself, and the PTTs would sign on the dotted line.

Brian knew that the United Kingdom was the key to Europe. Not only did 40 percent of U.S. voice traffic go through or end up there, but if MCI could establish a beachhead in England, it might act as a wedge to open up the rest of Europe. Brian was on a high from completing a deal for service to Canada that would allow MCI customers to call certain parts of the country at rates of 12 to 30 percent under AT&T's. The areas that MCI targeted for service included Montreal, Toronto, Ottawa, and Calgary, Alberta. These cities accounted for more than 85 percent of all traffic from the United States to Canada.

Worldwide, MCI had its sights set on the United Kingdom, France, Germany, Italy, Spain, Greece, Hong Kong, Australia, Japan, Brazil, Colombia, and Mexico. They accounted for nearly 85 percent of all phone traffic out of the United States. Still, the United Kingdom was the most critical.

Brian and his staff traveled to Britain with people from WUI. The MCI people looked down on the WUI folks. They were going to show these people how to negotiate the MCI way. Brian took the lead, confident that signing up the United Kingdom would be a done deal. Brian had heard that British Telecommunications, BT, the government-owned monopoly, was on the verge of allowing a competitor in the intercity market. That company was Mercury Communications. Brian believed that the British had seen the light and embraced competition. He viewed it as a political and social decision, and his approach was to deal with politicians who could put the squeeze on the right people at BT and force them to sign a deal with MCI. That backfired because BT officials believed it was a back-door approach, and instead of embracing MCI, they were alienated.

Most important, Brian didn't realize the basic problem that he was facing. *Nobody cared.* Nobody cared about MCI in the U.S. government, and nobody cared in the U.K. government. It wasn't political and it wasn't social. In fact, the last thing that the British Telecom officials wanted their citizens to see was that U.S. customers paid less for a call to the United Kingdom than a call in the other direction. Because MCI was so gung-ho about the new world of competition, Brian thought the rest of the world would be, too. That turned out to be very wrong.

Yes, competition was coming to the United Kingdom, but it wouldn't be installed for at least three to five years. Brian fought continually with someone in the WUI camp about how best to approach BT and the other PTTs. His name was Seth Blumenfeld, an employee of WUI since 1969.

Seth was born in the Bronx and raised in Yonkers, New York. After graduating college, Seth bucked a family tradition and decided not to become a doctor. Instead, he decided to go to law school. While he was in college and in law school, Seth belonged to ROTC, not out of any patriotic duty, but because it gave him thirty dollars a month beer-drinking money. He never thought in terms of joining the Army after law school—especially because the Vietnam War was heating up, and he didn't want to become a part of it.

During law school, he was commissioned as a first lieutenant and would become a prime candidate for Vietnam upon graduation. He was worried but figured that he could use his family's friendship with New York Senator Jacob Javitts to keep him out of the fighting end of the war. The senator would get him an easy assignment in the judge adjutant general's office, where the lawyers sat behind desks. The plan worked too well. The Army was so impressed by his credentials, especially the recommendations by Javitts, that they asked him to sign up for five years in JAG. Seth didn't want to waste five years of his life in the Army, but now he was stuck. He joined the infantry. That would only be three years, and maybe he could work his way over to JAG anyway.

Everyone in Seth's graduating class at Fort Benning was assigned to Vietnam except Seth. He was assigned to Fort Lewis, near Seattle, as a training officer for a new infantry concept. There would be six companies of six hundred Green Beret troops who would be self-contained fighting units with no need for any outside support in combat. After training these men, he waved good-bye to them as they left for Vietnam by boat. Seth took a two-week leave and went back to New York City to get married. Things were looking good until seven days later, when he got orders to take over one of the units. The commander of one of the units was unexpectedly granted a sole-surviving-son exemption, and a replacement was needed. Thirteen days after he was married, Seth was on a plane to Vietnam, beating his troops there by a week. He went into combat for thirteen months with 600 troops and came back with 112. Just before the Tet Offensive, he came home to his apartment across from Central Park in full combat uniform and had to sneak into the building because of 100,000 war protesters in the park's Sheep Meadow.

He began working for a law firm, then joined WUI in 1969. WUI was doing a booming business in Telex, which had several years earlier come into its own as a worldwide means of communication. Seth and a co-worker spent the next five years negotiating Telex contracts with the PTTs. WUI already had a cable agreement with the United Kingdom, and Seth's job was to open up the rest of Europe and the Far East.

Seth knew that WUI didn't have the resources to compete with ITT or RCA, which had set up offices in foreign countries to supply Telex. He also had the foresight to see that the governments of these countries would realize that Telex was a true money-maker and would take over these operations. So instead of WUI opening up its own offices, Seth decided to become partners with the PTTs, setting up and running the Telex offices and splitting the revenues with them. He was right about governments taking over the Telex operations. A few years later, governments paid RCA and ITT for their operations and nationalized them. In Chile, the Allende government had nationalized ITT's operations without compensation, and ITT and the CIA were accused by a Senate subcommittee in 1973 of discussing but not carrying out plans to prevent Allende's election.

By the time MCI bought WUI, Telex was a matured business. WUI and the others weren't making the money they once were because they were being hit by a one-two punch from external factors. The first was the passage of the Record Common Carrier Act that allowed Western Union Telegraph (WUT), the company that controlled 60 percent of the domestic Telex market, to offer international service. Because they could give their U.S. customers end-to-end service instead of having to stop at the border and use RCA, ITT, or WUI, they took a large chunk of these companies' market share. WUT had little trouble negotiating Telex contracts with the PTTs because there already were half a dozen IRCs around. The PTTs had no qualms about granting one more license, especially to a company as large as WUT.

The other punch came from "Telex pirates." Because Telex transmission was very slow, about thirty-six words per minute, it didn't require overseas cables with large capacity. A circuit that could handle voice, however, required a cable with a larger bandwidth. One voice circuit was equal to ninety-six Telex circuits, so pirates would lease one voice circuit and cram up to ninety-six Telex messages over the line at less cost than if they had leased Telex circuits. In the United Kingdom, all they had to do was buy or lease a Telex switch and pump the message into the United Kingdom's Telex network. Telex pirates appeared like just another international phone caller, and in the strict sense of the law, they weren't doing anything illegal—just clever. These pirates could undercut the IRCs by 50 percent.

One other thing caused a strain on WUI's profits—MCI's purchase of WUI. Employees had heard stories about MCI's tough management style, and they were anxious. Many people didn't know what MCI was planning to do, and they were scared. Morale among salespeople dropped. Many of them left, and others looked for new jobs. Rumors were flying that MCI would begin massive layoffs, and that only added to their anxiety. The rumors would turn out to be true.

The first month that Nate was president was the first month that WUI ever showed a loss. Nate couldn't believe it. He figured, well, that was a short-lived career. But he was reassured when he got a call from McGowan, who jokingly said, "Nate, even you couldn't have done it that fast."

MCI wasn't interested in Telex anyway. It wasn't a growing business. McGowan wanted to supply international voice, and he and Nate would rely on Seth and his contacts gained at WUI to do it.

Seth convinced Brian that his approach had been wrong. He had to be more subtle with the PTTs. "You have to play the game with them," he told Brian. He also told him that the negotiations would take years and that there was no one way to do it. He was also convinced that Brian's brash approach with the British had set back those specific negotiations at least a year.

Maybe it was his training in jungle warfare that taught Seth how to wait for the soft spot of his opponent before striking, because that's exactly what he did in all his negotiations. Although he was negotiating with many different countries, his actual strikes hinged on timing.

In Australia, Seth saw an opportunity arise out of the blue. That country built an undersea cable called ANZCAN (an acronym for Australia, New Zealand, Canada), which they had trouble paying for. At the last moment, AT&T, which had talked about picking up some of the costs, backed out of the deal. Seth heard about what AT&T had done and took the first plane he could to Australia. The Australians were down on AT&T, and Seth said MCI would pick up some of the costs that AT&T had at first promised if the Aussies would give MCI an operating agreement. It worked.

In Europe, Seth saw that he would have to breach CEPT, the Conference of European Postal and Telecommunications Administrations, a group that included thirty-four countries. CEPT members agreed that none of them would open up with an independent voice carrier. These countries had some agreements on Telex service that had fallen apart, mainly because the countries didn't trust each other, and Seth knew that.

Brian's basic approach was to address a CEPT meeting and discuss with them the advantages of competition. It was the same approach that had worked domestically with the FCC and Congress. Seth objected, saying it would just play into their hands. He reminded Brian that they had no interest in talking about competition. All you would do was draw them closer together because they would agree on one thing, Seth said: to keep MCI out. Instead, Seth proposed a divide-and-conquer approach. He knew that the countries really distrusted each other, and once he breached the CEPT agreement, his job of reaching other agreements might be easier.

Their mutual distrust was made clear to Seth during exploratory trips to the United Kingdom and France. United Kingdom officials would ask, "So how are things going with France?"

Seth knew that being absolutely truthful was his best ploy. He would answer, "They don't want to talk with me."

The U.K. officials didn't believe him. They figured he had a deal with France already.

The same thing would happen in France. "So how are things going in the United Kingdom?" they would ask. Again, he would tell the truth: "Terrible. They don't want to talk with me."

And they figured that Seth was just being sneaky, and he already had a deal with the U.K.

The more he told each side that he didn't have a deal, the more each side believed that he did.

During his first official meeting in France, Seth and Nate were talking with an official who asked, "How are things going with the U.K.?" Seth gave his usual response: "We're really not going anywhere."

Then the official said, almost in a speech: "We are a progressive administration; we believe in competition. We're the leaders in Europe and the world in innovative services, and as soon as you get a deal with the U.K., tell us because we want one, too." Seth tried not to laugh.

For several reasons, Seth picked Belgium to breach CEPT. First, they were generally conceived as being aggressive businessmen who made good decisions based on economics. Second, because they were a small nation, they had little in common with most of the CEPT members and did what they wanted to do.

Seth offered them a deal they couldn't refuse. He offered them the opportunity to be a "transit" country. This meant they would act as a "switch" for traffic coming into Europe from the United States. For that work, the Belgian Régie des Télégraphes et des Téléphones, referred to as the Régie, would receive payment based on the number of minutes of traffic that went through the country. It was only a couple of hundred thousand dollars a year, but they didn't have to do anything for it. It was found money for such a small country. Belgium agreed.

After Seth cracked CEPT, it was just a matter of time before other countries would follow. Still, he had to find the right button for each individual situation.

Seth was going back and forth every week negotiating with the United Kingdom. They were still the key, and he knew it. Unfortunately, the U.K. officials knew it, too. Seth had taken a patient approach, but finally, when Mercury got its license in 1984 and was looking for investors, Seth laid it on the line: "Gentlemen, it's obvious to me that you're not terribly interested in this entire affair. You are interested in using me to show that you're going to be an aggressive, competitive company at the time you feel Mercury is poised to compete with you. Then you are going to embrace, because you think Mercury will interconnect with me. I will be a major player and cause you harm."

He continued: "Here's what I'm going to do. I'm not going to be jerked around any longer. We've been doing this for two years, and we're not getting anywhere. I'm going back to my board and tell them we don't have an agreement with BT, and then I'm going to readjust my business plan."

Seth knew that if this didn't work, it would be all over, and he would be looking for a new job. So, with his best poker-bluffing face, he said, "I need the U.K. to be in this business, but I don't need you. I'm going to readjust my voice plan so you're not important to me. Yes, I'll wait three years, but you're leading me on for at least that long anyway. Here's what we're going to do. We're going to invest and take control of Mercury and then you're going to find out what real international competition is all about. You're going to have a nasty son of a bitch company right here in your own backyard. We're going to compete for your own traffic here."

His heart was pounding when he restated, "I know I can't be in this business without you now, but I *can* be in this business after three years without you, and you'll see what serious competition is all about." With that, he walked out.

The bluff worked. The next day, they started talking again, and within a month the deal was closed.

Ironically, Mercury had the same trouble with BT that MCI had with AT&T. BT controlled the local interconnections and balked at connecting Mercury's intercity network. Finally, Mercury was forced to take BT to court to secure the interconnections it needed.

As more countries signed, the easier it became to sign those countries that had been slow in agreeing. Although Seth relied mostly on his patience and finesse, he would be able to pressure some countries, like Italy and Japan, by sending traffic through transit countries with which Italy and Japan had agreements. He would point out to them that they would make more money if he sent them traffic directly instead of going through a third party. The traffic was going through whether they liked it or not.

The whole idea hinged on the system of *accounting rates* and *collection rates*, a complicated and mysterious concept upon which international rates are based.

Say, for example, a call from the United States to France has an accounting rate of $1.50. Theoretically, that's the rate that the PTT and AT&T have decided that call should cost. AT&T, however, may decide to only charge the customer $1.40 for that call. Now, the collection rate for such a call may be 75 cents. That's the amount the French PTT decided it wants as its cut. So, $1.40 minus 75 cents, and AT&T keeps 65 cents. From that comes its overhead and other costs, which are about 35 cents. So AT&T makes 30 cents profit.

Now MCI comes along and says it will only charge its customers $1.30 for that call, undercutting AT&T by 10 cents. France still gets the same collection rate of 75 cents—that never changes—and MCI keeps 55 cents. And from that comes its overhead and other costs, which equal about 35 cents, so it makes 20 cents profit.

Now let's say that MCI doesn't have an agreement with France and decides to go through Belgium as a transit country. MCI charges the same $1.30. France insists on getting the same 75 cents, and Belgium gets 40 cents for handling the call. This leaves MCI with only 15 cents left, which doesn't cover its costs. MCI loses money on transit traffic.

What it gets back, however, is credibility in the international voice market. It is showing countries that MCI is a viable company, serious about doing business. More important, MCI is showing that by cutting its rates below AT&T it can stimulate overseas telephoning from the United States, and that means more money for the PTTs. Domestically, MCI had proven that lower long-distance charges increase the number of calls, and Seth believed that the same thing applied internationally.

Moreover, if calls are stimulated from overseas to the United States, the PTTs give part of the traffic to MCI and not AT&T, and MCI will receive more money. The percentage is based on inbound traffic to those countries. For example, if MCI handles what amounts to 10 percent of incoming U.S. traffic, to a given country, that country gives MCI 10 percent of its traffic heading for the U.S. AT&T would only get 90 percent. What Seth ultimately hoped was that as MCI got more countries signed, it could negotiate for lower collection rates.

For the first four or five years, MCI's international voice service will not make any money. If it's lucky, and Seth is skillful enough, it will break even.

Still, the idea is positioning. If MCI can continue to sign countries and stimulate overseas calls, it will be perfectly situated in the coming years to take a piece of the international voice market that topped $5 billion in 1985 and will grow at about 15 to 20 percent annually.

Even while negotiations for the WUI purchase were going on, Brian had been running full out in his new job of worrying about the future of MCI.

Brian learned at McKinsey how to quickly size up a company's strengths and weaknesses. It became apparent to him and everyone else at MCI that the company's main weakness was local interconnection. Beyond lobbying the FCC for a lower rate, it was the only cost in its entire operation that MCI could not control. At the moment, MCI was paying the local phone companies 21 percent of its revenues, or $50 million, to connect its customers' calls. AT&T, which still owned the Bell companies, wanted even more money from MCI and others for those vital interconnections. An ENFIA agreement that had been reached in 1978 called for MCI to pay about $92 a line. Now it was $131, and AT&T wanted it raised to $293 a line when the agreement was up in April.

MCI was caught in a tough spot. As it added more customers, its interconnection costs increased. Three steps forward, one step backward. Moreover, as it got equal access in line with the pending divestiture, its costs would be raised to pay for the higher-quality connections until it would be paying the same price as AT&T.

Brian knew that MCI had to own and operate its own local distribution system. New technology was coming along, and maybe there was something around that MCI could use. The answer was already around, digital termination systems, or DTS—the same system that Xerox had just abandoned. This was the microwave network composed of small dishes atop buildings feeding information to one central dish on the tallest building in town. Like many others, Brian believed that Xerox was too early. There was not enough volume in high-speed data to support DTS. Now, that is. In the future, say five to ten years, there would be. However, long before that happened, MCI hoped it could use the DTS network to transmit voice messages as well. If MCI could lock up some licenses to operate DTS systems in major cities, it would at least have some kind of insurance against increasingly higher interconnection fees. Although it might not serve all of MCI's customers, it could at least reach the major business clients. And, unlike some other companies that applied for DTS licenses, MCI had its own long-distance network to connect the DTS cities. That meant it could control its costs for end-to-end service.

Based on Xerox's prototype system, the FCC had set aside frequency channels for DTS operation. And the beauty of it, from MCI's point of view, was that it was federally and not locally regulated. That made it easier to do business because MCI didn't have to deal with each municipality it wanted to build a system in, only with the FCC.

Even before Brian arrived, some MCI staffers had talked about DTS, but it was thought of as a business decision rather than a positioning decision. Now that MCI actually had the luxury of waiting for something to pay off in the future, it could look seriously at DTS. Brian convinced McGowan and Orville that MCI should look to a national DTS and begin to apply for licenses across the country. Other companies were doing the same thing, and it had to get its applications in.

MCI applied to operate digital termination systems in forty-six cities by 1983. The network would cost about $35 million. The application, like those from most other companies, was grander than reality. As it turned out, though, MCI did receive permission to build in thirteen cities, and by 1984, it would have two in operation.

MCI would deliberately take its time setting up DTS operations. They were playing a waiting game with the FCC. The FCC never intended DTS to be a method of bypassing the local telephone company with voice transmission. Because of that, it authorized frequencies in the 10 GHz band. They were okay for data transmission but not for voice. Because of the demand for DTS, based on the number of proposals it received, the FCC agreed to open up another frequency band once the 10 GHz band was used up. This band was 18 GHz, and it could be used for quality voice transmission because of its wider bandwidth. So MCI had no choice but to build 10 GHz systems and use those for data—a rather small market now—and wait for the newer bands to open up and use those for voice.

One thing that Brian McKinsey's training taught him was how to boil down a company's strategy to its simplest form. Intuitively, everyone at MCI knew it, but after realizing what DTS could mean to MCI, Brian summed it up with words and charts. He drew a " + " and in each corner wrote a different word: "VOICE," "DATA," "DOMESTIC," "INTERNATIONAL." No matter which of the first two you mixed with the second two, you had a business that MCI should be in. His job was to look into the future and continue to fill in the matrix.

Like a box of Cracker Jacks, Western Union International had a prize inside. The prize was a paging company called Airsignal that had radio licenses in about forty cities.

Airsignal was WUI's Siberia. When employees fell out of favor with WUI's management, they were banished to Airsignal. As a result, Airsignal had lain dormant for years with very little attention paid to it. And despite renewed interest in the paging business across the country, nothing much was going on at Airsignal.

MCI didn't have much early interest in Airsignal for its paging operations either. It had other value. Brian and Jerry Taylor—whom Brian had hired away from Carl Vorder Bruegge under McGowan's absolute-right-of-transfer rule—saw in it a way to enter another business using the local contacts and good name of Airsignal. This new business was cellular mobile radio.

Cellular mobile radio was a new technology developed largely by Bell Laboratories. It allowed people to make calls from their cars without the hassle of waiting for an empty channel or going through an operator. The old system of mobile phones was a disaster because it relied on one or two high-powered radio transmitters to cover an entire metropolitan area, in a thirty-to-fifty-mile radius, and only about twelve channels were available at any one time. During evening rush hours, for example, anxious callers had to wait their turn in line. Most cities had thousands of customers who couldn't even use their mobile phones when they wanted them the most.

Cellular technology would change all that. The system divided a city into little "cells" that ranged in size from a few city blocks to several miles. They were shaped anywhere from a perfect circle to something resembling a squashed blintz. Each cell contained its own low-powered transmitter just strong enough to serve the cell. Cells touched each other, and some overlapped slightly.

Adjacent cells used different channels, and there were more than six hundred in each city to choose from. Each channel could be used many times simultaneously as long as the cells were far enough apart. All the cell transmitters were connected to one central switching office much like land-based phones were connected to the central office of the local phone company.

Each cell transmitter sent out a special signal, and as you drove from cell to cell, your telephone automatically tuned to the strongest signal it heard. Your telephone continuously sent back a unique signal telling the central switching office where you were so that if a call came in, it knew where to find you amid all its cells. When a call was received, the transmitter automatically found a vacant channel, told your phone to ring, and you answered it and talked. Each mobile phone had its own phone number and area code, so callers didn't have to go through a mobile operator to call you.

Outgoing calls were handled just like any regular call: You dialed the number and were connected.

The ingenious part of cellular technology was how a call was handled as a car passed from one cell to another. As you moved to the outskirts of one cell, the transmitter sensed that your signal was fading, and it searched adjacent cells to see which one was beginning to hear your signal. When it found one, it automatically handed you off to the new cell. Neither side in the conversation heard any clicks or fading because the change-off was done automatically in a fraction of a second.

The cellular network can never be overcrowded because as more people subscribe to the service, the cells can be split into still smaller cells.

Everyone wanted the service, everyone but the FCC. It had studied the matter for more than twelve years before it actually okayed the service. The reason it took so long was fear. Cellular radio was more than just a new type of mobile phone service. It was a new type of phone service period. It was a way to bypass the local phone network altogether. There was no reason why people couldn't use their mobile phone in their office as their regular phone. It was exactly like a regular phone in quality and ease of use. The only difference was that it didn't have to be connected to wires in the wall.

Cellular technology, if it penetrated the mass market, would totally change the face of the nation's telephone industry. No longer would you have to wait for someone to wire up a new phone for your office. You could just buy a cellular phone and get service the same day. All it would take was a simple tickle of the computer keyboard to add your name and number to a cellular radio company's roster. Even industrial parks could get their own minicellular network, and the local phone company would be totally out of the picture.

The FCC didn't want to take a responsibility for these tremendous changes. It wanted to go slowly. It wasn't until 1982 that FCC Chairman Mark Fowler, a self-proclaimed deregulator appointed by Ronald Reagan, got cellular radio going. Fowler's philosophy and Jack Goeken's beliefs would have meshed well. Let the market decide. If it fails, so be it.

Well, it wasn't totally left to the marketplace after all. The FCC decided that each metropolitan area would have two licenses. One would go to the so-called wireline carrier, the other would be the nonwireline carrier. In plain English, it meant that the local telephone company would be guaranteed at least one license—if it wanted it— and the other would be up for grabs. The FCC made this decision under pressure from AT&T and the local Bell companies who were afraid of users eventually bypassing their network, leading to a deterioration of service for those who remained on the wired systems. Those who remained would probably be residential users, probably those too poor to buy into the new technology. Businesses would leave the local system for sure, if cellular gave them a better deal. And business customers accounted for more than 60 percent of a local company's revenues.

Cellular radio spurred discussion in the FCC and Congress for the first time on the issue of bypass and, more important, "Do the American people have a right to telephone service?" Should the government ensure a phone in every living room? Is it a national goal? Is it a necessity like food and housing, or is it more like a car—almost a necessity, but you can still take the bus if you can't afford one.

Brian wasn't worrying about any pending national debate. To him, cellular radio could be a way around the local phone companies just like DTS. It was a way to help control MCI's costs for local interconnection.

In the past, the FCC had stressed localism in granting licenses for TV and radio stations. Brian figured they would do the same for cellular systems. Airsignal, it seemed, would give MCI that extra edge over competitors. It was a local presence. As a strategy, it was sound. Unfortunately, the FCC changed plans. No longer was local presence an issue. Airsignal's local sales managers attending PTA meetings and lunching with the Rotarians didn't matter in the end.

Brian was new at MCI, but he knew Taylor's reputation as a strong start-up man—he had done a wonderful job starting Execunet and later residential service—and he wanted him to start up Airsignal. Taylor wanted it, too.

Jerry Taylor had responsibility for cellular radio and the paging business. The paging business traditionally was populated by mom-and-pop operations that took their time on projects, didn't know how to market, and generally ran their businesses inefficiently. They ran them like utilities. In effect, by virtue of their licenses they had a lock on their communities, so they ran their businesses like any other monopoly. Although Airsignal was the third largest paging company in the nation, it, too, was afflicted by the paging company malaise.

Jerry took strong measures. His first move was to fire most of the headquarters staff. Next he saw lots of paper shuffling, report writing, and memo moving and put a stop to most of it. He hired new sales-people from outside of the paging business who were not tainted by the old-fashioned notions of the business. Jerry knew that people didn't buy because of the technology; they bought because of the benefits, and he had his salespeople stress that in their pitches.

All paging companies leased their products. Jerry thought it was stupid to lease such a low-priced item as a pager, so he put a stop to it. They were $300 items, and all the work involved in leasing them wasn't worth the trouble in paperwork. It didn't matter to him that no other paging company was selling them outright. He did it anyway by negotiating a deal with Motorola to buy a large number of pagers at a low price. He figured out what price he needed to sell them to cover his costs, and he undercut everyone in the business including Motorola. By not leasing his products, he cut out insurance, maintenance, and all the other extra costs. If a client wanted a service contract, he would sell it to him.

Jerry began a series of what he called "Screaming Whore" ads, flamboyant moves to get people to buy pagers and use Airsignal's service. Taylor's goal was to take the technology out of it and use marketing techniques like those used by McDonald's or anyone else who sold to the mass market. Most paging companies talked about radio towers and new microchips; Airsignal's ads talked about benefits. "What does it cost to lose a phone call, Mr. Businessman?"

Later, other paging companies copied Jerry's techniques. It became common for customers to buy their pagers rather than lease them, and more and more ads were showing up with panache. Pagers became a consumer item with stores like Radio Shack selling $99 pagers to customers who used to buy CB radios.

Jerry was slowly building Airsignal and loving every minute of it. By June 1982, MCI filed for cellular licenses in twelve of the top thirty markets. At that time, the industry was caught up in cellular fever. Analysts were predicting a $6 billion annual market within the decade, and companies were scrambling to get license applications to the FCC on time.

The situation got so intense that the FCC was forced to award licenses by lottery instead of by comparative hearings for the markets outside of the coveted top thirty. In some markets, so many companies vied for licenses that the FCC encouraged joint ventures. They had brought it on themselves by guaranteeing one license to the local telephone company. They feared now that with so many companies trying to get the nonwireline license they would fight it out over several years and the local telephone company would have its system up and running and preempt *any* competition at all. In some markets, that would happen despite the deal mania that followed.

In the end, MCI would walk away with licenses in seven cities, a minority ownership in eight more, and a chance to control its future local interconnection costs.

Jerry Taylor picked up *The Wall Street Journal* one morning and read about J. Robert Harcharik, president of Tymnet, who had just quit his job. Jerry called Brian Thompson and said, "We've got to get this guy. He'll teach us about digital."

Although everyone at MCI knew the company had to get into digital transmission, they didn't know very much about it. Digital termination systems were fine, but it was small. In his obsession with filling the network's capacity, McGowan wanted to send large amounts of data as well as voice.

Harcharik knew about sending large amounts of data. He had been president of Tymnet, a subsidiary of a computer time-sharing business called Tymshare, for about three years. Tymnet leased long-distance telephone lines from AT&T and converted them into a packet switching network. Packet networks take lots of digital information from many different customers' computers and compress them into little "packets." When a packet is full, it is sent on its way around the network in bursts. Because they are sent quickly and in bulk, it is cheaper than just sending the information whenever it entered the communications system. It's sort of like waiting for a bus to be full of passengers before driving away. It's cheaper and more efficient than using several buses to pick up passengers as they arrive at the bus stop.

Tymnet charged customers less money than if they used AT&T's lines directly. Not only that, the data were sent more accurately.

Under Harcharik's leadership, the company went from $10 million in sales in October 1978 to $60 million in 1981. Harcharik was a driven man and had gone from company to company building them up, then leaving. His kick was climbing mountains while maintaining an overdeveloped sense of ethics. The memory of his ambitious salesman father dying of a heart attack when he was only forty-nine stayed with him all the time. Harcharik was always driven, but frightened at what ambition could eventually do to him. He was in constant emotional turmoil.

At age twenty-six, he and a friend had begun a firm called Comnet in Washington, D.C., a data communications company. He put up $4,500, $2,000 of which he borrowed from his stepfather. When Comnet went public, the stock cost $2.25 a share. Within six months, it rose to $60. The year before, Harcharik was making $14,000 a year. Now he was worth $5 million on paper. Two weeks later, though, the stock dropped to $30 and Harcharik felt sick. Not because of his losses. Hell, he was still a winner, but he heard about an elderly woman named Mrs. Cohen whose broker had put her life savings in Comnet stock when it was flying high at $60, and she lost half of it when it dropped to $30. Harcharik was bitter at Wall Street and what it did to people like Mrs. Cohen, and he became disillusioned with the whole process. Other things were going on at Comnet that he thought were unethical, and the pressure built up to the point where he had to leave. He walked away with $150,000 for five years' work and the memory of poor Mrs. Cohen.

Harcharik took a job with Informatics, a company that owned data bases. He proposed a joint venture between Tymshare and Informatics. It seemed like a good fit: Tymshare had the ability to move data and Informatics had the data ready to be moved. Informatics's board rejected the idea, but Harcharik was so impressed by Tymshare that he left his company to do the venture without Informatics. A year and half later, the idea bombed. It was a loser, and Tymshare folded it up.

During Christmas week 1974, Harcharik met Bill Combs, who was in charge of selling time on Tymshare's data network. Even though Harcharik's idea didn't work, Tymshare still wanted to keep him, so Harcharik cut a deal with Combs in which Harcharik would open up a Washington, D.C., sales office for Tymshare. A week after meeting Combs, Harcharik opened the office. His job was to sell data transmission time to the federal government. He built the business from $500,000 to $2 million in a year and a half and also organized a national sales force after rising to the rank of vice-president of sales.

In 1978, Combs left to become president of XTEN, Xerox's data transmission system. The two sat in Harcharik's room at the Howard Johnson's in San Francisco saying their good-byes. Combs explained about XTEN and how big it was going to be—so much bigger than Tymshare—and he told Harcharik, "I want you to come with me when I get it set up."

Harcharik said, "It sounds like a hell of a project. I enjoyed working with you. I hope it all works out for you. Meanwhile I'll be doing this."

As soon as Combs left, Tymshare offered Harcharik Combs's job. All he had to do was move to California. Harcharik turned the job down three times within a two-month period. The Comnet experience and all its pressures had nearly ruined his marriage, and he knew that if he went out West he would never come back and his already shaky marriage would end. He was doing okay living in Washington, watching his children grow and loving his wife.

A few months later, in September, Harcharik was sitting in a bar in Detroit with one of his regional managers. They had just come from Chrysler, their largest account—$100,000 a month—when Harcharik said he was going to call his boss, Warren Prince, and tell him that someone had to run Tymnet. The company had no leader, and it was going to hell, Harcharik thought amid the alcohol. He told Warren that he was willing to be acting president until someone permanent was found. He would come home every two weeks or so, and Warren said fine.

Harcharik went to California and never came back. He got caught up in the ego trip of being president of the company, and a month later he *became* president. He divorced his wife of eighteen years, something he would always regret.

Although Harcharik's personal life was a shambles, his professional life skyrocketed. After building Tymnet into a $60 million company, he won praise from everyone in the information industry. Unfortunately, as he was reaching his peak and grasping still further, he was stymied by Tymshare's president, Tom O'Rourke. O'Rourke was an entrepreneur and treated Tymnet like his baby. To Harcharik's thinking, it wasn't a baby anymore. The two fought until, finally, Harcharik left cold without any jobs lined up. The story of his leaving, which Jerry saw in *The Wall Street Journal*, was like an advertisement for Harcharik.

Bob Gant, who worked for Brian, knew Harcharik from Comnet. He called Harcharik and said, "We see you left. Would you be interested in talking to Brian Thompson here at MCI?" In typical MCI fashion, Harcharik paid his own way to Washington.

Brian told Harcharik that MCI wanted to get into data, but they weren't sure what it meant for the company. Harcharik told Brian some of the things he would have liked to do at Tymnet if he had had the money and if he could have convinced the management to let him do them.

In April 1982, Harcharik came on board. His job was to figure out what it was that MCI should do in the data business. Brian gave Harcharik about four months to roam around the company, discover the strengths and weaknesses of MCI, and see how data would fit into MCI's overall strategy. Harcharik thought to himself: "I'll take three or four months, look around the place, then come up with some ideas."

After six weeks, Brian went to Harcharik and said, "So when are you going to give us the plan?" and that was the first time that Harcharik learned what "MCI time" was all about. He had heard about it jokingly in the halls but now he understood what it meant. There was dog time, where one year of a dog's life is equivalent to seven years of a human, and there was real time, where one year equaled one year, and there was MCI time in which seven years of real time became one year of MCI time.

Although Harcharik could have used more time, he presented Brian with an idea that he had been thinking about for a long time. By the end of May, Harcharik showed Brian his plan for a "Digital Post Office," something he called MCI Mail.

Harcharik glued together the idea of MCI Mail from many different sources. One part came from his second wife, who was working at Hewlett-Packard, a company that made electronic equipment such as testing devices and printers. Unlike his first wife, his current wife had a career and was deeply absorbed in her work. She told Harcharik that he should see the high-speed graphics capability of an H-P printer that used laser beams to print characters. He saw immediately that laser printers could print signatures or reproduce a company's logo. Another piece came from Federal Express, which had proven that a time-sensitive-document business existed and that it was lucrative. Another part came from the purchase of Western Union International. The MCI Mail idea would embrace Telex as well.

The basic concept was simple. MCI Mail would mimic the Postal Service, but instead of using mailboxes, customers would use computer terminals. Harcharik believed that eventually all offices and homes would be equipped with computers instead of typewriters and that instead of paper letters, people would write electronic letters.

The Postal Service analogy would go even further. The hallmark of the U.S. mail is "universal termination." As long as a letter or postcard entered the mail system—from a box on the corner, from a post office, or from a letter carrier picking it up—anyone, anywhere, can receive it without cost. The sender pays the tab, and there is no cost to the sender until he actually mails the correspondence. In addition, no matter how long it took to compose the letter, the sender only paid for the final message that was sent. He was charged by weight. These concepts made MCI Mail different from current electronic mail systems that required each party to have a computer terminal. If the recipient didn't have a computer, he could receive an MCI Mail message by paper. The paper message would be sent by First-Class Mail or by a courier service. Also unlike other electronic mail systems, there would not be an on-line, per minute charge. You would only be charged when you actually sent a message, the cost pegged to the length.

The first name that Harcharik came up with was "Digital Post Office." That was shot down when focus groups said the word "digital" made them think of watches. Harcharik was going for the mass market with his idea, and digital was too esoteric. Finally, the simplicity of just plain "MCI Mail" was chosen. It was understood immediately.

After Harcharik presented his idea in May at a two-hour meeting with the senior managers, McGowan decided that it should be turned into an honest-to-goodness business plan. In December, with only one meeting in between, Harcharik presented senior officials with a business plan. Everyone thought it was a tremendous idea. It was high-tech, it was sexy, it had never been done before. It was everything that MCI believed it was: the innovator and leader in communications.

By the end of the meeting, McGowan was excited, flailing his arms, shouting, "Everyone will use this. It's terrific."

Orville, in his dry manner, said, "Mr. Chairman. Do I take it you're for this idea?"

And McGowan screamed back, unable to contain his enthusiasm, "Yeah, let's do it!"

Everybody got up, walked out of the room, and Orville, who walked out last, said with a half smile: "Okay, you sons of bitches. Remember when we lose $50 million doing it."

The next day, Harcharik became more frightened than he had ever been in his professional life. A guy showed up in his office with a funding authorization for $32 million, the amount he said he needed to get MCI Mail off the ground. What terrified him most was that they had actually given him all the money that he asked for. If it didn't work, it was his fault. There was no one else to blame. At Tymnet, he could always blame O'Rourke because he never gave Harcharik all the money he asked for, and he could say the project would have worked if he had gotten all the monies. Not only that, McGowan didn't ask for reports in the meantime, and he didn't have to check in either. MCI leased Harcharik space down the block from the MCI building to do his work. In other companies, you could blame the higher-ups for ruining your projects by meddling and changing things in midcourse. Here, at MCI, Harcharik was on his own with money in his pocket and a management that said, "We gave you what you wanted, now deliver."

Harcharik gave himself nine months to complete the project. October 15, 1983, was the date. His first job was to hire more staff. He needed about 150 people and already had about 10. One of them was Vint Cerf. He would be MCI Mail's version of Tom Leming, in charge of actually building the digital network.

Vint Cerf had spent most of his life as an academic and not as a businessman. In fact, Vint made a special point of warning Harcharik that he didn't have much business sense. On the other hand, he showed great enthusiasm for the idea and an absolute love for technology, and that's what clinched it for Harcharik.

Ironically, Vint had met with McGowan about a year before. Phil Nyborg, who was at the American Federation of Information Processing Societies and later the Computer and Communications Industry Association, both Washington lobby groups, was then working as Orville's assistant. He had known Vint for many years, mostly from his research work in computer science at Stanford. He invited Vint to speak with McGowan about a job as chief scientist. There wasn't a job open; it was just an exploratory meeting. Phil and Vint had been running into each other more frequently now because Vint had taken a position at the Defense Advanced Research Projects Agency (DARPA) across the Potomac River in Rosslyn, Virginia. He had been there for six years, working on packet switching technology, mostly learning how to connect the networks together.

Vint was fascinated by McGowan and impressed that he was willing to explain to him in great detail what MCI was about. Here was this nonbusiness type asking all kinds of dumb questions, and the chairman of a big corporation took the time to answer them. Although

Vint was awed by it all, McGowan's messy office with its papers all around was like home. He felt comfortable with him.

Orville was, of course, another story. His office was neat, organized, and rather businesslike. The two of them working together didn't strike Vint as odd, though. Coming from an academic environment, he quickly grasped the need for an organization to have a dreamer on one side and a down-to-earth practitioner on the other side. He had seen these marriages in university research teams many times.

After a couple of hours of talking with McGowan, they both concluded that because MCI didn't do any research, it didn't need a chief scientist. Even if it did, Vint wasn't sure he would want to work for them anyway. He was having a wonderful time at DARPA.

A year or so later, however, Phil called and said, "There's someone else I'd like you to meet. His name is Bob Harcharik."

Vint said, "Who's that?"

Phil answered, "Well, he's here from Tymnet, and he's doing some stuff for us."

Vint said, "Fine. I'm always willing to meet new people."

Vint had lunch with Phil and Harcharik. Harcharik explained that he was trying to build something called a Digital Post Office. For Vint, Harcharik didn't have to say anything more. That was such a grabber for Vint that he wanted to work for Harcharik. Vint knew it wouldn't be easy to design, but it would be a challenge. It was large, and he thought, "What a gutsy thing to do and what a great place to do it." He knew MCI's feisty reputation. Vint got excited, and within a month he joined.

Although he had no business training, Vint learned quickly about conducting projects in a businesslike manner, including completing them within budget. He had taught at Stanford for four years, and half of his salary had to come from grants for projects that companies and the government paid for. In a sense, it had been like running a business. The big difference now was that he was dealing with a large number of vendors who would supply MCI with its products and he had to get them all working together.

Within a month after joining, Vint had designed the architecture of the system. "Architecture" is the name given to the scheme of what fits where. It shows how the various products and services interact with each other and in what order. In his professorial fashion, Vint drew much of the plan on his big office blackboard, and when he explained it he looked much like the college teacher that he used to be. The system went over MCI's network, the same one that was used for long-distance service. The central hub, the place where the main computer that ran the system was located, was in Naperville, Illinois. Aside from being near the geographic center of the United States, Western Union International had a facility there and had extra room. It seemed a logical place to use.

Fortunately, much of what Vint needed to build the system was "off-the-shelf" products. Companies already had them, and they could modify them for MCI's specific need. Actually, it was Harcharik's plan all along to use as many ready-to-buy products as possible. That would make it cheaper than having someone specially design something, but more important, it allowed MCI Mail to be built rather quickly. Harcharik had bragged that he could do it in nine months, and he had to make his deadline.

By the end of January, Vint had decided what companies would get what contracts, and in February, he and Harcharik called the first meeting of all the vendors. The day before the February 11, 1983, meeting, Washington forecasters at first said the city would receive eight inches of snow. Washington is really a southern city, and even a few flakes close the town. Later, forecasters predicted more would fall. The contractors began to call Harcharik wondering if they should come in. He told them yes, nothing was going to stop this project. He knew that if he didn't set the tone from the beginning that nothing would stop the project, it would flounder, people would start to take their time, and it would end up like so many other projects that lingered and then died.

The next day 16.4 inches of snow fell, but everyone had come the night before, and they were all stranded at Blackie's restaurant attached to the Marriott Hotel a few blocks from MCI Mail's office. They all stayed overnight and got to drinking and knowing each other. A wartime camaraderie was born, and it set the standard that nothing would stop this project. Ironically, Vint was the only one who couldn't make it. He was snowbound about thirty miles away in the Virginia suburbs.

The meetings continued, about one a month. After the meetings, minutes were printed and distributed to the vendors so each would know what the other was doing. If they didn't, there would be trouble. Everything had to fit.

By late March, the system was far enough along to test but only on a rudimentary level. From the tests, the contractors could see where the problems were so they could figure out how to fix them. From then on, it was a matter of everyone programming his part of this massive computer network. By July, it was ready to demonstrate to the marketing and sales people. They weren't totally satisfied with what they saw. They wanted things a little simpler and easier to use.

That was the main problem: How do you design a sophisticated system yet make it so simple that anyone, without any computer training, can use it? Further refinements followed. Software changes came out every week.

Harcharik set September 26 as the day to unveil his baby. He would call a press conference and show the world that MCI could do the impossible. Not only would the project come in fifteen days ahead of schedule but would be done for $1 million under budget, $31 million.

But Harcharik didn't know that the night before the press conference at which McGowan would be the showman telling the world about this great new contribution to the information age, the laser printers that would print out the inaugural MCI Mail messages would decide not to work.

Gary Tobin and Bill Stern, who specialized in PR for MCI Mail, had begun setting the PR stage. They wanted publicity on a par with MCI Mail's importance to the company. Their job was to whet the appetites of reporters without telling them exactly what it was they were going to see. The whole project had been done in secret, and it wouldn't do to have it come out in dribs and drabs and steal the event's thunder. Reporters receive so many invitations to attend press conferences, especially those concerning some new widget, that they often ignore them. MCI had been lucky so far. Because of Tobin's understanding of overkill in calling too many press conferences, he made certain that MCI called very few. This way, when they did, it became special, and he could count on strong attendance.

Reporters who covered the telecommunications industry for trade publications and those from the mass-market media received a letter about two weeks before the press conference. It carried a Grand Central Station post office box return address but no other markings other than a September 13 postmark. After a personalized salutation, it said:

"On September 27th, this form of communication—the common letter—will be obsolete.

"Mark your calendar to get the full story."

And that was all.

A few days later, reporters received a Western Union Mailgram dated September 16. This time it read:

"LETTERS ARE FAST, MAILGRAMS FASTER. ON SEPTEMBER 27TH, WRITTEN COMMUNICATIONS WILL TAKE THE NEXT STEP FORWARD. WATCH ON THAT DATE FOR THE FULL STORY."

Even reporters who had seen other attention-getting devices were intrigued by this one. Nobody knew who it was from, and nobody knew what it was about.

About a week before the press conference, however, somebody did find out. A reporter for the *Chicago Sun-Times* learned about MCI Mail, perhaps through a telecommunications consultant named Harry Newton. Newton was the Oral Roberts of the telecommunications industry who not only advised clients on their telephone needs but gave speeches and seminars that whipped the audience into such a frenzy that they believed that communications could cure cancer if you dialed the right number. Newton had once worked for MCI during the early Execunet days and was a longtime acquaintance of McGowan. He was let go because McGowan found him too erratic to work with. In his enthusiasm, McGowan told Newton about MCI Mail, and it apparently spread from there.

The press conference, which would be held at MCI's Washington headquarters, would be sent by closed-circuit satellite hookup to New York, Los Angeles, and Chicago. This would be MCI's largest press conference ever and it had to work perfectly. Reporters who had never known anything about MCI would be there, and despite the leak to the *Sun-Times*, many of the details were still unknown.

One of MCI Mail's special features was that it could promise four-hour delivery of anything that you typed into your word processor or computer, complete with a signature of the sender. The text would be sent over the phone lines to MCI's main computer site in Naperville, Illinois, then transmitted over MCI's long-distance network to one of fifteen printer sites. From there, it would travel by Purolator Courier to the recipient. The plan called for McGowan to bring someone up on stage with him, chat for a moment, and then have that conversation typed into a computer for transmission. By the time the press conference ended, the reporters would see the printed messages delivered directly to the press conference rooms by a uniformed Purolator messenger. Although Federal Express had the overnight courier business locked up, four-hour delivery service would certainly be impressive.

The night before, the laser printers weren't working. The computer program was hopelessly screwed up, and the guy who wrote the software was on vacation somewhere in California. Vint was beside himself. He said to himself, "So much for my commercial career. It lasted four months."

He couldn't get in touch with the programmer, but he was able to find a fellow who worked for Hewlett-Packard, the builders of the laser printers. He got him out of bed and got him to the Rosslyn, Virginia, print site, just outside of Washington, and the two of them spent all night trying to get the program working. By the time that the press conference started, they had patched things together enough for it to work.

McGowan, Harcharik, and Orville introduced the product in great detail. The concept was simple. MCI Mail offered four products. The first was an "Instant Letter." It was delivered within seconds and could be sent between any computers or word processors. That cost a dollar.

The second product was the "MCI Letter." A message from a computer would be sent over the MCI Mail system to one of fifteen laser print sites, where it would be printed, stuffed into an envelope, and sent by First-Class Mail to the recipient. The letter could be printed on a company letterhead complete with a signature that the sender kept on file with MCI Mail. That cost two dollars.

The third product was an "Overnight Letter" that would compete with Federal Express's overnight letter. Federal Express's product had an advantage in being able to handle photos, drawings, and other illustrations as well as anything else that was relatively flat and could be placed in the large envelope. MCI's product was delivered by Purolator. It cost $6.00, well below Federal Express's $12.50 charge.

The last product was a "Four-Hour Letter" for $25. That was the most impressive product because no one had ever tried for such fast delivery. This was the product that McGowan was going to demonstrate.

He called someone on stage and dictated an unrehearsed message: "Ms. Dana Martin of Kiplinger Washington Letter is wearing a Timex watch. The watch shows 11:55 A.M. EST, which is two minutes fast," he said. Everything worked as planned. By the time people were getting ready to leave, the envelopes arrived in much less time than four hours with the printed message about Ms. Martin's errant watch.

The laser printer put McGowan's signature on the letter, and everyone was impressed.

Had he begun the demonstration a little later, however, it would have been a different story. Ten minutes after he told the audience about Ms. Martin's timepiece, someone in Naperville accidentally cut the power to the main computer system, and the entire MCI Mail system died. Nothing worked, and there was no backup power. McGowan didn't find out until later that he was minutes away from looking like a big jerk.

After the shouting was over, Harcharik had the job of trying to sell MCI Mail. That meant signing up as many customers as possible in as short a time as possible and getting them to use the service. In a sense, it was easy because there was no cost to sign up, and no risk to the user. On the other hand, he knew that because it was free to join, many people would do so with no intention of ever using the service.

The media had swallowed much of the hype about electronic mail and how it was the wave of the future. They looked skeptically on Harcharik's estimate of 200,000 users by the end of 1984 but were willing to give him a chance. Harcharik knew, however, that the press would be brutal if his plan failed to produce the large numbers of customers he had promised.

Harcharik had given himself a boost by cutting a deal with Dow Jones News Retrieval, a subsidiary of the publisher of *The Wall Street Journal*. News/Retrieval was an electronic data base that provided an electronic version of *The Wall Street Journal* and *Barron's*, one of Dow Jones's other publications. It also provided stock quotes, company profiles, and other business-oriented information. Customers paid a flat fee for the service plus a per-minute charge when they received information. News/Retrieval customers automatically received access to MCI Mail, and that gave the system 55,000 customers from the start. Any new subscribers to MCI Mail would also receive access to

News/Retrieval for free, although they paid for using the service just like regular News/Retrieval customers. This alliance with Dow Jones gave MCI Mail not only instant credibility but instant revenue as well. Anyone accessing Dow Jones through MCI Mail had a portion of his usage charges sent to MCI Mail.

Harcharik had hired a vice-president of sales named Ray Marks. He and Harcharik had worked together at Tymnet, and Marks was probably Harcharik's key to success at selling the service to the federal government. Their relationship was like a stormy marriage where husband and wife continued to love and respect each other above the screams and flying dishes.

The relationship began when Marks was selling computer hardware to the government, where he had established a strong reputation for knowing how to break into the lucrative federal market. He was introduced to Harcharik by a mutual friend, and as a courtesy to that friend, Marks reluctantly agreed to meet Harcharik in a hotel restaurant in San Francisco to talk about Tymnet. Marks was passing through the city at the time.

When he got to the hotel, he found that Harcharik wasn't there. He had left word that he would be at another restaurant, so Marks went there. When he arrived, he saw Harcharik with his staff sitting around a dinner table and there was no room to squeeze anyone else in. Marks told the maître d' to tell Harcharik he was waiting. Their friend greeted Marks and asked him to wait in the bar and have a drink. Marks doesn't drink.

He sat in the bar for an hour drinking coffee when Harcharik and their friend came out. Harcharik's first words were: "What makes you think you can sell this shit to the federal government? I certainly couldn't do it when I was there."

Marks thought to himself: "Screw you bastards. I didn't come looking for you." Then he said to Harcharik in an equally sarcastic tone: "Well, maybe you didn't know what you were doing."

"A nice relationship is shaping up here," Marks figured. "When does my flight to Minneapolis leave?"

Marks said, "Maybe I can't sell it. Maybe I should go back to doing what I was doing. I was very happy doing it."

Marks and Harcharik chatted some more. Marks wasn't impressed by Harcharik's abrasive challenge, and he thought he was a real jerk. "He may be good and he may be the president of Tymnet, but so what," Marks said to himself. He was impressed by Harcharik's physical demeanor, though; he was tall, thin, and aggressive-looking.

The next day, Marks was still pissed off but decided to look over Harcharik's operation. He talked to the employees, and he saw how the place was run. He couldn't put his finger on it, but he knew there was something special going on. Marks's last words to Harcharik that day were: "I heard you ran a pretty good organization, and I think you do."

Harcharik responded, "Ah, bullshit. You're just trying to patronize me." Marks realized immediately that Harcharik was one of those people who just couldn't take compliments, and he said, "I don't give a shit how you feel about it. I still think you run a good operation."

With that he left, and a few weeks later he began working for Harcharik at Tymnet. Marks figured it was either up in glory or down in flames with this guy, but either way it would be a hell of a challenge.

When Marks joined in January 1980, the government business went from zero to $500,000 the first year, $4 million the second, and about $16 million the third. Harcharik never said it, but he had the greatest respect for Marks. The feeling was mutual as Marks was able to see through Harcharik's abrasive shell to discover a sensitive man with a strong sense of ethics. Harcharik would establish unreasonable demands and appreciate it when you tried. He beat you bloody over quotas and deadlines, but conveyed his gratitude when it was over, no matter what the outcome. Beneath it all, Harcharik did a tricky balancing act: He really cared about people but never let it seem like it took a backseat to his aggressive business style.

Before Harcharik left to go to MCI, Marks and he had lunch. Harcharik told him if he ever came up with anything, perhaps they could work together again. Marks said fine, he would like that. He told Harcharik, "I like your style. I would like to work for you again." Harcharik said, "Ah, bullshit," and Marks realized again, God forbid he should pay the SOB a compliment.

Later, Harcharik called Marks and in his secretive way said, "We're going to build a digital post office."

Marks said, "Great! . . . What the hell are you talking about?"

And Harcharik laid out the plan, we're going to take the world by storm and do all these great things and blah, blah, blah. Harcharik was excited and he got Marks excited, but on later reflection he had second thoughts about whether it would work. Besides, he was doing well at Tymnet, making good money, but the truth was, he was a wee bored.

Things were going too smoothly. There were no traumas. All the tigers were tamed and he was ready for a change.

Marks hadn't made up his mind yet to join Harcharik when he suggested that he meet McGowan. Marks went to McGowan's messy office, and the first thing he saw was this guy with a coffee cup and cigarette in his hands. Marks liked him immediately. These were two of Mark's favorite things. If McGowan had been munching on a candy bar, Marks would have followed him through a burning building. The more McGowan talked and drew pictures showing the MCI dream, the more Marks believed that selling envelopes, as Marks referred to this crazy scheme, was the best thing in the world.

The two of them were talking, drinking coffee, smoking cigarettes, having a great time when Orville stuck his head in the door. "You've got to let him go. He's an hour late to see me already."

Marks then found himself in a quiet, neat office where God forbid you pull out a cigarette and drop an ash on the carpet. Still, Marks found a warmth to Orville beneath the structured environment. Marks walked out confused. He had never been assaulted by such opposite situations so close to each other.

The next day, Marks was heading for New York to visit Chase Manhattan Bank, one of Tymnet's customers, and in front of him on the plane was McGowan. They were sitting in the smoking section puffing their brains out. They didn't talk very much. McGowan was busy reading all his newspapers. When they landed, McGowan asked, "Where are you going?" Marks told him he was going downtown, and McGowan said he was going uptown. McGowan said, "Let's share a cab," to which Marks said, "I pay or you pay?" McGowan said, "You're going farther, you pay," and they both ended up going in separate cabs.

There was something in McGowan's attempt to weasel the free cab ride that intrigued Marks. Here was a rich man from a growing company trying to stick someone he hardly knew for the cab fare. That was chutzpah, but in a playful way. He joined MCI Mail and began building a sales force. Two months after the press conference, however, Marks went to Harcharik and told him that it may have all been a big mistake.

Harcharik believed his main professional flaw was that he was a good talker. He could talk people into anything—even bad ideas. He was beginning to wonder if MCI was just a product of his enthusiasm or a real moneymaking business.

MCI Mail spent $30 million the first year on TV and newspaper advertising. The TV ads portrayed MCI Mail exactly as Harcharik had wanted. One spot showed a time-lapse erection of a building-sized computer terminal adjacent to a post office. The idea was to convey to the viewer that MCI Mail was, as the slogan said, "the nation's new postal system." Another TV ad showed a father and son walking through a museum, looking at a mailman frozen in midmotion inside a glass showcase. He was the past.

Print ads emphasized MCI's price advantage over Federal Express's overnight rate ($6 compared with $12.50) and also let the reader know that a four-hour service was available.

For all Harcharik's hopes, however, MCI Mail had the look of a bomb. He had made some huge errors in forecasting the number of potential users and had also failed to see that people just weren't ready to communicate over their computers and word processors. The computer revolution was more like a slow-motion coup d'état.

As early as December 1983, two months after the introduction of MCI Mail, Marks realized that MCI Mail was not a mass-market product. For one thing, people who had computers didn't know how to use them. In most offices, people learned how to use their machines just enough to do what they had to do. If a computer was bought for word processing, it wasn't thought of as a tool for anything else. Harcharik had believed that computer users would think of it as more than that. In his despair, he had fantasies about going around to people and placing signs on their computers that said, "Asshole; this is your mailbox, too."

One Saturday morning, Marks walked into Harcharik's office and said to him, "Bob, nobody is buying this stuff. We've got to go out and sell it. People don't buy mail. They buy a solution to a problem, but they don't buy mail."

Harcharik walked out on him, saying, "That's not what I built. I didn't build an electronic mail system. I built an electronic postal system." To Harcharik, the difference was wide, although people on the outside—in the mass market—didn't see the difference between the two. Harcharik still stuck to his guns, saying that MCI Mail *was* a mass-market item, and it would work as he had planned.

Several months later, *The Wall Street Journal* ran a story that broke Harcharik's heart. In it, Harcharik admitted that MCI Mail was falling way behind revenue projections, even though he was still saying that it would show a profit in its third year of operation. He reiterated his belief that the time-sensitive-mail business, as Harcharik liked to call it, was an $8-billion-a year business, and it was only a matter of time before MCI Mail got its share.

The article pointed out that MCI had stiff competition in the electronic mail end of it including Telemail, from GTE Telenet, and OnTyme, from Tymnet, Harcharik's former company. Western Union had recently introduced a product similar to MCI Mail called EasyLink, which exploited WU's embedded customer base of Telex users. EasyLink also printed out paper messages for those recipients who didn't have computers. It was basically an add-on to its current Mailgram service, although the quality of the letter was poor compared to MCI Mail.

The most painful admission for Harcharik was that only 35,000 people had registered for MCI Mail and that only 35 percent of those people had actually used it at least once a month. The story also detailed MCI Mail's problem with letting people know they had an electronic message waiting for them. The piece even quoted Harry Newton, who said he received an electronic letter three weeks after it was sent. "It would have been faster for them to have sent the bloody thing to me on paper," said Newton.

Harcharik took the criticism hard. In a company like MCI, where bottom-line figures were the only thing that mattered, Harcharik was taking a great deal of abuse from those in the company who looked at Mail as a drain on the business. The kidding was good-natured but sometimes bordered on being nasty. Often, snide comments about Mail were heard at meetings. McGowan was willing to ride it out, but Orville—well, Orville was another matter.

Marks told Harcharik he needed more salespeople. He only had nine to cover the entire country, and people kept quitting because they couldn't make any money. The commissions were too low.

Over the next year, Harcharik changed the course of MCI Mail. He still believed in his dream, but now he was forced to be more practical and admit that MCI Mail was not a mass-market item—at least not yet. The new plan was to use an "agency program" to help sell the service.

Originally, agents were anyone who applied. They got a short course in MCI Mail, then were unleashed to sell the product. That didn't work. Too many wackos applied. In addition, there were too many people who would just sell the service, not paying any attention to the customer, and collect their commission. Another thing that Harcharik found was that even though MCI Mail was probably the easiest electronic mail system to use, people still had trouble using it. They didn't know how to use their computers, and MCI Mail customer service folks spent too much of their time hand-holding with users who would spend only a few dollars a month. It was not an effective way of using MCI Mail's resources.

Marks also looked into having computer stores sell MCI Mail. That didn't work either. For one thing, these stores wanted money up front each time they sold a customer the service. As Harcharik and Marks knew all too well, just because someone signed up, it didn't mean he would generate one penny of business for MCI Mail. Marks also discovered that the stores were unable to give customers the continued hand-holding they needed for MCI Mail. They were too busy.

After months of honing, the agency program began. The ground rules were simple: Agencies must have an existing computer business, such as a consultancy. This way, the agent has an interest in doing a good job because he is also interested in selling the customer some of his own services.

Agents sold to anyone from large corporations to individual users. They got leads on their own or from staffers manning MCI Mail's main number in Washington. The referrals from Washington went through one of MCI Mail's district sales managers around the country. That manager gave it either to one of his own people or to one of the independent agents. Either way, his commission was the same. That meant it was in his best interests to give it to the person who could best complete the sale and not just to one of his own salespeople. It also meant he would support the independent agents any way he could so he would receive the commission on sales in his area.

Most of the time, the district manager gave the lead to an agent while his own people were making cold calls, trying to fill in incremental business.

The next fix was to change the pricing schedules. Although it was a great marketing concept not to charge people to register, it wasn't paying off. If MCI could charge for the service, not only would it bring in instant revenue but it would weed out people who signed up and never used the system. It was expensive to register new sign-ups, send them an information package, and not have them spend any money. Marks believed that if you charged something, people would be more apt to use it. It would separate the real users from those who just signed up because it was free. Marks fought that battle; Harcharik still wanted it to be free, but eventually Marks prevailed. The question was how much to charge.

If you charge too little, it might still attract nonusers, but if you charged too much, it might turn away potential users who weren't sure if they wanted it or not and didn't want to waste money. At one meeting, someone suggested twelve dollars; another person said twenty dollars, and Marks said eighteen. The reason Marks gave Harcharik for proposing eighteen dollars is that many credit card companies charge their customers that amount. The real reason was that 18 was the numerical equivalent of the Hebrew letters that spell "Chai," which means "life." Eighteen dollars is a favorite amount for donations to synagogues.

Marks also believed that the Instant Letter charge of one dollar was too high after Vint tapped the computer's memory and found that most electronic messages had fewer than 7,500 characters, what was called the "MCI ounce." The price structure was such that the customer paid one dollar per MCI ounce, but because most messages were less, people felt gypped. Not only that, people had a tendency to save up until they had many short messages rather than waste the dollar. Moreover, OnTyme and Telemail were charging people less than a dollar for short messages. So Marks suggested a "mini-ounce" of 500 characters for forty-five cents, one dollar from 500 to 7,500 characters, and one dollar for each additional 7,500 characters. Harcharik didn't like it because it would cut into his revenue, but he reluctantly agreed to go along with it.

At the same time, the four-hour product was raised five dollars to thirty dollars, and the Overnight Letter cost was raised two dollars to eight dollars, still well below Federal Express's price. The best seller, the letter that travels by First Class Mail, remained the same at two dollars for up to three pages.

Marks also worked out a plan of discounts for high-volume users. This was done to attract more corporate customers, especially for the popular two-dollar letter. Next to the Instant Letter, the two-dollar letter brought in the most profit. The Overnight Letter copped little profit, and MCI loses money on the four-hour product because it must pay high out-of-pocket expenses to Purolator.

In a move to cut costs, Harcharik decided to charge fifteen cents a minute to customers who didn't live in an area served by a local MCI phone input and had to call in on AT&T's 800 numbers. The toll-free charges were becoming too great to bear, especially if someone signed on and didn't send anything.

Vint was also able to supply information about customers who never signed onto the system. These people were sent notices that their registrations would be terminated unless they paid the eighteen-dollar fee. Those that didn't respond had their names and passwords purged. Regular users received notice of the registration fee and had that charge added to their next bill.

MCI's aggressive marketing, advertising, and pricing fooled everyone. Competitors began to believe that there really was a huge time-sensitive market out there, even though there probably wasn't. MCI had tied up more than $100 million in its Mail system.

Federal Express followed. One year after MCI launched its electronic post office, they introduced ZapMail, a way of sending documents in only two hours. Unlike MCI Mail, ZapMail used a system of facsimile machines that took "pictures" of documents and sent them over satellite networks to the Federal Express near the recipient. From there, a courier would deliver it. All for $35 for one to five pages. ZapMail's advantages over MCI Mail were the faster service and excellent reproduction of pictures, graphs, and drawings, something MCI Mail couldn't do. Federal Express invested more than $100 million starting ZapMail, but it, too, discovered that a market didn't yet exist.

In the first year, volume reached only about 2,000 transmissions a day, and Federal Express was forced to lower its price from $35 to $25 for up to twenty pages. Still, it was bullish on the business and announced it would spend $1.2 billion upgrading the system over a ten-year period. Like MCI, Federal Express was willing to take short-term losses in a business they believed would pay off.

When ZapMail was announced, Marks told Harcharik, "If there's one thing we did, it was convince the world that there's a market for four-hour delivery."

MCI Mail would lose money for the next two years, with no profits in sight. In 1984, MCI Mail would lose $50 million, just as Orville had predicted.

Harcharik would be forced to change his plan. It was becoming clear to him that although MCI Mail was a good idea, it was too early. The marketplace had not developed enough for MCI to take advantage of it. And, unlike international service that would just be a matter of time, Mail showed no signs of being profitable. Harcharik entered a holding pattern. If he could maintain MCI's position in the electronic mail business until demand came along, it might become a leader.

On May 3, 1983, MCI announced that it had topped $1 billion in revenue for the fiscal year that ended March 31. (Unlike most companies, MCI's fiscal year didn't end in December but in March.) It was also the second consecutive year in which the company more than doubled its revenue over the previous twelve months. The stock, which had split once the year before, was poised for another split in August. Two splits in two years was rare, but MCI shareholders were willing to give McGowan anything he wanted, as annual meetings continued to sound more like revival meetings than business gatherings.

The credit for MCI's success lay with the management team that McGowan and Orville had established. While he was positioning the company for the future with international service, Mail, Airsignal, and increased network capacity, McGowan rearranged the senior officials and added a few more.

To an outsider, it was difficult to see how such a jumble of people with such varied backgrounds could work together. Job descriptions appeared to overlap, and there was no organized sense of how people were chosen or what their backgrounds were. They didn't fit into any usual corporative mold—they didn't all think the same way—and the only thread that held them together was a fierce loyalty to McGowan's dream of changing the face of telecommunications.

Two months earlier, Bert Roberts had been made president of MCI Telecommunications, the largest part of the company. It oversaw all of the company's long-distance services and was the biggest money-maker. It would not be an easy move for Bert. He didn't have the charisma of McGowan or the quiet charm of Orville. He remained a cold, calculating boss who would run his division with an iron hand, often blowing up at someone who had screwed up, but five minutes later insisting that they get on with business as if nothing had happened. Bert tried to be friendly, but he just didn't know how. He didn't feel comfortable dealing with people, and it would take awhile before he did.

McGowan and Orville knew that shortcoming when they entrusted him with the third most important job at MCI. They hoped they could mellow him a little. McGowan would smile and say that Bert would come around, that he would learn how to handle people. Orville was more apt to take "the Young Turk" aside, as he called him, and explain softly, "Bert, you just can't treat people like that." Orville was in his mid sixties and would want to retire within the next couple of years, and he and McGowan were both grooming Bert to take his place.

Gary Tobin would try as often as he could to put Bert before the media, but Bert often begged off, saying he was too busy. He believed that talking to the media was a waste of time and that he should be running a business, not talking to reporters. McGowan's lessons on how important publicity was weren't getting through to Bert at all.

Part of Bert's reluctance to open up came after one of his first public appearances as the new president. While addressing the New York Society of Security Analysts, someone asked him what MCI would do if AT&T lowered its rates. Bert said that MCI would follow and lower its rates as well. That didn't go over big. The last thing stock watchers want to hear is a promise that a company's revenues will decrease. Orville had to give first aid that afternoon when reporters and other analysts called to ask if what Bert said was really true. Orville had to assure them that MCI would not go lockstep with AT&T but study each matter as it arose before deciding. It was a humiliating lesson for Bert in the art of public speaking.

After that incident, Bert didn't talk to the press very much, despite attempts to get his face known to the world. If he took Orville's place, he would have to get out there in front of the crowds eventually.

Analysts looked at MCI's management team as a strong one. Nate Kantor was president of MCI International, Jerry Taylor was president of MCI Airsignal, Bob Harcharik headed data services, which included MCI Mail, Charlie Skibo was in charge of network operations, handling the switching circuits (Bert's former job), and Brian Thompson was in charge of corporate planning.

Carl Vorder Bruegge was still head of sales, Tom Leming controlled the microwave transmission services, and Wayne English headed the financial section. Ken Cox was in charge of the regulatory matters, and John Worthington remained as head of the corporate law department.

Some new people had recently joined. The first was Howard Crane, who would become Gary Tobin's boss. Orville wanted a senior person to handle public relations, and he wanted his own man and not Tobin, the logical candidate.

Crane had wanted to be a writer after seeing Babe Ruth's last appearance in Yankee Stadium and writing an essay for his school newspaper. After seeing his name in print, he decided on a writing profession and began as a sportswriter in Pensacola. After getting an offer from the *Long Island Press*, Crane headed North to begin work. While he was driving from Florida, the Brooklyn Dodgers and the New York Giants both announced their intentions to leave the Big Apple for California. New York sportswriters were out of work, and when Crane arrived at the newspaper, he didn't have a job.

After several unsatisfying writing positions on trade publications, he got a job at IBM writing technical manuals. That, too, was boring after a while, and he found himself finishing his jobs faster than his comrades and going to the movies in the afternoon. He was about to quit IBM when they opened up a new department. It was called public relations of data processing, and Crane found himself traveling around the country writing press releases and enjoying himself. This was the late 1950s and early 1960s and IBM was in the midst of transforming the world with new, innovative computers. It ceased being fun in 1969 when the Justice Department sued IBM for antitrust violations. From then on, IBM turned its attention to defending itself instead of putting out new computers.

The attitude toward PR also changed at IBM because of an article in *Fortune* magazine in 1965 about the development of the IBM 360 computer, the largest such project in IBM's history. Chairman Tom Watson, Jr., had agreed to open up the company to the magazine, and has regretted it ever since. The article described IBM honestly, in terms of real flesh-and-blood people. It showed their brilliance but also their foibles. From then on, Watson never trusted anyone in the press, and IBM put up a PR iron curtain with procedure manuals for dealing with media inquiries. It all revolved around the words "no comment," and IBM gained a reputation for being closemouthed and uncooperative.

Crane finally got so sick of IBM that he had to leave, and he found a job with a Philadelphia insurance company, INA Corporation, as a speechwriter. He was put in charge of advertising when his boss got fired but got fired himself after five and half years because he couldn't get along with his new boss.

In the spring of 1978, Crane ran into a friend of his in New York who had done some work for MCI about two years earlier. MCI couldn't afford to pay him, so they gave him some shares. His friend figured they were worthless and he put them away. Years later, they were worth more than $1 million. Through his friend, Crane met Carl and Orville. He had long discussions with Orville (whom he had known only slightly from Orville's days at IBM), who told him, "We may be out of business in six months, and I can't in good conscience ask you to take a job here." This was before the Execunet decision.

So Crane took a job at the Federal National Mortgage Association (Fannie Mae) in Washington and let Orville know he was around if a job became available. In August 1982, Orville called him out of the blue to offer him a job as vice-president of PR. Crane turned down the job because he didn't want to report to Bert. Of all the interviews he had, Bert's was the most uncomfortable. He also sensed that Bert thought PR was frivolous.

He did, however, take the job several months later when Orville raised the stakes and offered him a senior VP title. It was also becoming clear to Crane that Bert would head Telecom, and Crane would report directly to Orville.

Tobin had submitted a plan to Orville to consolidate all of the company's communications in one department and under one person. It would include public relations, the annual report, employee publications, and other items. Instead of Tobin getting the job as head of that unit, Crane, an outsider, got it, and Tobin worked for him.

It was becoming clear to McGowan that MCI needed to better manage the areas of public and regulatory policy. MCI was beginning to apply to the states for permission to offer intrastate service, and that needed coordination. In addition, more attention needed to be paid to legislation and the access fee matters at the FCC, especially with the coming of equal access. Ken Cox just couldn't handle the job anymore. Besides, he was only a half-time employee. Someone fresh and new was needed. That person was Gene Eidenberg.

Gene Eidenberg grew up in a New York, Jewish liberal, academic, Rooseveltian, Democratic party environment. He always wanted to enter politics, but his mother, Eve, a painter, thought he would be good at business because it required a lot of interpersonal contact and her son was a shmoozer. He always had that in the back of his mind even as he joined the political science teaching staff of the University of Minnesota and later became deputy mayor of Minneapolis. He had already gotten his Ph.D. in political science from Northwestern, and through his political connections, he became vice-chancellor of the University of Illinois, Chicago. Still a champion of liberal causes, he also served as chairman of the Illinois Law Enforcement Commission.

At that time, Gene met Chet Kamin in Chicago while Chet was an attorney for the governor and liaison to the Law Enforcement Commission. When that came to an end, Gene moved to Washington to work at HEW and later was secretary of Jimmy Carter's Cabinet. Chet was busy as MCI's attorney in the AT&T antitrust case. The two kept in touch, and in December 1980, after Carter had lost the election, Chet called Gene and said, "Gene, have you decided what you're going to do?"

Gene said, "Chet, it's the same old story. I don't know what I want to do when I grow up."

Chet said, "I want you to meet Bill McGowan."

Gene replied, "Who's that?"

"He's the chairman of this company that is taking on AT&T in the telephone business."

"Sounds nuts to me," Gene said, "but sure, I'll meet him. I don't see any sort of fit, though."

Like Gene's mother, Chet had already decided that Gene would be good at business and wanted to push him in that direction.

The three had dinner in Washington, and McGowan and Gene took a liking to each other. They talked about MCI and politics, and at the end McGowan said, "Why don't you come over tomorrow and meet some of my colleagues?"

The next day, Gene met Bert Roberts and some others, and to Gene those meetings had the cast of an interview, but Gene didn't know for what. At the end of the day, McGowan offered Gene a job working in Wayne English's financial department, as assistant treasurer. Gene was dumbfounded: "Excuse me?"

McGowan said, "Listen, I know you don't know the business but you'll learn and we'll go from there."

Gene was confused. Moreover, he was uncomfortable with the job and said, "Bill, it's not going to work. I don't feel the fit." McGowan wasn't all that specific with what he wanted, and in his gut, Gene felt it wouldn't work and turned down the offer.

Gene didn't know that McGowan often hired people based on what he felt they could do for MCI and not necessarily what specific spot they could fill at the moment. McGowan hired people based on his instincts. When he told Gene, ". . . . we'll go from there," it meant that Gene could reach whatever level he wanted in the company based on his performance and interest.

Gene then became a Fellow at the Institute of Politics at Harvard's Kennedy School of Government and later became chairman of the Democratic National Committee.

About six months later, Gene got a call from Chet inviting him to dinner with McGowan to talk about some legislation that affected MCI. "McGowan just wants to pick your brain," Chet said. They had a wonderful dinner, and after Chet excused himself to go the bathroom McGowan said, "That's too bad it didn't work out six months ago."

Gene said, "Maybe there'll be some opportunities in the future. I just didn't feel comfortable with it."

In December 1982, Gene and McGowan met once again. By then, MCI had acquired WUI, and the worldwide political implications of that move became clear to McGowan. The company had also become deeply involved in state politics through its dealings with state public utility commissions who oversaw intrastate service. In addition, MCI was becoming embroiled in Congress and the FCC over interconnection access charges, an issue that had taken on the flavor of a national debate. The matter of bypass, which Brian had dealt with on a technical level, was also becoming a political issue, and someone like Gene seemed like the right person to handle it. McGowan offered him a job as head of the regulatory and public policy division.

Before he said okay, Gene reminded McGowan one last time: "I don't have any experience in telecommunications."

McGowan said, "That is the recommendation. Are there any drawbacks?"

With that, Gene joined MCI.

One other new face had joined MCI. He would be the head of marketing and was looked upon as a "heavy hitter." His name was Ed

Carter, and he enjoyed a reputation as someone who could sell to the mass market using all the sizzle and pizzazz that people associate with marketing. Physically, he fit the role. He was big, rather imposing-looking, and hyper. His ego matched his size, and he could be standing still next to you but give the impression that he was still moving.

Carter had a varied background working for Avon for thirteen years, then Warner-Amex and Vicks, and at each place Carter felt like they didn't really understand what he was trying to accomplish. He had trouble getting along with the higher-ups and found himself on the street looking for work quite a lot. Carter knew Brian Thompson while Brian was in the subscription-TV business, and he introduced him to Carl. When the two met in New York, Carter got the impression that Carl would be retiring soon and was looking for a replacement. In the meantime, Carter would put together a marketing department. This was what Carter always wanted—to be the sales head of a high-powered, innovative company like MCI. He had wanted to be a salesman since he was a boy in North Carolina and sold his first newspaper on his route. "Dad," he said, "I love to sell people things." At MCI, Carter was ready for the challenge of his life. He would be selling telephone service in the era of equal access. It would be a whole new world, and Carter would be a part of it. He was ready.

When Carter joined MCI, however, he felt gypped. No, Carl wasn't going to leave any time soon, and Carter felt his talents were being wasted in marketing. Everywhere he turned, he ran into people who he believed didn't know the first thing about marketing. He felt contempt for them. As far as he was concerned, they were a bunch of kids playing a grown-up game.

From then on, Carter was bitter, but through his sheer strength and political savvy he built a marketing staff of 120 people, an empire within a company. He didn't get along with the other senior managers, and they fought continually. He never became a team player. He was an outcast, and for the first time, the happy MCI management family didn't seem so happy.

Mail, International, and new senior officials were costly, and McGowan had added still further drains. In February 1983, MCI had purchased the largest single amount of satellite transponders—twenty-four—in telecommunications history. Transponders are little relay stations in the air that amplify and retransmit messages, and the going rate was around $10 million each. MCI got a good price—about $7 million per transponder, for a total of $168 million—because the cable-TV industry, the largest single user of satellites, had just entered a slump and there was a temporary glut.

Orville, Wayne English, Bert, and Tom Leming were opposed to the deal, mainly because of the great costs, but also because of satellites' poor quality. Telephone calls over satellites sound awful because of the time delay. A signal must travel from earth to the transponder then back to earth, and that takes a fraction of a second. It doesn't sound like much, but telephone callers, especially Americans, like to talk at the same time. You can't do that on satellite.

McGowan, however, wanted the purchase. Aside from being a good deal (they could sell the transponders at a profit later), satellites would be a fast way to bring service to areas of the country that were not served by the existing network. It was to be a temporary measure because all MCI needed in order to service a remote area would be an earth station dish and a connection to the local telephone network.

Tom Leming would also embark on a mission to increase the size of the microwave network, planning to spend more than $1 billion a year for the next two years.

By the end of 1983, MCI had installed a fifteen-mile fiber-optic link between Los Angeles and Dominguez Hills, California, the sight of a WUI international switching center to the Pacific and Asia. Because of MCI's great buying power, Leming was able to bring down the price of fiber to a few cents a foot. He had also begun negotiations with Amtrak and other railroads to bury the fiber cables on their rights-of-way nationwide. Fiber optics are hair-thin tubes of special glass that carry laser beams. Because of their great capacity, one fiber cable can carry ten times more messages than the best microwave network and at a much lower cost. Another advantage is that a fiber cable can handle high-speed computer information that regular cable or microwave cannot.

Because of the increased use of digital information, especially by computers, MCI had begun changing its analog network to digital with the hope of having 85 percent of it digitized by the end of 1985.

It had also begun adding single-sideband radios to its network. SSB is a technique that doubles the number of telephone calls that can take place on any one channel.

McGowan continued to push hard for increased capacity of all kinds, even though it was expensive in terms of both money and the company's public image. Once again, McGowan looked like an obsessed man who couldn't get enough of this magical thing called capacity. He was betting the company once again, wagering that his investment in capacity would pay off, that the billion-dollar-a-year investment would not go down the drain.

He kept on about the information age and changing phone habits. McGowan cited surveys showing that young people didn't write letters anymore; they used the phone. He refused to be swayed by those who said that the United States would one day have a surplus of capacity, a veritable glut brought on by companies building thousands of miles of high-capacity fiber networks. For one thing, McGowan doubted that all those who said they would build would actually build—he knew how expensive it was to get into this business. Second, the coming information age would use all the capacity and still cry out for more. It would be that big.

The two-by-two matrix was beginning to change into something that looked like a dumbbell. On one side was CAPACITY: single-sideband radios, fiber optics, packet networks, digital radios, and satellites. It was connected to the other dumbbell that was labeled MARKET: paging, phones, Telex, international voice, and cellular telephones. In the middle was the MCI logo.

There were those who thought that MCI had overextended itself. Stock analysts began to think that MCI was spending too much on Mail and too much on the network. Some said MCI would never make back its investment. McGowan stuck to his belief that capacity was the only way to win at the telecommunications game. He believed that it was the only way for MCI to compete in the future, especially in the new phase of equal access in which all long-distance companies would be on a level playing field as spelled out in the AT&T divestiture agreement that would take effect January 1, 1984, and continue for the next three years.

Until now, the media and analysts had been good to MCI. Most articles were favorable and even upbeat. Now, however, people began to take a closer look and began to see past McGowan's quick smile and smooth talk. In August 1983, MCI took its worst beating on Wall Street. Late that month, an FCC order sent the stock dropping more than five dollars in just a few hours. It was a setback that spelled the beginning of MCI's fall from grace.

THE EIGHTH BUSINESS—

Equal Access
1983 TO PRESENT

1

MCI's positioning was going to be paid for from the company's revenues and from money raised by selling stocks and bonds in the public markets. In March 1983, the company had raised $400 million by floating convertible debentures. The stock market was healthy and MCI needed more money, so in May, Wayne presented the board of directors with a plan to go to the public markets once again.

The board agreed to Wayne's proposal but decided to wait until the first-quarter earnings were out in July. They knew that if the earnings were strong—and there was every indication that they would be—it would strengthen investor confidence and help sell the new issues.

MCI released figures on its most successful quarter ever: $331 million in revenues, and profits of $92 million, $10 million more than the previous quarter. The Street liked that news—especially the earnings per common share of stock of 48 cents, the highest ever.

Buoyed by its strong balance sheet, the board gave Wayne the authority to file for a public offering of $500 million. Drexel Burnham Lambert, Inc., the underwriter, said they could get a billion dollars, but Wayne didn't think they could. Just in case, though, he asked the board to allow him to go for that extra $500 million if Drexel was correct.

Wayne was hesitant because he thought the offering might be viewed by investors as a little flaky. Each $1,000 note paying 9½ percent annually was attached to eighteen warrants that allowed the buyer to purchase MCI stock at $55 a share anytime within the next five years. (Because the stock was slated to split in August, the warrant holder could buy a share for $27.50.)

The investor who only wanted straight debt could buy a unit and sell off the warrants. The investor who was interested in the stock because he believed the company would continue to grow could buy a unit and sell off the bond. Then there was the investor who wanted to play both sides of the street. He could keep the units intact. In theory, it allowed you to appeal to a broad spectrum of investors all at once. The idea had been brought to Wayne by Drexel, and they were confident it would work. Wayne wasn't convinced, but he was willing to give it a try.

Wednesday morning, MCI filed with the Securities and Exchange Commission for permission to offer $500 million in ten-year notes and warrants. That same day, Wayne began jury duty. At the end of the following day, Wayne telephoned Michael Milken of Drexel and said, "What's your book?" meaning how much interest is there in the offering.

Milken said, "Over two billion."

Wayne couldn't believe the response to the offering—and in so short a time. All he could say was, "You're kidding."

Wayne went to McGowan and told him about the book. He said, "Bill, we're going to go for the big one—a billion dollars—unless you reverse it."

McGowan said, "Fine. Do it."

Friday morning, Wayne got word in the jury waiting room that Drexel had sold a billion dollars' worth of paper. It was the largest public offering of any type, surpassing one two years earlier by AT&T that brought in almost $941 million.

MCI got $986 million from the offering after paying Drexel and other investment bankers about $14 million for their work.

At that time, Wayne felt he had accomplished all his five points. With a billion dollars in the bank, MCI would be in good financial shape for the next several years. No matter what happened to the market, MCI would have all the money it needed to expand its network and keep its unprofitable businesses like Mail, Airsignal, and International humming along.

Wayne didn't realize what good shape the company really was in. Had he waited only twenty more days, MCI probably wouldn't have raised a penny.

The dilemma of equal access continued to confront McGowan. MCI paid about 50 percent less than AT&T for its connections to the local telephone companies because it got inferior connections. MCI customers still had to dial extra digits, and the connections they did get gave poorer voice quality than AT&T's. In one sense, it wasn't a bad deal. MCI attracted a lot of customers who were willing to put up with poorer connections to pay less money. At the same time, MCI paid less than AT&T to the local phone companies for the access, and the money that it saved was enormous. By the end of fiscal year 1983 in March, MCI had paid $172 million for those connections, 16 percent of its revenues and its largest single expense. Interconnection charges came straight out of MCI's pocket, and it seemed sometimes that it might be better off with the lower quality connections and continue to undercut AT&T's rates.

On the other hand, without equal access, McGowan knew that MCI could not attract still larger numbers of customers who didn't want the inconvenience of poorer quality or extra digits.

It was out of his hands anyway. Judge Greene, presiding over the AT&T/Justice Department suit, ruled that once the Bell companies were separate from AT&T, it couldn't discriminate among the long-distance companies. As soon as it was technically feasible, the local companies would have to supply all carriers with the same access.

Equal access would be phased in starting several months after AT&T's divestiture on January 1, 1984, and continue until late 1986, when 80 percent of the nation's telephone companies would be set up to provide equal interconnection.

The FCC would set the fees. It had been struggling with the issue for years, even before divestiture was a real issue. Now, however, it had the added job of figuring out how to keep the local companies financially sound since they wouldn't receive subsidies from AT&T, which had kicked back a portion of its long-distance revenue to the local companies.

It was around this time that the FCC also proposed an "access charge fee" to be paid by consumers to make up for that long-distance subsidy. That not only stirred a national debate on telephone rates but caused a great deal of confusion because the FCC used the phrase "access charges" to refer both to the money paid by the long-distance companies and to that to be paid by consumers. "It was one of the stupidest things I ever did," FCC Chairman Mark Fowler told his staff. "We should have picked another name like 'the-cost-of-the-copper-wires-going-to-your-house fees.'"

Everyone knew that AT&T subsidized local phone service, but nobody knew to what extent.

The BOCs used the subsidy issue to coerce state public utility commissions into granting huge rate increases. Shortly after divestiture was announced, local companies in more than thirty states requested a total of $6.2 billion in rate hikes. It would double phone bills in many areas, and the BOCs were able to blame it all on divestiture. They said they would no longer enjoy their AT&T subsidy and would have to pay for new equipment to meet equal access requirements.

The state regulators believed them—at first—many granting whopping rate hikes in the heat of the moment. Others realized it wasn't true and granted lesser amounts to account for inflation and other factors. Many consumers began to blame MCI and the other long-distance companies for their spiraling rates, saying that if MCI hadn't come along and upset the apple cart, they wouldn't have to make up for "lost" monies by the BOCs. McGowan found himself in the position of calling the BOCs liars and saying that having a local phone company was a license to print money.

As it turned out, he was right. The first year after divestiture, the spun-off BOCs were financially healthy. The rate increases helped, but for the first time they were forced to operate efficiently and lean, just like real companies, and that made the difference. Many got into new businesses under the watchful eye of Judge Greene.

Ameritech, for example, began offering telecommunications consulting services. Bell South and NYNEX got involved in selling office equipment. Pacific Telesis bought some computer stores and formed Pacific Telesis International to launch foreign business in other countries. US West entered the real estate business, offering services for "wired buildings." All of the new companies were moving in the same direction: supplying customers with their total telecommunications needs, equipment, and service, except for long distance.

Investors liked what they were doing. The companies' stocks rose in 1984 for US West's low of 6.4 percent to Pacific Telesis's high of 14.9 percent.

There was also confusion as to how much effect AT&T's retention of the nation's rental phones would have on its revenues and that of the local companies. The question was how much would they charge customers who wanted to buy their rental phones. The FCC grappled with that matter as well.

Stock analysts were just as confused as everyone else as to what all this meant to companies like MCI. Even those who had been studying the industry for years found that it wasn't always easy to sort out the details.

One strong indication of MCI's financial future would be the cost of interconnection charges, and the FCC was watched closely for clues as to how much the carriers would pay.

On August 22, twenty days after MCI's public offering that raised $1 billion, the FCC released an order dealing with the interconnection charge matter. On page 43, it stated: "We further assume, based on estimates submitted to this proceeding, that nonpremium carriers would pay approximately $400–$500 in monthly carrier usage charges under the access charge plan." This was double what MCI, a "nonpremium carrier," was paying.

Tony Abell, who had been Orville's assistant until he became director of investor relations, read the order that night and knew there would be trouble the next day. That morning, he met with Orville, Wayne, Bert Roberts, and McGowan. They had to agree on what to say when the calls came in. They all decided to say that FCC's figures were conjecture and just an example of what *could* happen but not necessarily what *would* happen. They would point to footnote 16, placed right after the sentence, that read: "If this estimate of nonpremium carrier usage charges does not survive our tariff review process we shall adjust the surcharges accordingly."

Wall Street didn't care about footnotes. MCI stock fell from $20 to $15 a share in one day on 16 million shares, a record. As it turned out, MCI would eventually pay $315 per line, but the damage was done.

Abell was on the phone from seven in the morning until seven at night explaining to investors what was happening. The first day he answered sixty-three calls and another day fifty-one. He made about thirty-five one day and spent the following two weeks calling back people who couldn't get through to him. He would always keep the four-inch stack of pink "when you were out" forms to remind himself of how bad things could get.

Every day he would go through the pink memos and sort out the largest shareholders and call them back first. Individual investors didn't get called back for weeks. Institutional investors had glommed onto MCI as a hot stock in the past year and they owned about 40 percent of the shares. Abell had to take care of the bigger clients and not worry about the small, individual investors who owned just a few hundred shares.

McGowan was the largest single shareholder, about 6 million shares, and he was losing a million dollars a day. It never bothered him because he had never sold any stock. To him, the money never existed except on paper. Around this time, McGowan had allowed himself a house on Virginia Beach where he could go for weekends. It was also a place where his large family could meet at least once a year. Although he never sold any shares, he made a point of giving shares to his nieces and nephews to hold for their education. One of them was his twelve-year-old nephew Danny, a precocious youngster who delighted in reading the newspaper each day to see how much he was worth. Danny's parents told him he had fifty shares, even though he had more. If they told him the truth, he probably would have quit school.

They were sitting at the shore and Danny said to McGowan's brother Joe, "Uncle Bill's not worried about the company?"

"No, Danny," said Joe, "he's not."

"Well, how come I'm losing my ass?" piped Danny.

McGowan wasn't worried. He believed that what he was doing was right. Spending money building the network, increasing capacity, would be the only way to make money. And although it caused the company's equity to drop a billion dollars, McGowan still believed that the Over-The-Counter market was the only way to do business.

Unlike the New York Stock Exchange, McGowan viewed the OTC as the only truly competitive way to do trades because it didn't rely on specialists to set prices of stocks. Instead, brokers punched into a computer network all the prices that investors were willing to pay for the stock and all the prices that people were willing to sell the stock for, and the matches were made. To McGowan, it kept the stock fluid and easy to trade. That meant more people would be willing to buy and sell it, the brokers made more money because they got paid by the trade, and MCI was given great visibility. The OTC had a premier section called the National Market System, which included companies like Apple, Intel, and MCI. For a company like MCI, it was being a big fish in a little pond.

The OTC was the future of trading stocks, according to McGowan, because it symbolized the essence of the free market—just like MCI. The OTC hadn't always been prestigious. In the early 1970s, it was called the under-the-counter market because of all the cheap, fly-by-night firms that were traded on it. It wasn't until large companies like MCI and Apple came along that it gained any credibility at all.

McGowan felt so strongly about it that he took an active role and became a member of the Board of Governors of the National Association of Securities Dealers, the NASD, in January 1983. The NASD oversees the OTC market.

For MCI, the OTC was too efficient, however. On the New York Exchange, specialists might be able to stem the downward move of a stock, especially if it was found out that hysteria was based on investors not reading the fine print. On the OTC, however, the free market took control and Danny was losing his ass.

What happened to the stock had a profound effect on morale at MCI. For the first time since Execunet, MCI was no longer the darling of Wall Street analysts, investors, or the public. It appeared to be a scam that had gone sour. Even the employees, most of whom had joined several years earlier during the up, up, up period, began to see their shares go down, down, down, and with it the chance to make a million dollars like the old-timers who worked around them.

The situation got worse. Sprint had just been bought by GTE, a telecommunications conglomerate that had vowed to spend a billion dollars or more to expand its long-distance network. MCI and Sprint had been neck and neck for the past few years, coming to within five percentage points of each other in revenue only four years earlier. Sprint, however, couldn't sustain its growth because the Southern

Pacific Railroad couldn't afford to invest in Sprint the large sums of money the company needed. As a result, MCI's network grew and was able to build capacity and take on more and more customers. Sprint ran out of capacity many times, having to halt their expansion.

Gus Grant, president of Sprint, had beaten McGowan and MCI on many different turns. Sprint built the first coast-to-coast long-distance link, had the first credit card service, and even offered its customers a network that could end your call anywhere. It did that by leasing excess capacity from AT&T, and although it was expensive, it helped gain new customers because they could call anywhere in the United States. MCI insitituted its own version called "Omnicall" months after Sprint.

If GTE had pockets as deep as it thought, Sprint would be a real threat to MCI. McGowan used to make jokes about Sprint, calling it Splint. Now the joke was over.

And then there was AT&T, which would divest itself of its local phone companies in a few months. AT&T offices had signs saying "One-One-Eighty-Four," the day it would begin its new life. The employees were getting psyched. McGowan knew that there would be confusion at AT&T after the January 1 divestiture, but that wouldn't last forever. Eventually, the behemoth would be tamed, and it could devote much more of its attention to the long-distance business.

There were still more competitors. The FCC ruled that all long-distance companies must sell their excess capacity to others. MCI bought it from AT&T, and some companies bought it from MCI and Sprint. Although McGowan believed that the "resellers" would eventually disappear because they didn't control their own network and thus their own costs, they were able to take a chunk out of the carriers that owned networks by buying excess capacity at bulk rates—like WATS lines—and selling it to the customer at lower rates than the company they bought it from could.

More than 350 resellers sprang up almost overnight. One of the most aggressive was Allnet, a Chicago company begun by an ex-MCI salesman named Mike Richer.

Mike Richer was an MCI district sales manager in Chicago from 1975 to 1978. He left the company during the time when the courts forbade MCI from adding any more customers to their Execunet service, and Richer got bored. After a period of intense selling, he was reduced to calling current customers only. He couldn't solicit any new business.

Around this time, he got an offer from Livingston Communications, Inc., to be vice-president of marketing. The company was the largest distributor of Northern Telecom PBXs. At Livingston, Richer resurrected an old friendship with Mel Goodman, one of the company's founders. They had known each other when Richer was a branch manager for Litton, the company that tried to go head-to-head with AT&T in the telephone switching business in the early seventies but failed, partly because of AT&T's illegal actions. Much of the Litton case came out during the AT&T/Justice Department trial, but Litton had filed its own suit and won an award for $276 million eight years later. Goodman served as Litton's general counsel and helped liquidate its remaining inventory.

Richer and Goodman saw that the laws were beginning to change. The FCC had decided that it was okay for someone to lease lines from MCI and Sprint and resell them to others. Soon after, they would apply the same rules to AT&T lines as well.

Richer took his ten-year-old son and traveled for six weeks around

the West in a camper. All the time, the idea for taking advantage of the
new regulations was brewing in his mind. After the trip, he spent
another month fine-tuning his plan, and in March 1981, he and
Goodman founded a company called Combined Network, Inc. The
name came from the combined networks of MCI and Sprint. Not only
could they offer small customers a price below MCI and Sprint, but
they could also give greater range. MCI didn't go everywhere and
neither did Sprint, but by combining the two, Richer's company could
go many more places than either of the companies. MCI had mid-
western cities that Sprint didn't, and Sprint had a lot of West Coast and
East Coast cities that MCI didn't.

MCI didn't make it easy for Combined Network. They promised
lines, then didn't deliver. They missed deadlines on purpose. MCI
wanted to keep its own private lines instead of selling them to resellers
because it was less trouble, and they made more money. It was a
business MCI didn't want to be in but was forced to by the FCC.
Consequently, MCI put people in those jobs who didn't know the
business and could not do the best job possible. What did MCI care?
Richer couldn't take MCI to court because their foot dragging wasn't
blatant, and it would be impossible to prove that they were flagrantly
violating FCC rules.

In essence, MCI was doing to Richer what AT&T had done to
them. While never coming out and saying no, it dragged things out to
the point where it became impossible for Richer to be in business.
Legally, MCI could claim that it didn't have the capacity, and it would
be impossible to prove otherwise. Although MCI had given Richer
some of the lines he wanted, they were of the metered line variety and
not the private line variety that he wanted. The costs of metered lines
were expensive compared to private lines.

The whole matter became moot after a few more months anyway
because now Richer could get all the lines he wanted from AT&T. It
had a lot more capacity than MCI and was more willing to do
business.

Combined Network took off. They could offer prices about 20
percent lower than MCI or Sprint because they were buying lines in
bulk and selling them well below the price of direct-dial service.
Richer also came up with another big advantage over the others: six-
second billing increments. A caller on MCI or Sprint paid his bill
based on one-minute increments. If a call lasted one minute and thirty
seconds, he would pay for two full minutes. On Combined Network,

he would pay for exactly one minute and thirty seconds. It was a strong marketing tool and worked great in ads. Later, after Combined Network changed its name to Allnet, its TV ads showed a man hanging up a phone and money continuing to fly out of it. Psychologically, it worked. Consumers hated paying for something they didn't buy, and more important, many of them didn't know that MCI and Sprint billed by the minute and that made them angry.

Allnet continued to grow, and it went public in April 1983. By the end of its fiscal year in September 1983, revenues reached $143 million compared with $34 million for the year before. It had a profit of $5 million compared with $822,000 the year before. It had more than 130,000 customers, and they could originate calls in more than 35 cities.

McGowan said publicly that resellers like Allnet couldn't last. If they didn't own their own facilities, they couldn't control their costs, and as prices for leased lines and interconnection charges rose, they would be forced out of business.

That might be true, but in the meantime companies like Allnet were taking customers away from MCI, and they were making money at it. The reselling business became so lucrative that companies sprang up all over the country to serve certain cities or just the state they were in.

It seemed that every week dozens of these companies got started, many of them on a shoestring, and they all made money—at first.

With the divestiture of AT&T on January 1, 1984, came the realization that the fever couldn't continue. The divestiture would eventually bring it all to an end and no one would be immune—not Allnet, not Sprint, and not MCI.

Although the figures wouldn't come out for a few months, MCI's quarter ending September 30 would be the first time since Execunet that it didn't increase its profit. Revenues increased to $396 million for the three-month period, but income dropped $3 million, to $51 million. Earnings per share dropped, too.

It was just the beginning. It wasn't just a fluke quarter. In the year that would end March 31, 1984, net income would drop to $155 million, a $15 million decrease from the year before. And the drop by quarter would continue as well.

McGowan wasn't worried. He knew that MCI would pull through. It was just a matter of time before it would attract more customers because of equal access. And, as the network grew, the company would rely less and less on At&T leased lines to terminate calls to areas where MCI's network didn't reach.

Orville was concerned but didn't see it as anything but a temporary situation. He thought of MCI as going through a dark tunnel for about two years. Then it would enter light once again.

Their confidence, however, didn't spread to everyone. The losses had a profound effect on MCI. It led to a company-wide depression. No longer was it the cocky upstart that could do anything it set its mind to. No longer was it growing like mad, doubling its revenues every year and splitting its stock on cue. MCI was a mature company, but many employees weren't willing to accept it.

Nowhere would the depression be felt more than with Bert Roberts, who began to withdraw more and more from others. Unlike McGowan and Orville, who kept their doors open and always answered their own phones, Bert had his secretary run interference for him. He often kept his door closed, and junior officials in the company had to get appointments to talk with him. He kept away from the media.

He would blow up at meetings and walk out in a huff. Instead of mellowing him, McGowan and Orville saw Bert become even more curt with people and more difficult to deal with. One reason was that he wanted to drastically change the company's basic structure. McGowan and Orville wanted it, too, but it wasn't the right time yet.

Bert wanted it now.

New Year's Day, divestiture day, was anticlimactic. Nothing extraordinary happened. Telephone service continued as usual, and America spent the day watching football on TV. At MCI, Ed Carter was formulating his marketing plans for equal access. McGowan knew it would be a one-shot deal. As far as he could see, the entire $40 billion long-distance business was up for grabs. Whoever could sign up the most customers when equal access came to their cities would keep them. Without equal access, MCI would continue to hold 3 to 4 percent of the market share, but with equal access he thought MCI might be able to get more than 20 percent.

MCI had always been perceived as a strong marketing company. Whether they were or weren't didn't really matter. They gave that impression, and that's what counted.

AT&T, on the other hand, wasn't looked at as a company with good marketing skills. It never had them at all because it never had to market its products or services. It relied on its monopoly status and consumer identification of the company name. Judge Greene had decided that the Bell logo would stay with the local phone companies, despite AT&T claims that it would hurt them not to have it. As it turned out, just the name AT&T was enough. Coupled with a new logo showing a blue globe with white lines, AT&T was off and running.

The equal access rules were stacked in AT&T's favor. Judge Greene had given the BOCs three choices to handle customers who didn't choose a long-distance company: (1) The local companies could send a tape-recorded message each time a long-distance call came in telling the customer that he didn't have a long-distance service anymore; (2) local companies could distribute unassigned long-distance calls to all the long-distance companies in that area on a prorated basis; or (3) local companies could send all default traffic to AT&T. All the BOCs chose the last option. It was easy, cheap, and caused the least disruption to customers. Even though the local companies and AT&T were separate, in the minds of consumers they were still the same, and the local companies didn't need the hassle.

AT&T ads played on this advantage. Andy Griffith got on TV and told people that they didn't have to do anything if they didn't want to. He was only talking about phones; consumers could continue to lease them instead of buy them. The inference was there, however, that in general, people didn't have to do anything about long-distance service either.

AT&T's ads stressed quality over price. The strongest slogan was: "Everyone says they're cheaper, but no one says they're better." It had great appeal.

Tom Messner, from the advertising firm of Ally & Gargano, continued with the MCI account. The ad showing the running money meter was still the mainstay of the campaign, but he had come up with newer approaches.

One of his most successful creations was a spoof of one of AT&T's most successful commercials, titled "Joey Called." In the AT&T ad, an elderly black couple is sitting at the kitchen table and the woman is sobbing into a handkerchief. When the husband asks why, she says, "Joey called." The father is worried about Joey and asks if he is all right. She says, "Yes, he just called to say he loved me." It was rated one of the top ten commercials of the year. It had everything: a message, warmth, poignancy.

Messner's ad, titled "Parents," used similar-looking actors and exactly duplicated the set, the camera angles, and the lighting. The woman is sobbing and the husband asks, "Have you been talking to our son long distance again?" The woman nods her head and continues crying.

Man: "Did he tell you how much he loved you?" The woman nods her head again.

"Did he tell you how well he's doing in school?" She continues crying.

"All those things are wonderful. What on earth are you crying for?"

With that, the woman says, "Have you seen our long-distance bill?"

The announcer then says, "If your long-distance bills are too much, call MCI. Sure, reach out and touch someone. Just do it for up to 30, 40, even 50 percent less."

The ad broke every rule of direct-response advertising. It didn't put the product up front first, and it spent time on negatives. It worked, however, because it spoofed one of AT&T's most successful ads, which also happened to be one of the corniest ads on TV. The public also liked the way it made fun of AT&T's "Reach out and touch someone" slogan.

Now with divestiture, Messner wanted something new, something stronger than he had ever done. He thought about a debate between McGowan and AT&T Chairman Charles Brown. The advertising would begin in January with McGowan going on TV and publicly challenging Brown to a TV debate, with MCI paying for a half hour of TV time. The second ad would be one that talked about Brown accepting the challenge and what would happen next or talk about Brown not accepting the challenge and what that meant. The third leg, if Brown accepted, would be the debate itself.

McGowan liked the idea, pending approval by the company's lawyers. They advised him not to do it. They said it would lead to legal problems. So, with equal access coming up, Messner needed something else. For the past year or so, he had kicked around the idea of a celebrity endorsement. MCI was now large enough to pay for a star and also had enough credibility that a celebrity wouldn't be afraid of putting his name next to it. He had been talking about it for a year, and now was the time to do it.

Messner picked his prototypes, the type of celebrity he would like to get. They included Charleton Heston, Marlo Thomas, Willie Nelson, Merv Griffin, and Wilt Chamberlain. Messner wanted people who were recognizable, hadn't done any other commercials, and were MCI customers. That would allow them to say something like: "Most companies give you their product to use and then pay you to say how much you liked it. With MCI it was the opposite. I began using it on my own and now they're paying me to tell you how I like it. It's great." Messner had reports from the field sales offices that these people were customers. Some of the reports turned out to be bogus. In other cases, the stars wanted too much money. Little by little, the list narrowed.

The first celebrity signed up was Merv Griffin. His company was an MCI customer. He did a series of low-key commercials. In one of them, he told how he had heard about MCI but didn't sign up right away. He continued to use AT&T. "Then I remembered a piece of advice my grandmother gave me years ago. 'Mervin,' she said, 'don't be a jerk.'" The Merv series didn't do all that well. Messner believed it was because Sprint put on a lot of its commercials at the same time and diluted Merv's impact.

Ed Carter didn't think that was the problem. He said the ad was terrible, that Merv wasn't right for the part, and he blamed Messner. That was the beginning of a feud between the two that led to Messner leaving the account that he had nurtured from the beginning. Messner couldn't handle what he saw as Carter's massive ego and his belief that he could run things better than Messner and everyone else.

A series with Burt Lancaster was much more successful. It too was low-key and serious with Lancaster explaining that AT&T was more expensive than MCI, so why use AT&T? "After all, a phone call's a phone call," he said.

Another showed Lancaster in his kitchen, and while he pours coffee he says, "Are you still using AT&T instead of MCI for long distance? Well, I hope you're happy because by not using MCI's more modern, up-to-date system, all you're doing is taking money out of your pocket and handing it over to AT&T." As he picks up the coffee, he says, "Not that they don't appreciate it. They do. In fact, every month they send you a thank-you note. It's called a bill."

MCI paid Lancaster about $750,000 to do ten commercials, and it paid off. Lancaster had just the credibility that worked.

Lancaster was followed by Joan Rivers, who was signed for eight commercials. They were the opposite of Lancaster's ads. They were funny and irreverent. It was Rivers at her wackiest and most self-effacing. She made fun of AT&T's operators, who were now under orders to be extra nice to callers and also to say, "Thank you for using AT&T." Rivers said, "Have you noticed how friendly AT&T has been lately? Sure, now that you have a choice of long-distance companies," and then in her squeaky voice she mimicked an operator: "'Hello, thank you for calling and have a nice day' . . . and why? Grow up! It's not because they love you. It's because they're afraid you're going to call MCI." Then she went on to an unflattering interpretation of a phone operator.

In another ad, she used the line made famous in her nightclub acts: "Can we talk?" After explaining about MCI, she says, "There's still a few of you out there who aren't using MCI. Look, you can do what you want but don't call me and complain about your phone bill. Call MCI. They can do something about it." Then at the top of her lungs: "I have done all I can!"

Using Rivers was a risk because her loud voice and off-color jokes irritated a lot of people. It turned out, however, that she didn't turn off the audience at all. Even people in traditionally conservative parts of the country liked her. And subbing for Johnny Carson on *The Tonight Show* gave her high recognition factor.

MCI was forced to take the operator ads off after the CWA, which represented the operators, took offense at the commercials. The operators dared Rivers to try one shift just to see how hard the job really was. For months, they picketed *The Tonight Show* when she was there and also her nightclub engagements. For months, she resisted but finally agreed to take them up on the offer.

MCI couldn't run ads just about equal access because only a few cities at a time would be getting it. In fact, only parts of certain cities would get it at the same time. This made national ads about equal access impossible to do. MCI had to market equal access in a very narrow way. When the Bell Operating Companies listed the first city to be changed over to equal access, it turned out to be Charleston, West Virginia, but nobody knew exactly why.

It would be here that the first head-to-head battle would take place among the long-distance companies.

MCI didn't know anything about Charleston, West Virginia, except that it was the state capital. As he headed down to Charleston on a reconnaissance mission for the company, Don Campbell, who worked for Howard Crane in PR, thought about why Charleston was chosen. He had called Chesapeake & Potomac Telephone Company for an answer, because it was their equal access equipment that would be used, but he didn't get an adequate answer. The only thing he could figure was that some arcane schedule on switching modernization just happened to be set on Charleston when the equal access rule came around. As a result, Charleston switches were the first ready for action.

From a marketing point of view, Charleston was a good pick. It was a medium-sized city, about 80,000, that didn't sprawl. That made it easy to identify your potential customers. It was fairly isolated, situated between mountains, which meant its media were self-contained, and the long-distance fighters could not only focus their advertising but measure its impact with precision. Charleston was the perfect test market.

On his first trip to Charleston, Campbell appeared on a public-TV discussion show about the changing world of telephones brought about by AT&T's divestiture. He drove outside of Charleston to the studios, which were located in the town of Nitro, named for its main product, nitroglycerin. He found himself on a panel with the West Virginia PR man from AT&T, a representative from C&P, and a member of the state's Public Service Commission.

During the hour-long show, the C&P representative answered about 95 percent of the questions because they were local in nature. "How much will my phone bill be raised? What happens if I don't pick a long-distance company? Do I have to buy my own phone?" Campbell fielded only one question, and it was a sophisticated one. He believed it was a plant, but he didn't know from whom.

In the following months, Campbell found himself spending more time than he wanted to in Charleston. Being a big-city boy, he didn't like Charleston with its one decaying main street and new downtown mall that housed the stores from the one decaying main street. In the evenings, he found himself eating in a near-empty Marriott dining room, going to the bar for a drink, and listening to the waitresses tell him that it wasn't always this slow: "You should see this place on a Friday night!" After that, he would go back to his hotel room and watch cable TV.

The people in Charleston couldn't believe all the attention they were getting. As the July 15 date for equal access got closer, news crews from all the networks roamed the streets doing interviews with people and getting their views on being the first to get this great thing called equal access. Even newspaper reporters were amazed to see "Charleston" on the dateline of wire stories that didn't have anything to do with something that the state lawmakers did that day. It was also the first time these reporters had been wooed by so many PR flaks. They actually got calls from big companies that were willing to spend time explaining what this all meant. They found themselves enveloped in something big. Campbell made certain that he introduced himself to all the media in Charleston and let them know that he was available twenty-four hours a day for them to ask questions, even though he would be home in Washington most of the time.

When Campbell tried to hire a local PR company, he found that the only one in Charleston was already on retainer with AT&T. So he hired two women who had just started their own company. They had few clients and they were small ones, but they were local and spoke the language. Dan Wallace from MCI's Pittsburgh office came into town and hired seven salespeople and one clerical person.

Campbell wanted MCI to shoot the opening salvo at the battle of Charleston. He didn't hear anything from Sprint, but he was afraid that AT&T might do it first. He scheduled a press conference for April

12. Campbell and Tobin agreed that having the chairman of MCI might impress the folks in Charleston. Certainly, the chairman of AT&T would never come to such an event. Although he wasn't certain if it would be lost on the media or not, two of McGowan's senior vice-presidents would be there, too: Ed Carter in marketing and Charlie Skibo, head of network operations. It was a standard MCI PR ploy: Show the people you're talking to just how important they are to you. Tobin knew how tired reporters were of talking to flaks who were sent to press conferences, so he always got McGowan or someone at the top to come and speak.

On the morning of April 12, McGowan boarded the company plane at Dulles Airport outside of Washington. A year before, when MCI was still on a roll, it had bought a Falcon-50 jet that once belonged to a Middle Eastern sheikh who had fallen on hard times. He left his mark on the plane, though. On the back wall, a map of the world had the Middle East as the center. On maps printed in the United States, the Western Hemisphere is in the center and Asia is split at one end and continued at the other end.

MCI officials spent half their lives on planes, but the Falcon wasn't a cost-cutting measure; it was one of convenience. It would allow them to reach more places in less time. Orville was put in charge of who could use the plane, but despite his vigilance, it was used frivolously by some senior members who liked the status of flying on a company jet. McGowan used it quite a bit, but also flew commercial jets if it worked out that way.

On the plane, McGowan thumbed through background material on Charleston prepared by Tobin and Campbell. He learned that 34,000 phone users in Charleston would get equal access in July, and that was roughly 40 percent of the total number of phones in the city. He also discovered that the entire town was only worth $10.5 million in long-distance revenues.

He knew that Charleston would be important because it would teach MCI about equal access marketing, but he didn't go overboard. "It's only Charleston," he said as the plane landed. "I don't have that tingly feeling."

The TV lights were set, the print reporters were seated, and the press conference began. McGowan put on his usual "just another guy" self as he explained what MCI was doing in Charleston and what equal access was all about. He called Charleston the "New Hampshire primary of the equal access campaign," a slogan that Tobin dreamed up. It was catchy, and many reporters used that quote in their stories.

He explained that some of Charleston's residents and businesses would only have to dial one digit, then their long-distance number for service with any carrier of their choice. They could use a push-button or rotary phone. He talked about how this was all brought about by divestiture and explained the benefits.

McGowan introduced Carter, who detailed MCI's strategy. Carter was his usual self, too. He was forceful, hard driving, and sweated profusely as he explained that MCI had decided to do away with its monthly fees, which ranged from five to ten dollars. It had not been an easy decision.

At a meeting only two days before, Carter and Bert Roberts had insisted that MCI's monthly fees were driving away new customers. MCI had been losing customers since January, when Sprint abolished its monthly fee. "We've been passive and stuffy about making changes," Carter said, "and we've lost momentum." McGowan sat and listened to the pitch. Unlike most meetings he attended, he put down his reading material and listened closely. Usually, McGowan found meetings boring and sat and listened with only half an ear. He often read industry newsletters and rarely stayed at meetings more than two hours. If they lasted longer, he believed people were just posturing and not really saying anything that was well focused.

This time they were talking about real money. If the monthly fee was lifted for MCI's more than 1 million customers, it would cost the company about $70 million a year. At the end, McGowan reluctantly agreed to drop the fees but said, "Just be sure to look at ways to diminish the hit we're going to take." It was his way of saying, "I gave you the responsibility and the authority, now don't screw up."

Along with the dropping of fees, Bert Roberts and Carter wanted MCI to begin volume discounts. Sprint's customers received a discount on their total bill if it exceeded $25 dollars, then another discount if it was over $75 dollars, and so on. It was a good marketing tool, especially because Sprint would add the customer's entire bill, then subtract some money at the bottom. Bert and Carter were convinced it was correct to sacrifice profit for market share, and McGowan went along on the volume discounts, too.

Carter announced that MCI was sending ballots to all those who were in equal access exchanges. About 35,000 letters were sent. The ballots explained equal access and asked people to sign an agreement that MCI would now be their "dial-1" carrier. If the cards were returned by May 31, the caller would get sixty free minutes.

The balloting issue was critical to MCI's equal access campaign. Although the local phone companies were bound by law to let their customers know three months in advance of equal access that they had to choose, Carter knew that callers would still view them as part of AT&T and would not leave AT&T. He was fighting the strongest market force ever—inertia—and the requests for decision by the local phone companies were weighted in favor of AT&T.

Charlie Skibo went on next. He explained what MCI's network was all about and how they were able to offer savings of up to 40 percent below AT&T. He showed slides and graphs showing where MCI's network reached and how it was connected to the local telephone systems. He was forceful but just a bit nervous.

Campbell got word that Bell Atlantic, the parent company of C&P of West Virginia, had hastily called a press conference. Bell Atlantic hadn't planned one, but now that the media were in Charleston, they didn't want to waste the opportunity.

At the press conference, C&P officials played it straight and matter-of-factly. They showed a list of the eight long-distance companies that were authorized to handle traffic out of Charleston. AT&T was first, but Tom Burns, C&P vice-president, was quick to point out that the companies got their positions chosen by lot and AT&T just happened to come out first. Even though it was true, it didn't look right and everyone was skeptical.

Burns explained their side of the equal access issue. He described what they were obligated to provide to the carriers and the public. Like other Bell Operating Company officials, he wasn't sure of what was going on. This was the first time they were on their own, away from Ma Bell, and they weren't sure of themselves. He insisted that C&P would fulfill all of its obligations. "If we don't," he added, "the carriers will not be bashful in telling us."

6

AT&T was ready for the fight. It continued its massive TV commercial campaign featuring Cliff Robertson, who told consumers that unlike its rivals, AT&T was the only company that served small-town America with its own lines and with operator service. He would look into the camera and say, "What would long-distance service be without person-to-person calls?"

Robertson was the perfect spokesman. He carried himself in a distinguished manner, and although he was a star, he was never associated with the glitter of Hollywood. In the late 1970s, Robertson helped expose a check-forging scheme by Columbia Pictures President David Begelman. It added to his public image of an honest man, even though he paid a big price. He didn't work in Hollywood for four years.

His ads emphasized AT&T's history of high quality rather than price. Robertson did, however, mention price in one commercial where he chided AT&T's competitors for saying they were just as good as AT&T. "You get what you pay for," he said. It was the first time that AT&T's commercials hinted at competition. It was also a move away from the warm and cuddly "Reach out and touch someone" campaign of past years that had been so successful.

AT&T turned out to be better marketers than MCI expected. Orville was most surprised at how fast they had turned from a service company that didn't have to market to one that could. In May, while the

Charleston sign-up period was still in effect, AT&T filed with the FCC for permission to start a campaign called "Reach Out America," which would reduce its rates by about 6 percent. The plan would allow callers one hour of night and weekend calls anywhere in the United States for $10.00. Additional hours would cost $8.75. AT&T had already put the plan in place in about eight states for intrastate calling, and it was a hit.

The FCC ordered the 6 percent cut because AT&T no longer had to subsidize the local phone companies. It was the first time in fourteen years that the FCC had ordered such a cut. It was AT&T's idea to cut its rates 6 percent by using the Reach Out America Campaign. Not only did they satisfy the FCC but it became a marketing gimmick. MCI, of course, tried to prevent Reach Out America, saying that it was predatory pricing because it was priced below costs. Their argument was unsubstantiated, and the FCC granted AT&T's request.

In direct response to AT&T's move, MCI dropped its fees in July by about 6 percent. All the other competitors followed. Allnet adjusted its fees and so did Sprint, ITT, SBS, and the others. Market share became the Holy Grail, and companies were willing to do anything to get it.

The madness didn't end with long distance. AT&T had just received permission to charge fifty cents per call for operator information (after two free calls a month), so MCI cut a deal with the local telephone companies that handle the calls to do the same for them. But MCI would charge forty-five cents, five cents less than AT&T. The Bell companies charged twenty-five cents for the service to everyone, but McGowan was willing to take less profit just to undercut AT&T by 10 percent. Subtracting the cost of the long-distance call and some equipment that MCI had to install to handle the information requests, its profit on each call was only a few cents. The other long-distance companies followed MCI's lead on operator assistance also.

A flurry of marketing campaigns never before seen in long distance began. Sunday newspaper inserts gave those with scissors one hour of MCI telephone time if they bought Cheer. In all, MCI and Procter & Gamble printed 30 million coupons promoting MCI service along with P&G products. Sprint offered five dollars' worth of calls if you bought a box of Shredded Wheat. (Sprint discovered that the demographics of their customers matched the demographics of Shredded Wheat eaters.) AT&T had already begun working a deal with General Electric that gave purchasers of small appliances a certificate entitling them to seven dollars' worth of calls.

Allnet began giving customers five dollars if they changed from another carrier to them. They called the plan "Second Thoughts," and the five dollars covered the fee that the local phone companies charged customers for changing their primary equal access carrier after the initial sign-up.

AT&T began "Opportunity Calling," which gave callers who spent more than fifteen dollars a month dollar-for-dollar savings when they bought products shown in a special catalog. The customer could first buy the products at any store and then get a rebate, or the customer would get money certificates first and then buy the product. Opportunity Calling was not successful. It was too complicated; the customer had to do too much. Moreover, AT&T had to keep track of billing and how many credits people had and that was expensive.

TV, newspaper, and magazine ads continued to bombard customers as MCI spent its $60 million budget, which was up 50 percent from the year before. AT&T spent about $200 million. In Charleston, MCI spent $500,000 alone.

All this sideshow activity, however, didn't work out as expected. In some cases, it drove customers away. Consumers, who were confused to begin with, became even more confused. Many of them were so bewildered that they did nothing and got AT&T service by default. Charleston customers were getting a double dose and were getting annoyed at being called all the time by salespeople and tired of emptying their mailboxes crammed full of offers and coupons. Many of them stayed with AT&T because it was the only way they could show their displeasure with all the craziness around them.

Everyone knew it couldn't last forever. It was only a matter of time before companies would pay the price for all the advertising and giveaways. More important, interconnection charges for equal access lines were $750, more than twice the $315 price companies paid for the older, unequal connections.

By the middle of the year, analysts were saying that a shake-out in the long-distance business was imminent. Companies were beginning to show signs of financial failure. MCI stock was still falling. It was now hovering around $7 a share with no signs of stopping. Even AT&T's earnings were suffering, and Chairman Brown told shareholders that it might not be able to deliver a dividend. Some smaller companies had already folded. Others merged with their enemies in order to stay alive. SBS laid off 14 percent of its workers.

Bert Roberts kept even more to himself, and others at the company were becoming defensive as well.

MCI managers had always prided themselves on controlling their costs. Now it appeared they had lost control. They were riding a treadmill that wouldn't slow down.

McGowan continued to keep his cool, but there was something that scared him more than any short-term financial losses.

A strike against MCI by employees at Western Union International was reaching a boiling point. With the media's attention focused on Charleston, the union was preparing to square off with MCI in that city and show them on national TV as the most vicious union-busting company of all time.

When MCI bought WUI, Nate Kantor inherited union problems. MCI had prided itself on not having unions, but now they were forced to deal with the matter. McGowan had made it clear that unions were obstructionists, and they had no place in a company like MCI. He blamed the Communications Workers of America for much of AT&T's slowness and resistance to quick change, and he didn't want that to happen to MCI. It all stemmed from his childhood when he worked for the railroad. His father, an engineer, was a union representative for about a year, and to young McGowan unions added nothing to the business. Unions forced wasteful rules on the railroad and kept them from cleaning house of unproductive workers. He thought unions had a place in industries that were blatantly unhealthy or unsafe—like steel mills or coal mines—but they didn't belong in other companies.

When Nate Kantor took over Western Union International, he brought his management style with him. He was a tough manager who ran his division by the numbers. It was a holdover from his Army training. Of all the MCI senior officials, Nate always developed the best business budgets and came in closer than the others. Precision was his goal, and he knew how to cut costs to the bone. He could be ruthless when necessary.

The first month that Nate took over, August 1982, WUI lost money.

The only thing to do was cut costs, and that meant cutting people. As far as Nate was concerned, it was the only way. The company was fat with people. WUI had 1,556 people, and about 600 belonged to Teamsters local 111. In September and October, Nate fired 30 managers and about 70 union workers. That immediately saved the company $50,000 a month.

While that was taking place, Nate divided the company into two parts under the new name of MCI International. One side was called MCI International Telecommunications and concerned itself with international voice traffic. The other side kept its old name of Western Union International and was the Telex part of the company. It was also the unionized section.

In April, MCIT moved to Rye Brook, New York, in Westchester County, and left WUI in lower Manhattan. It was becoming clear to union president Daniel Kane that MCI was going to kill them off by a standard warfare technique of divide and conquer. Or, at the very least, cut them off and let them die by themselves.

When the union began making noise about the layoffs, Nate was too far away to handle the job, so he named Ron Spears senior vice-president in charge of WUI operations. In essence, he gave Ron a company.

Ron Spears, like Nate, was a West Point graduate. He spent twelve years in the Army artillery. He left the military because he couldn't advance in the ranks as fast as he wanted. He left and joined AT&T's long-lines division, the long-distance company, in 1977. AT&T had a management problem at the time. They had a group at their fourth and fifth levels of management (AT&T had about fourteen levels) who were ready to retire and had no one to replace them except younger junior executives who were still green. So they hired a bunch of men, thirty to thirty-two years old, who would stay a few years and then move up to fill the void. Ron was one of them. After a year, however, AT&T wanted to lump the younger managers and the Army grads together, which meant that they wouldn't be making the money they thought they would make, and some of them resented what they saw as a lowering of their status. Ron was one of them, and he was angry.

He saw an ad in the *Washington Post* calling for someone with experience building computer models of network needs. In other words, someone who could figure out what switches were needed where, how many, and what type. If a company couldn't forecast where its resources were going, it would waste money and have an inefficient network. MCI had placed the ad. Ron called the company and asked for whoever was in charge of the network. He knew that you didn't go through the personnel office; you went straight to the person placing the ad. Ron had been doing that exact work at AT&T, and he was hired.

He began working in the department headed by Bert Roberts, who was then senior vice-president of operations. He and Bert had similar natures. They were aggressive, abrupt, quick to boil over and show their anger. Ron was impressed with Bert's brilliance and how he could cut through the bullshit and get right to the heart of any problem. He envied Bert's ability to see clearly and fix a bad situation, even if it meant doing something painful or unpleasant. He learned a lot from Bert.

He also learned a lot from Nate, who worked for Bert at the time. Nate took Ron under his wing and watched out for him. He would counsel Ron, often telling him to settle down, not be so competitive and abrasive. Being among people who were much older, Ron felt he had to prove himself all the time to make sure the higher-ups were noticing him. Nate would tell him, "Just do your job, and the rest will be obvious."

As director of network engineering, Ron proceeded to restructure the network. He was surprised when McGowan would call him on the phone wanting to know about the technicalities of the network. He didn't think that chairmen knew, or even cared about, such matters, but he learned that McGowan was different. He wanted to know everything. In fact, Ron had trouble doing his job because McGowan kept wanting to know what was going on. It wasn't until McGowan was busy in 1980 with the AT&T antitrust trial that Ron was able to finish restructuring the network the way he wanted to, including bigger switches and different routing of calls.

As soon as Ron took over WUI in July, he ordered another layoff, about seventy-five people. The contract was up in less than a year, and Ron's strategy was to keep constant pressure on the union up to the deadline. There was another layoff in October, about twenty-five people, and then there were small layoffs every 90 to 120 days. Ron kept the pressure on. He was sending a message to the union that when contract time came around, MCI would do what it had to do to get things cleared up. The contract hadn't been touched in thirty-five years.

In January, Ron briefed McGowan and the other senior managers.

He went through his proposal article by article and told McGowan, "If I get everything I want, *everything*, then I will give them the pension." Pensions were always a sore point with McGowan, and he didn't want to give in, but he said, "Ron, do what makes the most sense." No one interfered with Ron. Nobody told him how to conduct the negotiations or what to do, not Bert, not Orville, not McGowan. They gave him a free hand.

In February, Ron gave Kane a proposed contract. Every article had been changed. MCI wanted to reduce pay and pension benefits and slash job security clauses. Job security was the sticking point. Both sides wanted it their way.

MCI's offer was typical. Compared to most companies, MCI paid poorly. McGowan didn't believe in paying high wages, and that extended to executives as well, who were paid well below their colleagues at comparable firms.

Kane knew MCI had the upper hand. Starting with 600 union members when MCI bought the company, he now was representing only 400. After eight weeks of negotiating, Ron had cut that number to 320. Ron made it clear that he didn't want a strike, but Kane wouldn't give in and neither would Ron.

On April 2, Kane called a strike.

It was a violent one. About fifty-five workers continued to work. Some of their homes were vandalized, and they were assaulted on their way to work. Car tires were slashed and windshields were broken. Spears was prepared to hang tough. He would replace all the strikers if necessary, and they wouldn't be taken back. He had already hired forty scabs.

Kane had organized many of West Virginia's unions to picket MCI's offices in Charleston. With the media's attention focused on that city because of equal access, Kane was assured of coverage. He would also embarrass MCI and expose their union-busting tactics. He had also gotten agreements from the United Mine Workers, the West Virginia Education Association, the state AFL-CIO, and the Communications Workers of America to back a boycott of MCI in that state by discouraging customers from signing up.

A rally in Charleston was set, and McGowan was worried. The company's public image could not stand what was going to happen. Both sides were still talking and in fact were getting close to a settlement, but Kane kept up his pressure.

Newspapers and magazines ran stories about MCI and the strike, and for the first time ever the company was being portrayed as the bad guy.

McGowan finally intervened. He called Nate: "There will *not* be a rally. If there is a rally in Charleston, there will not be a contract signed."

Nate called Ron and told him what McGowan had said. Ron said, "You can't do this."

Nate said, "This wasn't a two-way conversation. I listened. He told me 'No rally.' He wants it off."

Ron called Kane. They had a two o'clock meeting, and Ron thought he had a proposal that Kane would buy.

"Dan, there's a rally in Charleston today."

"Yes, there is," said Kane.

"Call it off."

"I can't."

"Dan, call it off. If there's a rally in Charleston, don't bother coming to the two o'clock meeting."

"You can't do that."

"There won't be a meeting. We've got nothing to talk about. Either you're in control or you're not. If you're not, say so. But this rally has nothing to do with you, me, and this fucking strike."

"I don't think I can," Kane said.

"There won't be a two o'clock meeting."

Kane called back in fifteen minutes and said, "I'm trying," but the wheels were in motion, and they were hard to stop. Kane had trouble locating the organizers. He had set the rally up two weeks before, and it was ready to roll.

Kane wanted the strike settled, and so did MCI. MCI had the upper hand until Kane organized the rally and the boycott. At that point, Ron would have given Kane plenty to stop it.

Unfortunately for Kane, his advantage disappeared quickly. He had done one more thing to try to improve his bargaining position, and it backfired. WUI had agreed to provide Telex services for the Summer Olympics in Los Angeles. All labor unions had agreed that the Olympics were off limits. No matter what was going on around the country, national union leaders had come together with Olympic officials and given their word that no union would picket the games.

Kane broke that agreement by saying his local would picket the Olympics. "Not one delivery man, not one reporter, not one athlete, not one coach, not one spectator will enter those Olympic facilities without first having to bust through a picket line," Kane vowed publicly.

Actually, that was good news for MCI. Nate and Ron didn't want to service the Olympics anyway. It seemed like a good idea at first, but it was turning out to be more expensive than they had figured. They were hoping that Kane's action would prompt the Olympic committee to invite MCI to leave, but the committee didn't.

That threat got the Teamsters into trouble. Jess Carr, who ran the West Coast Teamsters, looked like he was out of control. Kane had embarrassed the union, and it was clear that he would receive no more support from the national membership. Without that support, Kane didn't have any way to continue the strike. Moreover, he was now being pressured by the union's upper echelons to settle the strike.

Now Kane was in deep trouble, and he had no choice but to swallow his pride on the East Coast and the West Coast.

At two o'clock, just as the rally was to begin, someone climbed to the podium and said, "The rally is off."

Ron and Kane met that afternoon as scheduled and reached an agreement. The next day, it was signed.

Tobin went to Charleston that day and told reporters that WUI had no relation to MCI and that MCI was not involved in the strike negotiations. Because of Nate's structure in setting up the two divisions, Tobin's statement was a "PR truth."

In the end, each side had moved closer to the middle ground, and both claimed a victory.

MCI's main advantage over AT&T was that AT&T was large and subject to FCC regulations more stringent than those imposed on other carriers, including MCI. AT&T had to wait longer for its rate requests to be approved by the FCC, it was subject to a maximum profit margin rate, and it couldn't offer equipment to its customers except under a separate subsidiary.

The FCC kept these rules in effect because AT&T still dominated the long-distance market, holding more than 90 percent of the market share, and it would destroy growing competition if it was set loose. As senior vice-president in charge of regulatory and public policy, Gene Eidenberg's job at MCI was to keep AT&T boxed in by regulation as long as he could.

Now that MCI was becoming a $2 billion company, and GTE, a $14.5 billion company, had bought Sprint, it was getting more and more difficult to show the FCC that the companies were still handicapped and that competition hadn't really arrived. The FCC wasn't buying it anymore, and it was beginning to cut AT&T loose. (Although GTE owned large local phone companies throughout the United States, it was permitted to buy Sprint because it didn't dominate the local phone scene in any one region of the country, according to Judge Greene. Sprint and MCI were treated the same by the FCC.)

Eidenberg's tactics for handling the regulatory process were different from those employed by MCI in the past. The company had gotten what it wanted by raising its voice, being abrasive, and demanding its rights. It litigated at the drop of a hat.

Now MCI was a huge company. It couldn't cry wolf very much longer and complain that AT&T was trying to push it out of business. For the first time, MCI was on the other end. It was being sued by people who felt ripped off by this $2 billion company: customers who didn't get good service; employees who were caught in the sales layoffs with the excuse that they weren't doing their jobs when the truth was that the company was changing its marketing thrusts and didn't need them anymore; and large customers who paid for calls that were never completed. (In unequal access areas, there is no "answer supervision," so the billing computer doesn't know when a call is answered. MCI began its billing timer arbitrarily after six rings or so. MCI's contract says customers can get their bill corrected, but many didn't know it and paid for calls that weren't completed.)

MCI's attitude changed. It became less confrontational and more smooth. Its responses to the FCC became less spontaneous and more thought out. Eidenberg made his views known by politicking, lobbying, and taking the right people to lunch. Although he headed MCI's legal shop, he wasn't a lawyer and that was an advantage. Rather than getting bogged down in the legal details of any issue, Gene was able to see what was really behind the briefs and petitions, and deal with them from a political point of view.

McGowan knew that AT&T would do the smart thing in Charleston. They would let MCI, Sprint, and the other carriers grab a large market share, and then tell the FCC, "Look at how their market share has grown. If you don't deregulate us, we're going to lose money. It's not fair. We can't compete." Eidenberg knew that AT&T would do the same thing in the states that were just beginning to permit intrastate competition. There, too, Eidenberg's goal was to keep AT&T tied up with regulation as long as possible, even though it meant a state-by-state campaign. Toward the end of August, Don Campbell walked into Gene's office and said, "Virginia has completely deregulated AT&T." It was the first state to go that far.

Gene said, "You know, AT&T has a chance to act predatorial, but if they're smart, they won't."

He was right. AT&T was smart. So was McGowan. When Charleston's results were in, MCI had grabbed about 12 percent of the market, and AT&T used it as proof that equal access was really equal and that the other carriers were finally able to take care of themselves. The FCC listened carefully, and it was another point for AT&T. McGowan took issue with that, saying that MCI had to spend a half-million dollars to get these new customers, and their average bills were only about $35. If MCI had to do that all over the country, it would lose money.

More important, 70 percent of the people in Charleston didn't pick *any* carrier, and AT&T got them without lifting a finger.

Eidenberg spent much of his time trying to get the local phone companies to change their rules about equal access notification. In Minneapolis, the next equal access area, Northwestern Bell sent all its customers a ballot that listed choices for long-distance carriers. Customers who didn't choose were given to a carrier on a pro rata basis. If, for example, 30 percent of those returning the ballots chose MCI, then the next 30 percent who didn't respond would be assigned to MCI, unless they objected within sixty days. Almost three-quarters of those in Minneapolis did choose, and about 25 percent chose MCI, double the number in Charleston. Clearly, balloting by the local companies was the way to go. Not only was it cheaper for MCI but it seemed to work better than MCI doing its own balloting. The main reason was credibility. People paid attention to their local phone companies.

Gene continued pressuring the FCC to change the equal access rules, but it wasn't until a few months later when McGowan attended a symposium about telephones that things happened. McGowan was on a panel with Randall Tobias, AT&T Communications chairman, Tom Bolger, chairman of Bell Atlantic; and others. McGowan did what he did best. He laid out the problem for all those who attended, including the news media.

He said, "We assumed that equal access meant equal, the way the English language expresses it. We at MCI and the other carriers find ourselves in a process heavily biased in AT&T's favor. I am not here to point fingers, although if I crook my finger a little, don't be surprised." Tobias was sitting next to him.

McGowan blasted the default traffic issue and complained that Bell companies didn't give MCI the necessary customer information it needed to do its direct-mail and ad campaigns. MCI was permitted to purchase the name, phone number, and address of those in equal access areas. AT&T had that information plus usage data and information about those with unlisted numbers. He reiterated the complaint that the phone companies switched customers to equal access on a piecemeal basis, which made it impossible for MCI to get the most from a blanket advertising campaign.

Technically, he said that AT&T had all the "tandems" it needed but that the local phone companies weren't prepared to install them for the other carriers when they needed them. Tandems are lines that connect the long-distance companies' "point of presence"—the location at which the carrier's network enters the local phone company's service area, or LATA—into the telephone central office. The areas that Judge Greene designated as LATAs (local access transport areas) may be as large as a state, and just because MCI brought its network into that LATA didn't mean that it could get connections through the LATA to the phone customers. MCI and other carriers had to wait for those links to be built.

Bolger complained that the Bell Operating Companies were caught in the middle. There was no way they could accommodate all the requests for equipment. Besides that, while he and the other companies were spending huge sums of money on that equipment, AT&T already had plans in the works to bypass the local companies and go directly to the customer for private line service. The money spent on installations might go down the drain.

Despite Bolger's correct assertions, McGowan had still stolen the show. It was one of his most flamboyant attacks yet against the FCC, AT&T, and the Bell companies. It got results, too.

A few days later, FCC Chairman Mark Fowler called McGowan and said he wanted to come over and talk with him. His office was only a block away.

Fowler had read an account of the meeting and also heard about it from his staff. He said, "Is all that true? What you said?"

"Yes," McGowan said.

"All of it? Without exception?"

"Yes."

Fowler said, "Okay."

That afternoon, the FCC put out a statement that they would look into the matter, especially the part about default traffic, the most important issue in making equal access equal.

Bert Roberts had been working hard on his new structure for MCI. He had wanted to decentralize the company for many years, and he was getting impatient with how long it was taking. Bert had stormed out of a meeting after he thought it was going to be about reorganization but turned out to be about something else. He was being stalled, and he didn't like it. That only made him more angry and short with his colleagues.

Even at the Monday morning meetings that Orville had established for senior managers to update each other on the latest news, Bert mostly kept to himself. In his day-to-day activities, he relied heavily on MCI Mail's instant electronic letters. It was fast, efficient, and didn't require personal contact.

Orville was supportive of decentralization and so was McGowan, but McGowan wasn't convinced that the right time had come yet. Orville trusted William's instincts for timing.

Actually, the company had been decentralizing for a long time. The field personnel were given so much autonomy that Orville had to close his eyes to much of the duplication that he saw going on. It violated his sense of order and decorum. Still, he believed so strongly in letting managers run their own shops that if someone on the East Coast duplicated something on the West Coast—if he reinvented the wheel—that would be okay.

Bert had been working with Orville and Orville's assistant, Bob Pons. Bert didn't warm up to Pons and on many occasions had accused him of snitching to Orville about trivial things. As far as Bert was concerned, Pons was Orville's boy. It was all during Bert's bad period, and Pons was the recipient of much of his anger and impatience. After several months, however, he did win his trust. Bert didn't let many people close to him, but Pons became one of the few.

Pons was one of the few people at MCI who knew exactly what the reorganization would entail. The plan was to divide MCI into seven regions that would exactly match the spun-off Bell companies. This was crucial. Bert knew that MCI had to control its local interconnection costs, and that meant "managing" the Bell companies closely. That couldn't be done from Washington. Interconnection costs in equal access areas were now $750 a line, more than twice as much as an unequal access line when MCI customers had to punch in all the extra digits. By the end of the year, MCI would have spent almost a *half-billion dollars* for the interconnections, close to *one-quarter* of the company's revenues. The other great drain was the cost of leased lines that MCI got from AT&T so it could give its customers access to areas that MCI's network didn't reach. Leasing lines would cost MCI $343 million, almost 18 percent of its revenues. The cost of leasing lines would diminish as MCI continued to enlarge its network. Still, MCI *had* to control these costs if it was to survive. Other companies weren't, and they were disappearing.

Ironically, MCI would become the Bell companies' best customer because it was buying all those interconnections. Charlie Skibo had just ended a year-long trek with his network operation field personnel around the country meeting with BOC personnel. He discovered that when trouble arose in getting interconnections, the MCI people didn't know whom to talk with at the BOCs. The problem was one of communication and trust. The Bell companies still looked at MCI as "those people" who broke up Ma Bell. Many of the Bell managers had hoped to move up the ladder from the Bell companies to the corporation. With the divestiture, movement was nearly impossible. Skibo knew he would have to change that attitude because now the local companies would be receiving large amounts of money from MCI, and MCI, in turn, would be relying on the Bell companies for its success in equal access. He set out on a get-acquainted spree, introducing himself and his people to the companies that would be crucial to MCI's future.

MCI was still suffering from a reputation for giving poor customer service. Customer service, which came under Carl's sales division, was a joke. He had never worried about customer service, and now that MCI had more than 2 million customers, it became impossible. In the past, it didn't matter. Now, with increased competition, it began to make a difference. With equal access, all companies would have the same-quality connections. Making sure the customer was pleased would make all the difference. Decentralization could make it possible to give good customer service. Like many companies, MCI would have to get closer to the customer it had grown apart from over the years.

McGowan hoped that by dividing MCI along the exact geographic lines of the BOCs, MCI would get closer not only to their customers but to the Bell companies as well. Because they served the same areas, MCI's new presidents would have the same interests and share the same local problems as the BOCs.

One reason that McGowan had delayed the reorganization was that he didn't know how the Bell companies would unfold. Nobody knew which companies would be able to shake off the AT&T prejudices and work with MCI and which would be willing to meet them halfway. McGowan would have to send the toughest managers to handle the toughest Bell companies.

All around him, McGowan had seen something at MCI that appalled him. It was bureaucracy. McGowan had prided himself on having a company that moved quickly and didn't take long to make decisions. He was fond of comparing the efficiency of his company with others. Now, with ten thousand employees, it was getting harder. As the company grew, it began to slow down. People weren't willing to take risks anymore. They were getting shy about making mistakes. McGowan was a strong believer that people should be allowed to make errors. If they weren't, it meant they weren't doing anything but hiding out and collecting a paycheck.

MCI was also attracting a different kind of employee. In past years, there was a chance to break new ground and make lots of money on stock if the company worked out, and this attracted bright, talented, aggressive people. Now, with the battles over and the industry settling in, people joined with few expectations of making a big splash. MCI was just another place to work.

It *used* to be a great place to work, people kept telling McGowan.

Somehow, McGowan had to implement the reorganization at just the right time and in just the right way to bring back that spirit. His plan was to wait until things got unbearable, then use the reorganization to shake things up.

By early August, rumors were flying around the company about a reorganization. The scuttlebutt centered on who would get the seven presidents' jobs. These would be great jobs because each president would have complete control and would be responsible for profit and loss. Unlike other company decentralizations, the amount of revenue support they got from headquarters would be relatively small.

When the news came out on August 22, some choices were surprises while others were expected.

Brian Thompson took charge of the Mid-Atlantic Division, the area served by Bell Atlantic. Brian was flattered that the job was offered, but what he really wanted was Orville's job when he left. He believed he could do it. Brian knew he would miss being at the upper echelon of a large corporation and the prestige that it brought.

NYNEX, the Bell company in the Northeast, had a reputation for not cooperating with long-distance carriers. Kantor's skills as a tough manager would be needed to bring the telephone company in line. Nate took the job with reservations, although like a good soldier he took it without complaint. His only regret was that he couldn't see MCI International—his baby—through. He had started it, and he wanted to finish it. Seth Blumenfeld took over his job at MCI International.

Ron Spears was a surprise because he was so young. He was given the Midwest Division out of Chicago. McGowan believed that Ron proved during the strike that he was a mature, strong manager.

Charlie Skibo was given the Southwest Division in Atlanta. Skibo, however, had second thoughts about it. He wasn't all that sure that decentralization would work, though he was willing to give it a try.

The Southwest Division was given to Frank Harkins. Who? Not many people in the field knew who Harkins was. He had joined MCI only two years earlier by way of Western Union International. Harkins had been vice-president of North American Phillips and was with W. R. Grace. He was a solid manager. At MCI, he was senior vice-president of planning and administration, but he was never part of the "inner circle."

Jerry Taylor was given the largest region: West Division. It covered fifteen states from Minnesota to Washington and south to Arizona and New Mexico. It mimicked US West, the old Mountain Bell and Northwest Bell areas, and was considered one of the more progressive Bell companies. Like Nate, Jerry had misgivings about leaving his old job. He wanted to see Airsignal through to where it would begin to make a profit and become a strong division within MCI.

On the West Coast, McGowan threw a curve: Gene Eidenberg, who had never been a businessman until he joined MCI, got the area that covered Nevada, California, and Hawaii, the same area as Pacific Telesis, the old Pacific Telephone area. Of all the new presidents, Gene fit into the West Coast life-style. He was still a hippie at heart and would get along well in lotus land. Whether he could run a business was unknown.

McGowan chose these people for two important reasons. First, he trusted all of them. They all had good instincts. Second, by dismantling his senior staff at headquarters, he was sending the strongest single message to the field that this reorganization was for real. It wasn't like other companies that promised decentralization but still ran things from home base. By showing that he had no one around him anymore, he showed that he meant it. Instead of having a headquarters-driven company, MCI would be driven from the field.

As much as possible would go out. Very little would stay in Washington. Of course, dealing with the FCC would stay, and so would the litigation still pending. MCI Mail and Airsignal would remain as well because they were small and needed tender loving care to grow.

It wasn't easy for McGowan to give up his control, but he believed he had to do it in order for the reorganization to work.

On August 28, the new presidents met for their first meeting. McGowan spoke first and explained that the plan actually took root about three years ago when some administrative and task functions had been given to the regions. He admitted how he had been urged by Orville and Bert to do it about a year ago, but he waited because he wanted to see equal access get a little further along. He also didn't see enough talent in the company. When Orville came to him with a list of two people for every president's job, he decided to go ahead.

McGowan said, "We have bureaucracy. Compared to other companies, it's not much, but it's not as little as we would like to see ourselves having."

He noted that AT&T hadn't done anything to change people's minds about what it was. "We're looking for a local presence."

After a few more minutes, he opened the floor for questions about the structures of the divisions. No one said a thing. They looked like they were in shock, and McGowan said, "Would you like me to structure it for you?" He smiled. Then the questions began.

Orville talked about what they had to do between now and when the reorganization was to take place, January 1, 1985, one year to the day after AT&T's divestiture. He discussed how McGowan had decided that MCI would now get its fiscal year in line with most other companies and have it the same as the calendar year. That would require all the new presidents to get their budgets ready in only four months.

Bert talked about organizational structure. He gave several different plans and said each president could decide how he wanted to run his own shop. "One reason behind this reorganization is to eliminate bureaucracy. Go slowly to prevent too many levels."

The presidents were divided into study groups. The groups would decide what functions would be decentralized, given to the field, and what would remain at headquarters. McGowan was savvy enough to know that nobody liked to give up power, so he warned them it was better to err on the side of putting too much into the field than too little. The groups included finance, state regulatory, law, purchasing and material, human resources, network operations and employee communications/media, and public relations and marketing.

Carl Vorder Bruegge and Ed Carter were not at the meeting, even though sales and marketing would be affected. Their absence was deliberate.

Next, the meeting dealt with staffing. Bert warned, "We can't get into a bidding war." Harcharik was petrified that his Mail division might be gutted, all the good people wooed away by the divisional presidents. Orville wanted to guard against that and said that all requests for anyone in Harcharik's shop must go through Harcharik first. The same went for Airsignal.

Bert said the company had to be careful of people's sensitivities, and he brought up a story in a recent *Washington Post* that talked about the reorganization and possible layoffs at the Pentagon City office. The story triggered morale-breaking rumors, and McGowan and Orville were forced to make a special tour of the building to reassure employees that the story was not correct. It may have been the most exercise McGowan had in years. As it turned out, the story was accurate enough, in that many people would be laid off at headquarters and Pentagon City because their jobs wouldn't exist anymore. Many would be offered jobs in the new divisions.

During a presentation by Human Resources Vice-President John Zimmerman about moving expenses, Howard Crane worried about how the reduction brought on by the reorganization would look to the press. Bert argued that AT&T's recent announcement of layoffs of eleven thousand people got very little press attention. He was quickly corrected by McGowan and others who said it got a lot of notice and didn't look good.

Amazingly, everyone had thought that the news of the reorganization would get a big reaction. After all, MCI's numbers were bad, going to get worse, and the company was going to restructure itself. To outsiders, when a company reorganizes itself so radically, it's usually taken as a sign that it has lost control and the move is a last-ditch effort to survive. In a way, at MCI, it was, but nobody outside the company really noticed. Either nobody noticed or nobody cared.

Bert told the new presidents that sales commissions would be frozen and the ad budget would be dropped by $25 million. "We're in one of the tightest budget periods we've ever experienced."

Orville told all presidents to send weekly reports over MCI Mail. He would discontinue the 8 A.M. Monday breakfast meetings on October 1.

McGowan closed the meeting, reminding the new presidents to look for more than one person for each open spot and not to be fearful of hiring good people. He knew most bosses were afraid of hiring good people. He knew most bosses were afraid of hiring someone who could eventually take their place.

He said, "Nobody will be criticized for making the wrong decision or hiring the wrong person. You will only be criticized for not making a decision, for letting it drag on."

Orville remained quiet on one important point: what to do about major accounts. McGowan wanted these large customers to be handled by headquarters. The presidents, naturally, wanted to get them for themselves. They were great sources of revenue. The issue was left up in the air, but to McGowan it was still crucial, and only about five people in the company knew that in two days he would try to do something about it.

The financial outlook for all long-distance carriers was becoming bleaker. Even AT&T had predicted that it would lose money for the month of September, the first time in more than a century. For the quarter that would end September 30, MCI would show a loss in revenues and profit. The profit didn't worry McGowan. He always believed that as long as the revenues were growing, a company's profits would eventually follow. This time, however, the revenues fell, too. Most of that was caused by the elimination of the monthly fee, but it also meant the company had not been attracting enough new corporate accounts. Equal access was great, but it was expensive getting small users who spent less than $100 a month.

McGowan knew what the problem was: MCI didn't have any salespeople who could walk into a General Motors or an Exxon and sell them service. These people had all left during the sales staff shuffles of the Grow Like Mad period, and now MCI was left without any seasoned salespeople who knew how to go after large corporate accounts. Not just get them, but keep them.

McGowan had a solution, but it was a radical one. He wanted to cut a deal with IBM in which the computer giant would do a joint marketing and information swap with MCI. For MCI, McGowan saw many good things. IBM would lend credibility to MCI that it didn't have. Its salespeople could walk into a large corporation if they had the

IBM name attached to them. McGowan also knew that IBM's real competitor was not Digital Equipment Corporation, Control Data, or any of the other computer companies. It was AT&T.

AT&T and IBM were both fighting for the same market—the office of the future. And both wanted to provide end-to-end service for their customers. That meant computers coupled with communications. AT&T had the communications but not the computers. IBM had the computers but not the communications. With MCI in concert with IBM, they might beat AT&T.

AT&T had recently made some moves into the computer area with its introduction of a new personal computer and office networks that could connect them together. It had also been gaining strength in computer programming.

IBM had recently made some strong pushes in communications. It had purchased ROLM, a maker of telephone PBXs, and it was also strengthening its control over Satellite Business Systems, SBS. SBS had never made a profit. In 1983, it lost more than $123 million. SBS was formed as a communications company that would specialize in sending high-speed data, but that market didn't grow as fast as expected, and the three partners—Comsat, IBM, and Aetna—had reconfigured the network to handle voice traffic in order to go after an existing market and raise some revenue. Now Comsat wanted out, and IBM was prepared to buy its one-third share and place one of its top officials at the helm of SBS.

For years, no one could figure out why IBM held on to its stake in SBS. IBM never backed losers, and SBS was clearly a bomb. Now it was becoming clear. SBS would provide IBM with the communications network it needed to compete with AT&T. Moreover, the FCC had just lifted restrictions that prevented joint marketing by IBM and SBS. Soon, they could walk into a company and sell it computers and satellite communications.

IBM's problem was that it didn't understand the telecommunications industry, didn't know how to deal with the local phone companies or the regulators, and that would impede its plans. McGowan believed that IBM could get that expertise from MCI. In addition, MCI's network was far superior to SBS's in quality and geographical range. If IBM went to a company and sold them end-to-end service, MCI's network would be the best vehicle.

McGowan was willing to take the risks involved in such a move. He knew that he might have to give an IBMer a seat on the board of directors. McGowan had always enjoyed a crony board that didn't give him any trouble. An outsider could make it more difficult for him to get things done. He also ran the risk of IBM wanting a small piece of MCI, maybe 10 percent, then continuing to gobble up MCI little by little, just as it had done with ROLM. It started with 15 percent, then 23 percent, then the whole thing.

That's what worried Orville. Having worked at IBM, he knew they liked to control anything they owned. He told William, "Once you open the door, it's very difficult to close it." He didn't like the idea of IBM getting mixed up with MCI. He thought it would destroy MCI's corporate culture. He was hoping that IBM wouldn't be interested.

After three months of pounding by McGowan, Orville finally agreed to call IBM's chairman, John Opel, whom he knew, and arrange a meeting. On August 30, Orville and McGowan traveled to IBM's headquarters in Armonk, New York, and talked it over with Opel and several others, including Vice-Chairman Paul Rizzo.

McGowan got the impression that Opel wasn't aware of how serious the SBS problem was. Perhaps the information wasn't reaching him. Orville got the impression that IBM just wasn't interested.

The meeting was congenial, but nothing concrete was accomplished. Orville breathed a sigh of relief, though he knew that Opel would be leaving soon and that President John Akers would take his place. Akers had a reputation for being more open to new ideas. He wanted to do everything possible to get IBM to react more quickly to the marketplace, and he also understood that communications was the key.

The main benefit of the meeting was that word leaked out that IBM and MCI had met. Rumors spread that IBM wanted to buy MCI, and MCI's stock rose a few dollars to its highest point in months.

12

McGowan was right about the reorganization. It had lifted morale, especially among headquarters employees, who began to jockey for positions in the field. People *wanted* to move; they wanted new challenges. They looked at each division as a brand-new entrepreneurial company that had no limits to growth. Bob Pons landed a tough job. He was tapped to head customer service in Nate Kantor's Northeast Division. That was a demanding assignment. Because of the overtaxing of New York Telephone, MCI customers had terrible problems with service.

Don Campbell went to work for Brian Thompson in his PR shop. Little by little, the offices of MCI's Washington headquarters became vacant. The exodus had begun.

Ed Carter was left behind with nothing to do. Even though nobody admitted it, the reorganization would kill two birds with one stone. One bird was Carter.

Because all the marketing would be done on a regional basis, and MCI made no national TV buys, there was little for Carter to do but act as a consultant to the divisions. When January 1 rolled around, Carter would find his 120-person staff cut in half. Sixty took jobs in the divisions, and they didn't need Carter anymore. Some of the presidents told Carter to butt out. They didn't like him or his manner of business.

Tom Messner of Ally & Gargano had taken himself off the MCI account because of Carter. The two just didn't get along.

In recent years, Carl was being blamed for poor customer service and not doing better in large accounts. He took the bad-guy rap, even though it hurt him. He knew that he had done what had to be done during MCI's crucial growing phase, although it had hidden consequences now. Carl could stay as long as wanted. Nobody would ever fire him. Certainly not McGowan. For all his tough talk, he never fired anyone.

Wayne English, who had accomplished all his goals, was now ready to step down, and Bill Conway was prepared to take his place.

McGowan began remembering when MCI was just a small band of individual companies. Now it was one large company, almost $2 billion, and dividing it up into divisions had a certain symmetry to it. After all, the company began with separate divisions, and it now ended with separate divisions. It had come full circle.

Beyond all that, though, McGowan had something else in mind. He was building a new age company—a field-driven company. MCI would be composed of seven companies, all of them in the same business but each doing it in its own way. And each had complete responsibility for profit and loss.

MCI would be something new, something no one had ever seen before. Not only had McGowan established a new business in the United States—the competitive long-distance business—now he was establishing a new kind of business model.

There had been great talk lately about what to do about huge conglomerates that were failing because of their bulk and slowness. They were like dinosaurs dying because they didn't fit in their environment anymore. Many, in fact, were starting to sell off their subsidiaries—especially those that were unrelated to the company's main line of business—in an attempt to get themselves focused on the business they knew best.

If MCI worked, it could be the prototype for other companies to follow, and McGowan would be remembered as someone who always knew the business.

EPILOGUE

The new presidents performed pretty much as expected. Ron Spears was highly aggressive, pushing the Bell companies in his area to serve MCI's needs. He also began using creative promotions such as pledging $1 million for the Heart of America Challenge to bring sailing's America's Cup back to the United States. Nate Kantor, the old military man, spent many months running his "boot camp" making sure his team knew exactly what he wanted before making their formal attack on the Northeast area. Jerry Taylor, who had always managed by "love," was slowly building his team of loyal people who had to get a handle on the largest MCI region. So far, he hadn't done anything special, but past experience showed that he would.

Brian Thompson was doing splendidly, but that was no surprise. Aside from being a competent manager, he was given one of the best regions to begin with. Frank Harkins, the reliable workhorse, had built one of the strongest regions from a managerial point of view, placing solid administrators in critical positions. It was still too early to tell how imaginative they would be.

Gene Eidenberg . . . well . . . it was too early to tell about Gene, too. He was still learning how to run a business. It would take him awhile, but when it came to the political aspects of running his region, he didn't have to learn much at all.

Charlie Skibo surprised everyone when he decided to leave his job as president of the Southeast region. He was offered the type of job that he had wanted all his life, and he couldn't turn it down. Charlie left MCI to become president of US Telecom, the division of United Telecommunications (formerly United Telephone) that handled long-distance service. US Telecom leased most of its lines but was planning a large fiber-optic network to service its customers. The new position gave Charlie the chance to run his own national company *and* make more money. He couldn't pass it up. Charlie was replaced by Dan Akerson, who had been at MCI for two years.

Back at headquarters, Ed Carter, senior vice-president of marketing, had resigned. His stormy relationship with the other senior managers had been strained beyond repair. They couldn't stand his condescending attitude toward them and MCI anymore, and Carter believed his ideas weren't appreciated. It had been made clear to Carter that he was no longer welcome. After the company was decentralized, there was little for him to do anyway, and after a while he got the message. Even though Carter was a brilliant marketer and had taken MCI into new areas—such as selling residential service through Amway distributors—his large ego and contempt for the people at MCI were too much.

Carter established his own consulting firm in Washington, D.C., and now that he was gone, Tom Messner of Ally & Gargano returned to the MCI account.

As far as managers were concerned, though, one bright spot *had* begun to appear. Bert Roberts, who had been in his shell for so long, was coming out. Now that the decentralization had been accomplished and he was assured of taking Orville's place as president upon his retirement in September, he was less anxious and easier to be around. He was becoming a *mensch*. He was feeling more comfortable talking to the media and to those in the company. For all his business bravado, Bert was actually a shy person, and he was beginning to overcome it. That, and the lessons from McGowan and Orville, seemed to be paying off. He might be able to fill Orville's shoes after all.

Around the same time that Orville had planned to leave, Tom Leming announced his retirement, too. He had promised to leave when he was 65 years old, and his birthday was coming up in a few years.

Meanwhile, telecommunications companies were still faltering. Allnet was planning to merge with another reseller, Lexitel, Corp., making the new company the fourth largest long-distance carrier behind AT&T, MCI and Sprint. For Allnet it would mean an infusion of much-needed cash. For Lexitel, which operated in fewer than ten states, it would mean extending their reach nationally. Mike Richer would take a back seat, and his partner Mel Goodman would become chairman of the newly formed company.

Strong speculation arose that GTE wanted to sell Sprint but that they couldn't find a buyer. Gus Grant, who was Sprint's founder and former president, was now engaged in building a nationwide fiber-optic network as head of a company called Fibertrak. It was jointly owned by Santa Fe Southern Pacific Corp. (formed by the Santa Fe and Southern Pacific railroads) and the Northern Southern Corp. Grant was interested in buying some of the fiber-optic segments that Sprint had already installed.

If Grant was successful in building Fibertrak, it would extend eight thousand miles along railroads' rights-of-way and link more than fifty cities. It would cost $1 billion. Grant's plan was to become a "carrier's carrier," leasing circuits to long-distance carriers and not to the end user. If he was successful, the high-capacity fiber circuits might cause a communications glut, a lowering of long-distance costs, and a price war among the surviving players. The only question was whether he could get all the money he needed.

Early indications were bad. Grant had failed to sign enough large customers to begin building the network on schedule, and the project was put on hold. His hopes of starting construction grew dimmer each day.

Internationally, MCI was now serving about forty countries. In Japan, the Nippon Telephone and Telegraph Corp. (NTT) lost its monopoly status established by the government in 1952. The government now owned all of NTT's stock and was to begin selling it to the public in 1986. The FCC, meanwhile, had broken another monopoly by permitting private companies to establish their own satellites for international service. That was once the exclusive domain of Intelsat, the international satellite consortium of countries to which the United States belonged. In Great Britain, newly established long-distance company Mercury Communications was planning domestic and international service in competition with the now former monopoly service British Telecom. Mercury had fought BT in the courts in order to get interconnections to the local phone network—just like MCI and AT&T—and won.

In the United States, MCI and AT&T were still brawling. On April

15, 1985, the two companies had returned to the courtroom. A year and half earlier, a federal appeals court in Chicago had thrown out a lower court's decision to award MCI $1.8 billion in antitrust violation damages. AT&T *was* guilty of anticompetitive actions—that part wouldn't change—but at issue now was the amount of the award. For that, a new trial was necessary.

Based on a new profit/loss study, MCI's lawyers claimed that AT&T should pay MCI $5.8 billion (trebled under antitrust law to $17.4) because that's how much damage AT&T's actions had caused. Buoyed by their previous wins, MCI's lead counsel, Chet Kamin of Jenner & Block, believed that a jury would agree with that figure.

AT&T thought the amount was outrageous, and its new chief counsel, Blair White of Sidley & Austin, who replaced George Saunders, said that MCI's studies were totally unrealistic. AT&T's studies, White said, would show that MCI's real damages were really about $10 million.

McGowan was not the least bit pessimistic about asking for such a high figure. As usual, he caught the rest of the company up in his enthusiasm.

Some of the BOCs believed McGowan, too. US West had already settled its share of any damage award—all the BOCs would be liable for a prorated part of any AT&T payment—by paying MCI $63 million and agreeing to assign equal access default traffic more fairly.

Before the trial began, analysts were saying that MCI might receive from $10 million to $300 million before trebling, and as the trial commenced, MCI's stock inched higher, ready to explode if it indeed won a lot of money.

MCI's witnesses tried to show that their profit/loss study, prepared by Bill Conway, was an accurate portrayal of the facts. They told the jury how AT&T had kept MCI from entering markets at critical times in the company's development. Economist Dr. William Melody, who authored the most crucial parts of the study, testified that in a perfect world, MCI would have taken in $12.8 billion in revenue from 1973 to 1983, instead of the $3.1 billion it collected. Melody stated that his assumptions were based on MCI entering markets earlier than it did.

AT&T's Blair White, however, skillfully shot down Melody's assumptions by showing the jury two telephones—one a Touch-Tone, the other a rotary dial. He pointed to thirteen cities that Melody said MCI would have served had it not been thwarted by AT&T's actions.

Then he told the court that those cities didn't have Touch-Tone service at the time MCI offered its Execunet service, which needed Touch-Tone phones to work. White said Melody included those un-Touch-Toned cities in his study. He showed that MCI's study was based on a "perfect world" and not the "real world." White told the jury that the highest amount of damages that AT&T should pay was $36.4 million.

That was it. MCI had messed up big time. It had placed all its hopes on a flawed profit/loss study, and White had discredited it. MCI couldn't adequately defend the accuracy of the study.

Moreover, MCI's lawyers failed to factor in one important aspect of human nature: greed. It seemed to the jurors, the lawyers found out later, that MCI was being greedy. Here they were, a $2 billion company, and they were claiming that they were injured to the tune of almost $6 billion. MCI hurt itself by asking for so much money. Jurors chosen from the general public just weren't prepared to award that kind of dough, and they didn't.

They awarded MCI $37.8 million, trebled to $113.3 million. It was close to the $36.4 million figure that Blair White in his closing statement told the jury AT&T actually owed MCI. The jury totally threw out MCI's profit/loss study. They didn't believe it one bit. To them, it was just a bunch of numbers with nothing to back it up. They believed AT&T and not MCI. McGowan sat in the courtroom, and his heart sank when the verdict was read. It was a clear victory for AT&T. They had whittled down a $1.8 billion award to $113.3 million, and they could even appeal that if they wanted to.

On the plane ride back home, McGowan and the others didn't talk all that much. Mostly, they drank wine and thought about what had just happened.

Later on, McGowan complained that Judge John Grady, who had also presided over the original antitrust trial, failed to give the jury correct instructions. It might be a basis for an appeal, but down deep he doubted MCI would appeal the decision.

For the first time in a long time, McGowan had been humiliated. Sure, MCI had beaten AT&T, and yes, AT&T was guilty, but maybe, after all, MCI had cried wolf just one time too many. Or worse still, maybe McGowan hadn't learned the lesson he had taught AT&T—not to be so smug and arrogant to the point where you hurt yourself and your cause. Asking for so much money certainly seemed the height of insolence.

Still, in McGowan's usual blind optimism, he looked ahead to next year when MCI and AT&T would meet again in court. This case was called Antitrust II by MCI lawyers and would cover AT&T's alleged antitrust actions for the years *after* April 1975. MCI had asked the court to award a billion dollars, but McGowan would probably settle out of court for a lot less.

Even though MCI won more than $100 million, it was considered a defeat. MCI needed more money to grow, and a large award would have helped. Still, the company had something positive to help balance it. Because of McGowan's screaming and yelling, the FCC had announced that it would order the Bell Operating Companies to change the way it handled default traffic. Until now, all but a few of the BOCs had turned over to AT&T those customers who didn't choose a long-distance company. Now the FCC said that customers who didn't select a company would be distributed to companies based on market share. If, for example, MCI had 5 percent of a market, 5 percent of the default traffic would be routed to MCI. It was fair to everyone.

Still, McGowan knew that wouldn't be enough to keep MCI alive. Despite MCI's commitment to a positioning strategy that would give it control over local communications, McGowan was planning to sell MCI's cellular mobile and paging business, Airsignal. He had little choice. MCI desperately needed more funds to plow into its main business—long distance—and owning paging and mobile phone services was distracting the company's attention. Eventually, McCaw Communications Companies, Inc., a Bellevue, Washington, firm would buy Airsignal for $120 million and add it to its cellular holdings in Seattle, Kansas City, Wichita, Oklahoma City and Austin.

But McGowan had to do even more. He was forced to change the entire face of the telecommunications industry once again.

On June 25, 1985, stock trading was halted on IBM and MCI by company request. The two companies had struck a deal that was the end result of their first meeting almost a year before. The agreement called for MCI to buy Satellite Business Systems with 45 million shares of MCI stock valued at $360 million. McGowan's company got the failing SBS, debt-free, for 16 percent of MCI. IBM also got warrants to buy another 7 million shares, bringing their stake to 18 percent. In essence, IBM became the largest single MCI shareholder. (They had to keep the shares at least three years, and they had to buy out Aetna's share of SBS.) Until then, that title had belonged to

McGowan. The deal also permitted IBM to purchase up to 30 percent of MCI without seeking approval from MCI's board of directors.

While many people saw it as nothing more than a sellout to the world's largest computer company, others saw it as one of the shrewdest moves in business history. For one thing, it guaranteed MCI's survival for a few more years. It meant that MCI could now more easily attract large investors, something it desperately needed. It also added 200,000 SBS users to MCI's customer base. More important, the deal gave MCI entry to large accounts that would now be attracted by the power and strength of IBM. From a competitive point of view, it nearly preempted any small long-distance companies from the industry, especially those that didn't have their own networks and were strictly resellers.

McGowan was counting on IBM's interest in MCI to dig into its pockets now and again to pay for MCI's network growth. He knew that IBM wouldn't let MCI falter if they had a piece of the action.

For IBM, it was a chance to understand the telecommunications industry. They had failed at running SBS, and they were admitting it. Not only that, but if MCI performed the way it had in the past, it was a plain and simple sound investment for IBM. It also gave IBM guaranteed access to a worldwide network for its own use.

As McGowan and IBM's vice-chairman, Paul Rizzo, spoke to reporters, who had been assembled on short notice, Orville at first refused to go into the room. He stayed outside and looked very sad. He didn't like the deal. He believed that IBM's stuffy influence would wreck MCI and kill the unique management style that had been built up over many years. He remembered what he had said to William when the negotiations began: "Once you open the door, it's difficult to close it." He feared that IBM would eventually gobble up all of MCI.

The event made the front page of most major newspapers. Here, for the first time, was the only entity that could actually challenge AT&T. The two driving forces of the information age were computers and communications. IBM had the computers, MCI had the communications, and they were going against AT&T, which had the communications but was still behind in computer technology— although they were catching up quickly. The event was being heralded as the start of a new chapter in the history of the information age.

The main drawback for MCI was that AT&T could now argue that it should be completely deregulated in the face of this new twosome. The competition wasn't weak anymore. The FCC was slowly loosening its reins on AT&T, and this would surely speed it up. The purchase upped MCI's market share to around 6 percent. AT&T, however, still had about 90 percent.

Unlike Orville, McGowan wasn't afraid of IBM buying up the rest of MCI. He believed that IBM had discovered it couldn't run a telecommunications company and would leave him alone to run MCI. He knew that he might have to put an IBMer on his board of directors but thought he could live with that.

To McGowan, it was all a big risk that he had to take if MCI was to survive.

Jack Goeken had done a similar thing nearly four years earlier. After ten years of work, he had finally gotten his air-to-ground pay telephone system called Airfone up and flying. Airfone allowed passengers to pick up a cordless telephone, one of several placed throughout the cabin, and place calls from their seats, paying for it with their credit cards. It took Jack longer than he expected to iron out the technical and legal bugs, and revenues were flowing too slowly. He needed money.

Through a Western Union lawyer—whom Jack knew because he had opposed his original MCI application before the FCC—Jack got WU interested in Airfone. He sold them 50 percent of the company. Airfone was in bad financial shape, but with that cash infusion Goeken might be able to keep it alive a little longer.

Both Jack and McGowan were trying to save their dream.

Update for This Edition

Since the hardcover version of *On The Line* was published in March 1986, MCI and the telecommunications industry have continued to undergo vast changes. GTE Sprint and US Telecom merged in the summer of 1986 to form US Sprint, the nation's third largest long distance company. Charles Skibo was named president and Ed Carter became the head of marketing. Although Carter didn't fit in at MCI, his marketing genius shined at Sprint. Because of his efforts, Sprint was able to add about a million new customers in 1986.

Bob Harcharik kept his word about retiring young and left MCI Mail. He bought a boat, which he named *Grand Finale*, and was last seen sailing to Hilton Head, South Carolina, and points south. Vint Cerf, MCI Mail's technical wizard, left soon afterward and began his own consulting firm. Ray Marks, Mail's vice president of sales, went to work for GTE Spacenet, a satellite communications company, as vice president of marketing. Tom Leming left MCI when he reached 65 and bought a vineyard in California.

In August 1986, Western Union sold its share of Airfone to GTE for about $39 million. It also bought Jack Goeken's remaining shares of the company for an undisclosed amount. Jack's latest venture, Railfone, a system for telephoning from trains, was being installed aboard Amtrak cars.

Orville's wife died of cancer shortly after they moved to California in preparation for his retirement. He agreed to a position as vice chairman, although he has limited duties.

By the end of 1986, competition in the long distance business had reached a fever pitch. All major companies, AT&T, MCI, and US Sprint were suffering financial pressures. AT&T was forced to lay off 27,000 people, 9 percent of its workforce. MCI cut 2,300 people, about 15 percent of its workers. MCI started buying back its own shares in an effort to stabilize its plummeting price. AT&T continued squeezing MCI and US Sprint by lowering its rates in accordance with government orders. Both companies had to respond by lowering their rates to remain competitive. Analysts were forecasting lower profits and tough futures for all three competitors.

On December 21, 1986, Bill McGowan suffered a massive heart attack and was rushed to Georgetown University Hospital in Washington. He spent more than two weeks in the intensive care unit before being allowed to go home. His illness was kept secret until a newspaper reporter learned about it shortly before McGowan was to be discharged. About six months earlier, McGowan had married Chicago entrepreneur Sue Gin in a private ceremony at his Virginia Beach, Virginia, vacation home. His brother Joe officiated. Like his illness, McGowan had chosen to keep his marriage a secret, even from his closest associates.

McGowan's recovery was slow. In mid-April 1987 Orville was named acting Chairman and acting CEO, leading to speculation that McGowan was more ill than had been suggested by company officials. It wasn't until May that it was disclosed that McGowan had undergone a heart transplant on April 25 at the Presbyterian-University Hospital of Pittsburgh. It was not known if he would ever return to work.

INDEX